ENVIRONMENTAL THEOLOGY

# Hope
# for the Land

## *Nature in the Bible*

### RICHARD CARTWRIGHT AUSTIN

John Knox Press
ATLANTA

*Abbreviations*

ILL      Inclusive Language Lectionary
JB        Jerusalem Bible
KJV     King James Version
NEB    New English Bible
NJB    New Jerusalem Bible
RSV     Revised Standard Version

**Library of Congress Cataloging-in-Publication Data**
(Revised for book 3)

Austin, Richard Cartwright, 1934–
   Environmental theology.

   Includes bibliographies and indexes.
   Contents: bk. 1. Baptized into wilderness —
bk. 2. Beauty of the Lord — bk. 3. Hope for the land.
   1. Nature—Religious aspects—Christianity. 2. Muir,
John, 1838 – 1914. 3. Edwards, Jonathan, 1703 – 1758.
I. Title.
BT695.5.A97 1987     231.7      87-45550
ISBN 0-8042-0869-7 (pbk. : v. 1)
ISBN 0-8042-0859-X (pbk. : v. 2)
ISBN 0-8042-0861-1 (pbk. : v. 3)

# Contents

Acknowledgments    v
Timeline for Biblical History    ix

**Introduction    1**
1. Abuse of Nature    1
2. Hearing the Word    8

**Part I. Liberation    17**
3. Hebrews in the Land    20
4. Covenant Promise    28
5. Jesus' Baptism    37

**Part II. Creativity    43**
6. God Creating    45
7. Image of God    51
8. Moral Creativity    60
9. Sexual Anxiety    70
10. Seventh Day Delight    78

**Part III. Sabbath Ecology    87**
11. The Land    89
12. Rights for Life    97
13. Jubilee    106
14. Jesus' Kingdom    115

**Part IV. The Fall    127**
15. Beautiful David    129
16. Solomon's Technique    140
17. The Serpent    150
18. Horses and Chariots    157
19. Pollution    164

**Part V. Ecological Visions    177**
20. Comparisons    179
21. The Day of the Lord    190
22. Redemption    200
23. Abundance    209
24. Peaceable Kingdom    218
25. The Lamb    227

Suggestions for Reading    235
Series Relationships    237
Notes    240
Index    253
Biblical Citations    258

# Acknowledgments

Scripture quotations from the Revised Standard Version of the Holy Bible, copyright 1946, 1952, and © 1971, 1973 by the Division of Christian Education, National Council of the Churches of Christ in the U.S.A. are used by permission.

Excerpts from **The New English Bible**. Copyright © the Delegates of the Oxford University Press and the Syndics of the Cambridge University Press, 1961, 1970. Reprinted by permission.

Excerpts from *The New Jerusalem Bible,* Copyright © 1985 and *The Jerusalem Bible,* Copyright © 1966 by Darton, Longman, & Todd, Ltd. and Doubleday, a division of Bantam, Doubleday and Dell Publishing Group, Inc. Reprinted by permission of the publisher.

Excerpt from "The Historical Roots of Our Ecological Crisis," White, L., Jr., *Science*, Vol. 155, pp. 1203–1207, 10 March 1967, Copyright 1967 by the American Association for the Advancement of Science. Reprinted by permission.

Excerpts from *The Message of the Psalms* by Walter Brueggemann, Copyright 1984, Augsburg Publishing House. Reprinted by permission.

Excerpts from *Exodus and Revolution* by Michael Walzer, Copyright © 1985, Basic Books. Reprinted by permission.

Excerpts from *Sexism and God-Talk* by Rosemary Radford Ruether, Copyright 1983 by Beacon Press. Reprinted by permission.

Selections from *Cry of the Environment: Rebuilding the Christian Creation Tradition*, edited by Philip N. Joranson and Ken Butigan, Copyright 1984, are used with permission of Bear & Company, P.O. Drawer 2860, Santa Fe, NM 87504.

Excerpts from *The Liberation of Life: From the Cell to the Community* by L.C. Birch and J.B. Cobb, Jr., copyright © 1981 Cambridge University Press. Reprinted by permission.

Excerpts from *Prairie Smoke* by Melvin R. Gilmore, copyright 1929 Columbia University Press. Reprinted by permission.

Excerpts from *The Politics of Jesus* by John Yoder, Copyright 1972 by Wm. B. Eerdmans Publishing Co. Reprinted by permission.

Excerpts from *God and the Rhetoric of Sexuality* by Phyllis Trible, Copyright 1978 by Fortress Press. Excerpts from *The Land* by Walter Brueggemann, Copyright 1977 by Fortress Press. Reprinted by permission.

Excerpts from *Deep Ecology: Living as if Nature Mattered* (1985) by Bill Devall and George Sessions, Gibbs M. Smith, Inc. Reprinted by permission.

Excerpts from *The Great Code* by Northrop Frye, Copyright 1982 Harcourt Brace Jovanovich, Inc. Reprinted by permission.

Excerpts from *God in Creation: A New Theology of Creation and the Spirit of God* by Jürgen Moltmann, English translation copyright © SCM Press Ltd., 1985, *Science in Christ* Copyright © 1969; *Od Testament Theology, vol. 1* by Gerhard von Rad, Copyright © 1962; *The Prophets* by Abraham J. Heschel, Copyright © 1969. Reprinted by permission of Harper & Row Publishers.

Excerpts from *Inclusive Language Lectionary*, Year A, Copyright © 1983; Year B, Copyright © 1984; Year C, Copyright © 1985 by the Division of Education and Ministry, National Council of the Churches of Christ in the U.S.A.

Excerpts from *The Tenth Generation: The Origins of the Biblical Tradition* by George E. Mendenhall, Copyright 1973 by The Johns Hopkins University Press. Reprinted by permission.

Excerpt from "Headlights at High Noon: A Silent Spring in Eastern Europe" by James Bovard, April 26, 1987, *The New York Times*. Copyright © 1987 by The New York Times Company. Reprinted by permission.

Excerpts from *Meeting the Expectations of the Land*, Copyright © 1984 by Wes Jackson, Wendell Berry and Bruce Colman and from *The Book of Job*, Copyright © 1987 by Stephen Mitchell. Published by North Point Press and reprinted by permission.

Excerpts from *Gaia: A New Look at Life on Earth* by J.E. Lovelock, Copyright 1979; *Israel: Its Life and Culture* by Johs. Pederson, Copyright 1926; *On Literacy* by Robert Pattison, Copyright 1982; *The Compact Edition of the Oxford English Dictionary*, Copyright 1971; "The Lamb" by William Blake in *Songs of Innocence*, Copyright 1967. Reprinted by permission of Oxford University Press.

Excerpts from *Saint Francis: Nature Mystic: the derivation and significance of the nature stories in the Franciscan Legend* by Edward A. Armstrong, Copyright 1983; and *Letters from Prison and Other Essays* by Adam Michnik, Copyright 1985. Reprinted by permission from the University of California Press.

Excerpts from the John Muir Papers, Holt-Atherton Pacific Center for Western Studies, University of the Pacific. Copyright 1984 Muir-Hanna Trust. Reprinted by permission.

Excerpts from *Genesis: A Commentary* (OTL) by Gerhard von Rad, Copyright 1961 by Westminster Press. Reprinted by permission.

Excerpts from *Our Demographically Divided World*, Worldwatch Paper 74, by Lester R. Brown and Jodi L. Jacobson, Copyright 1986. Reprinted by permission of the Worldwatch Institute.

# Dedication

In Memory of
Emma Cartwright Stroup, 1876–1971,
and
Russell Cartwright Stroup, 1905–1977.

When I was a young boy at their dinner table,
my Uncle Russell would read the Bible beautifully,
and Emma, my grandmother, would
discuss the readings with enthusiasm.
My love for the Bible grew from this soil.

# Timeline for Biblical History Discussed in *Hope for the Land*

| Century B.C | Events | People | Literature |
|---|---|---|---|
| 13th | Exodus from Egypt | *Moses* | 10 COMMANDMENTS |
| | Liberation of Canaan | *Joshua* | |
| 12th | | | |
| 11th | | | COVENANT CODE |
| 10th | United Monarchy | *David* | YAHWIST NARRATIVE |
| | | *Solomon* | |
| | Israel     <Divided Monarchy>     Judah<br>(northern)                   (southern) | | |
| 9th | *Ahab, Elijah* | | |
| 8th | *Amos*<br>*Hosea*<br>Fall of Samaria, 721 | *K. Hezekiah*     *Isaiah*<br>                *Micah* | |
| 7th | | *K. Josiah*     *Zephaniah*<br>        *Jeremiah, Ezekiel* | DEUTERONOMY<br>HOLINESS CODE |
| 6th | | Fall of Jerusalem, 587 | |
| | | Exile, "Babylonian Captivity" | JOB<br>PRIESTLY NARRATIVE |
| 5th | | *Second Isaiah* | |
| | | Nehemiah returns to<br>Jerusalem | |
| 4th | | | |
| 3rd | | | |
| 2nd | | | |
| 1st | | | |
| 1st | Jesus' ministry<br>Paul's ministry to Gentiles | | PAUL'S LETTERS<br>MARK, LUKE,<br>  MATTHEW<br>GOSPEL OF JOHN |
| A.D<br>100 | | | |

# Introduction

## 1. *Abuse of Nature*

Many who love the earth are concerned that biblical tradition may have motivated the human abuse of nature which now threatens the survival of life on this planet. Unintentionally, we who have gone forth in Jesus' name to save the world may also have contributed to its destruction. Modern Christians, therefore, need to express clearly a theology that supports life in all its complexity and environmental interdependence, so we may serve our Lord's interest in all creation.

During the 1960s Western society awakened to the fact that technological manipulation of nature, with its uncontrolled side effects, threatened fundamental life systems. In 1966, on the day after Christmas, a professor of history at the University of California spoke to the American Academy for the Advancement of Science on the topic "The Historical Roots of Our Ecological Crisis." Lynn White, Jr., at the close of his eloquent address, made a sobering accusation against a seemingly unlikely offender. "Christianity," he stated, "bears a huge burden of guilt." His historical analysis and his moral conclusion are now widely accepted among environmentalists.[1]

The vast power that modern culture wields over nature, White suggested, is the consequence of a nineteenth-century fusion of speculative science and pragmatic technology. This joining of creative energies resulted in turn from the democratic revolutions which had reduced social barriers between the philosopher and the artisan. Behind these developments were Western traditions of science and technology that had produced the Scientific Revolution of the seventeenth century and the Industrial Revolution of the eighteenth. And long before that, White affirmed, Western Christianity had encouraged the early emergence of technologies such as the moldboard plow, a tool that revolutionized agriculture in northern Europe. Christianity supported early scientists in their conviction that trying to understand natural processes—"to think God's thoughts after him" —had moral value. White argued, in fact, that the distinctive creation stories of the Bible lie at the very foundation of scientific tradition, because they convey assurance that the world was made for humanity:

> God planned all of this [earth] explicitly for man's benefit and rule: no item in the physical creation had any purpose save to serve man's purposes. . . . Christianity, in absolute contrast to ancient paganism and Asia's religions . . . not only established a dualism of man and nature but also insisted that it is God's will that man exploit nature for his proper ends.[2]

Wherever biblical monotheism spread, it challenged the animism prevalent in popular religious awareness. Believing that spirits inhabited trees, springs, hills, and other features of the landscape, common people had traditionally empathized with their environment and had sought to placate it while they used it. "By destroying pagan animism," White pointed out, "Christianity made it possible to exploit nature in a mood of indifference to the feelings of natural objects." Ronald Reagan, he noted, recently expressed this cultural indifference:

> The newly elected Governor of California, like myself a churchman but less troubled than I, spoke for the Christian tradition when he said (as is alleged), "when you've seen one redwood tree, you've seen them all." To a Christian a tree can be no more than a physical fact. The whole concept of the sacred grove is alien to Christianity and to the ethos of the West.[3]

White's argument has flaws. For example, if Christian imagery was so influential to the development of Western technologies which now overwhelm nature, why was there such a long hiatus between the time of Jesus and the seventeenth century when the pace of scientific discovery began to escalate? Nevertheless, the final prescription of White's address is sound: "More science and more technology are not going to get us out of the present ecologic crisis until we find a new religion, or rethink our old one." Although some have taken his words as a pretext to dismiss Christianity, White himself wished to rethink our faith. He recommended the example of Saint Francis of Assisi, who preached humility "not merely for the individual but for man as a species" and who recognized that all creation exists to glorify God, not just to serve human society. Saint Francis, White hopefully proposed, might serve as the "patron saint for ecologists."[4]

\* \* \*

While White spoke in Washington, D.C., I was spending my first Christmas in the Coal River Valley of southern West Virginia, where my own advocacy for nature was awakening. Earlier that year I had left a pastorate in the stylish Georgetown neighborhood of Washington to lead the Presbyterian Church's largest Appalachian mission project, within the poverty-stricken coalfields. Although I was an urban person, this was not my first rural experience. As a child I had attended a boarding school on a farm near Washington, where after morning classes we worked the fields. Later, graduating from theological seminary in New York City, I had organized a "larger parish" of five small churches in a farming and mining area of western Pennsylvania. I had gone there merely seeking the freedom to be creative, but I found myself on a strange and shocking battlefield. Modern technology in the form of giant shovels, bulldozers, and other strip-mining equipment was at war with the earth to extract coal. The people who lived among these once-beautiful hills often became casualties along with the landscape.

When I reached the West Virginia coalfields in 1966, I had equipped myself with an understanding of Appalachia's economics, the sociology of poverty, and the role of the church in community organizing. During the "War on Poverty" I was to be a lieutenant on the front lines. The battle against poverty, however, was disrupted by intense crossfire from the other battle, the assault of human technology upon the land. With a ferocity made desperate by hard times, those with capital were dismembering the hills, using dynamite and bulldozers to harvest coal cheaply. Meanwhile the displaced underground miners huddled in their "coal camp" shacks, threatened by rockslides from the strip mines high above them and also by rising water that rushed from the denuded hills through creekbeds choked with debris. The spring of 1967 brought a devastating flood. Some church members joined a successful effort to obtain a state law regulating strip-mining, but after the law was passed the state government was too weak to enforce it. The hills surrounding my house were soon under attack by a strip-miner who was also a state senator. After five years' ministry, I took a leave of absence to lead a campaign against strip-mining in West Virginia; this effort failed. Later, I helped to organize a national campaign for a federal law regulating strip-mining for coal, which met with success.

These struggles in unfamiliar terrain drove me to plumb the depths of my own faith and to search the Scriptures for guidance. I felt called to fight this human assault upon the earth. When I resumed my formal ministry I obtained permission to specialize in the relationship of Christian faith to environmental concerns. I began to see biblical evidence, previously overlooked by most Christians, that places nature in covenant history, in moral responsibility, and in the promised kingdom. My first insights—the germ of this book—appeared in a 1977 essay called "Toward Environmental Theology."[5]

\* \* \*

Because the Scriptures express moral relationships among God, humanity, and the full range of life and life-support on this planet, they can help inform our faith and guide our conduct amid the modern environmental crisis. Hebrews developed a complex understanding of the relationships among species sharing the same habitat—a moral perspective, not a technical theory—which I call a *biblical ecology*. Liberation is my opening theme. God began work of salvation by rescuing from oppression and sin those who would come to know and serve the Lord; and the biblical memory of liberation includes not just oppressed people, but also oppressed lands. The words *covenant* and *promise* apply to the range of created life as well as to human beings.

I then explore the moral character of creativity. Unlike Lynn White, I see in the Genesis creation stories a God who delights in all life and who gives men and women the vocation to nurture the world's abundance. This creativity, including but transcending sexuality, is the ongoing artistry of a vast congregation. Many creatures and natural forms build life, coming together in awareness, nourishment, and delight.

Biblical ethics do not attribute holiness to features of the landscape. Instead they draw all of life—domestic creatures, wild creatures, and the land itself—into the politics of the covenant relationship where each has distinctive rights and duties. Stories of "the fall" express how such moral relationships have broken apart to yield sin, oppression, and pollution. Jesus' call for a new kingdom is a call not to withdraw from the world, but to make these relationships right. The heart of the biblical hope is a desire to reestablish a nurturing ecosystem of peace among all peoples and with all species, so that each may live while all worship the Lord together.

I am indebted to several scholars who have contributed to my biblical reflection. In 1962 George Mendenhall published his seminal thesis, "The Hebrew Conquest of Palestine," which suggested that the tribal confederation of Israel had resulted from peasant revolts against Palestinian feudalism, revolts stimulated by Hebrew invaders who carried a message of responsible freedom under YHWH, the Lord. I build from Mendenhall's work to suggest a biblical "liberation theology," including the land itself as well as its inhabitants.[6] Among contemporary biblical scholars, Walter Brueggemann has most thoroughly explored the role of land in the development of Hebrew faith, community, and ethics.[7] Land is an active partner in biblical religion. Brueggemann's insights contain a moral vigor which I have found inspiring. My thinking on the place of nature in biblical ethics remained incomplete until I read John Howard Yoder's study *The Politics of Jesus.*[8] Yoder suggests that Jesus' call for a new kingdom revived the biblical *jubilee,* the year to restore

equity among persons and moral relationships with the land as
well.

Imagining a biblical ecology requires overcoming hierarchical patterns of thought in order to convey more lively relationships; I would not find this possible without help from
contemporary feminist theologians and biblical scholars, and I
am especially grateful to Rosemary Radford Ruether and Phyllis
Trible. George Landes, Professor of Hebrew at Union Theological
Seminary in New York, has reviewed this manuscript, gener-
ously commenting on my use of biblical material and assisting me
with points of translation. The mistakes which remain are mine,
but at least there are fewer of them.

I gladly use these fruits of modern scholarship to assist my
interpretation of the Bible, though I caution the reader that since
I am not an academic scholar I may have overlooked some
research. The dialogue between God and the Hebrew people was
expressed in events and conduct as well as words; thus I find
inspiration not just in the words of Scripture but in the events
glimpsed through the official text. Like any biblical study, this
one is selective. While I attend to the history and images that cry
out with relevance to our environmental crisis, I pass by many
passages that do not call so insistently. I prefer not to argue with
other viewpoints, though I occasionally mention another perspective to clarify my position. I strive to listen honestly to the
Scriptures and to write fairly for the reader.

I love the beauty of Scripture, not just its cognitive meaning but also its emotional color. When quoting, I select among
several English versions. The majestic King James Version (KJV),
which has graced and shaped the English language, was published in London in 1611; I have quoted the Westminster Study
Edition (1948) in order to set prose in paragraphs and poetry in
verse. American scholars, who prepared the Revised Standard
Version (RSV) in 1946, 1952, and 1971, used ancient Hebrew and
Greek biblical manuscripts to correct the King James Version
and modernize its usage. English scholars followed similar principles to produce the New English Bible (NEB) in 1961 and 1970,
often with graceful results. Roman Catholic scholars working in

Jerusalem from ancient texts created a modern French version and then an English version, the Jerusalem Bible (JB), in 1966; it provides stimulating alternatives because the phrasing is not influenced by the King James Version. The New Jerusalem Bible (NJB), 1985, has revised this text and reduced sexist language. *An Inclusive Language Lectionary* (ILL), 1983–85, revises many RSV passages to remove sexist language. Sometimes I construct a fresh rendering, though since my facility with biblical languages is limited, I review such translations with a competent scholar. I alert the reader if a version is my own.[9]

I commonly emend biblical quotations to remove pronouns that suggest the Lord has gender: changed words appear in brackets and the reference includes the note "alt." In my own writing I also avoid using gender-specific language to refer to the biblical Lord, but I do not change words from other writers whom I quote.[10]

# 2. *Hearing the Word*

John Donne (1571–1631) was a poet of love and a lover of words during the most formative period of the English language. He became also a lover of God's Word and a leading preacher. In one sermon he addressed God concerning God's own words:

> My God, my God, Thou art a direct God, may I not say a literall God, a God that wouldest bee understood literally, and according to the plaine sense of all that thou saiest? But thou art also (Lord I intend it to thy glory, and let no prophane misinterpreter abuse it to thy diminution) thou art a figurative, a metaphoricall God too; A God in whose words there is such a height of figures, such voyages, such peregrinations to fetch remote and precious metaphors, such extensions, such spreadings, such Curtaines of Allegories, such third Heavens of Hyperboles, so harmonious eloquutions, so retired and so reserved expressions, so commanding perswasions, so perswading commandments, such sinewes even in thy milk, and such things in thy words, as all prophane Authors, seeme of the seed of the Serpent, that creepes, thou art the Dove, that flies. O, what words but thine, can expresse the inexpressible texture, and composition of thy word.

Even in this rapturous praise, however, Donne noted that God's word may not seem equally expressive to everyone. If two persons were considering a portion of Scripture, Donne observed, "one [might] wonder, that all should not understand it, and the other, as much, that any  man should."[1] Today Donne would encounter even more persons perplexed that anyone could understand God speaking through the Bible; many of these, in fact, now also doubt it is worth the effort to try. Donne would today meet others who cling anxiously to a biblical literalism, fearful lest one shrill note of contradiction shatter the whole splendid crystal vase of truth. He would not feel at home with either. I imagine Donne would search instead for those persons, whatever their theology, who could still be surprised by God's words and delighted by what they heard.

Donne understood that the God manifest in Hebrew and Christian Scriptures finds lyrical, powerful expression through words. When read with an openness to fresh discovery, the communications of the biblical Lord awaken the hearer, arouse strong emotions, suggest far-reaching meanings, and stimulate purposeful response. They forge a relationship marked by a quality I have called "moral beauty." Although all of us would probably consider ourselves well acquainted with words, since we use them with such versatility in our daily discourse, we rarely encounter words' affecting power—their capacity to enlarge both heart and mind. In the Bible, however, we can find a compendium of such rare occasions, moments of special communication experienced by people remote from us in time and different from us in culture.

Much of the Old Testament, as well as the Gospels in the New Testament, emerged from cultures steeped in oral tradition. Stories and sayings were handed down by word of mouth. Sages, storytellers, poets, and teachers, skilled in transmitting these prized words that transcended daily life, relied on stylistic devices to aid memory. Using rhythm, rhyme, repetition, and vivid characterization, they artfully engaged listeners' feelings to convey the insights that made such narration so valuable. Because the language was engaging, people savored the words, much as David did in the Psalms:

> How sweet are thy words to my taste,
> sweeter than honey to my mouth! . . .
> Thy word is a lamp to my feet
> and a light to my path.
> (Psalm 119:103, 105, RSV)

Words tied the past to the present, so that feelings and insights flowed memorably to the hearer. These powerful words that transcended the commonplace to communicate emotion and meaning were properly considered divine. They had the capacity to change people's hearts and lives, as the Bible records:

> For, as the rain and the snow come down from the sky
> and do not return before having watered the earth,
> fertilising it and making it germinate
> to provide seed for the sower and food to eat,
> so it is with the word that goes from my mouth:
> it will not return to me unfulfilled
> or before having carried out my good pleasure
> and having achieved what it was sent to do.
>                                                    (Isaiah 55:10–11, NJB)

In many cultures, however, writing gradually supplanted the active functions of oral tradition. When the past was thus reduced to written words, part of the people's emotional relationship with it was lost. Literary critic Northrop Frye explains that "the ability to record has a lot more to do with forgetting than with remembering; with keeping the past in the past, instead of continuously recreating it in the present."[2] In ancient Greece Plato had inaugurated another use of language which would set the style for philosophical and religious reflection during the Roman and medieval periods: he wrote down words as the outward expressions of inner thoughts. When the thinker stands back from the thought, Frye comments, "the intellectual operations of the mind become distinguishable from the emotional operations."[3] Such reflection stimulated abstraction and the development of logic. When Jews and early Christians carried the biblical tradition into the Greek-speaking world of written reflection, they conformed to Platonic tradition and used the forms of doctrine and theology to express their convictions rationally. These forms eventually became authoritative over the language of story; and in the Christian era, the rational frame of mind came to rule even the interpretation of Scripture.

A third use of language, different both from storytelling and from abstraction, sprang up in the sixteenth century.

Northrop Frye writes that Francis Bacon, a leader in the scientific revolution, first employed language to document objective observation. Renaissance scientists who were intent on observing and manipulating the natural world scorned traditional reasoning, with conclusions implied in the premises, as a circular intellectual game isolated from the world. *Things* were now "real"; ideas and ideals, once the "real" world of philosophers and theologians, faded. Language came to be understood as properly descriptive of an objective natural order which we experience through our senses. So that they might use words precisely, scientists sought detachment from objects under their scrutiny: neither emotions nor prior knowledge should invade their observations. Language, like data, was deemed most truthful when not charged with extraneous meaning or personal feeling.

The God of the Bible—whose word went forth but whose face remained hidden—did not fit tidily into scientific communication. Human experience of this God was usually intangible and ambiguous; the Lord was not available for dispassionate examination. Although John Donne could embrace the sublime mystery of God's word, some intellectuals attempted to modernize God's image, proposing either a remote cosmic clock maker, or a generalized foundation for existence. Skeptics later came to doubt the relevance of even these images.

* * *

The first Bible I read was the newly-published Revised Standard Version New Testament, received on my twelfth Christmas from my Uncle Don, who suspected I might need help. This was a troubled time. My recently-divorced parents were competing for my favor, and the stirrings of adolescence were causing me anxiety. That spring I marked biblical passages on human sinfulness, on sexual regulation, on not loving the world, and on girding oneself with the whole armor of God. The words I heard as God's were those offering a clear, even rigorous standard that I might adopt as protection from the confusion around me and within me.

A few years later I heard God's call to faith and ministry.

Then biblical words of promise, hope, and purpose were the words
I savored. Sitting in the bass section of the church choir, I reveled
in God's joyful word interpreted by Bach's music when we sang
"God the Lord is sun and shield." During my college years and in
seminary, desperate to understand, I wrestled with Paul's letter
to Romans just as Jacob wrestled with God's angel, until it
blessed me with insight. Still later, as a young pastor preparing
a sermon, I often became so absorbed by the text I was studying
that I would veer off in an entirely new direction. To my congregation I would preach—and also to myself—a word I had just
heard.

   My love affair with the Bible has now continued for forty
years. As in any long, stimulating relationship, some beauties
fade, but new delights appear. I take issue with a few of the passages which in my youth I marked; now a more mature lover, I can
acknowledge some disagreements. However, when in prepara-
tion for this book I read the full Bible again—for perhaps the
fourth or fifth time in my life—I was astonished to encounter
scores of passages I had never noticed before, passages that
excited me with their beauty and drove my thought forward to
new insights.

   I have come to understand that the "word of God" is
personal. The connecting force in God's word is not truth or
doctrine, but the personality of God engaging particular human
personalities. The Old Testament is awash with God's passions,
including both love and anger, expressing a Being of abiding
purpose who sometimes changes mind and strategy. Some have
found this "anthropomorphism" in the biblical accounts offensive, but it is the heart of the recorded meetings. God is not a
principle, however lofty, but a *personality* revealed through expressive actions, a Being complex enough to appear, at times,
contradictory. This distinctive personality, more than any other
characteristic, separates YHWH, the Lord, from all human idols
whether carved crudely from wood or crafted with the translu-
cence of philosophical abstraction. All of us inevitably mix some
idolatry with our faith: since the process of knowing God is
interactive, we shape the faith which we make our own. Never-

theless, as our relationship with God develops, our appreciation of the Lord's character may clarify.

Jesus Christ is the word of God at its most personal and expressive. Though there is much about God which we learn elsewhere, for Jesus did not teach everything, in Jesus we meet God directly, made flesh for us, made plain and personal. We treasure Jesus' teachings, but we are saved by the death which is God's most radical expression of love for us. We are shown, in Jesus, the living God who condescends to us. The Holy Spirit, of the Three whom Christians acknowledge to be God, may seem to manifest the least personality. *Spirit* is an elusive word, but it always represents God engaged with the world. The Spirit dwells within other lives, expanding and enriching them; its personality comprises all the new characteristics of those it has touched. In this way God continues to condescend, bringing life to a beloved world.

Therefore, when the church calls the Bible the Word of God, it is both remembering and anticipating. Particular stories and sayings have entered the canon of Hebrew and Christian Scriptures and have survived numerous editings because they have been "word of God" to some who heard them, helping to bring persons together with the Lord in relationships of meaning and purpose. The church cherishes and disseminates these Scriptures in confidence that they will, often and again, fire the imaginations of new hearers despite the widening gulf of time and cultural difference.

No one text inspires every believer, and there are some passages which, in a particular age and culture, may inspire none. Insight results from a complex interaction involving the needs and dispositions of an individual, cultural and religious influences, and God's own gracious approach. A Scripture may become "word of God" when it actively inspires an individual or takes on symbolic meaning for a group, an age, or a culture. Martin Luther, for example, had surely read Paul's letter to the Romans many times before the one time when the phrase "the just shall live by faith" (Romans 1:17, KJV) caught his imagination and transformed his outlook, becoming his distinctive word from

God. Because Luther's spiritual struggle mirrored the need of his age, his rediscovery of this text made it God's word for his generation as well.[4]

It is therefore not surprising that precisely when a text is "word of God," it may take on different meanings for different persons. All can agree on a matter of indifference; passages that seem to affect no one are not, in that age, items for dispute. When a word from God, however, speaks to many in one age, those who are touched by it may disagree with one another over nuances of such a precious insight. This is the word of God at work—the Spirit animating different personalities and consequently affecting society. The record of human experiences within the Bible leads us to expect such variety; so also does the history of those who have loved God's words during the two millennia since Jesus.

This perspective is different from "relativism." We are met by a living God who is not simply the product of cultural or religious imagination. Yet the words of God require engaged listening, for they make little sense within that dispassionate, objective language which scientists use and modern culture values so highly. God's words have a moral beauty that gives them power distinct from the energies physics can measure. They are not, to be sure, bullets from beyond which hold their shape perfectly as they pierce our consciousness. Rather, they bring together personalities: ours with God's, ours with those of others who hear the words. They require apprehension, the "ears to hear" for which Jesus pleaded. When we apprehend something beautiful and make it our own, we modify it in the process. We create as we are created.

Our culture blesses us with language, images, training, and experience, without which our awareness would be rude indeed. All this cultural equipment, however, tends to define what we can hear, helping us to notice some meanings and teaching us to ignore other possibilities. The history of biblical religions proves that culture profoundly affects the human dialogue with God. Themes that seem central in one age may nearly vanish in another. It is also clear that this God, so restless and demanding, whose word interrupts the busy flow of human life to insist on justice and compassion, has changed society. The words of the Lord, over and again, have shaken a complacent society to its foundations, or called together those most desperate to build a new life. It is worth our while to listen for God's word.

The chapters that follow share some familiar biblical words which have taken on new meanings for me. I hear new things because I have been living, alert and anxious, on the war-torn frontier where human society confronts the other creatures who share this planet with us. It is troubling to hear meanings which the church does not appear to have heard before. Are these "voices" no more than vibrations from my own anxiety? Am I, perhaps, obscuring the environmental problem by addressing it with words from an archaic, irrelevant faith? Or does God wish me to speak for the forms of life who cannot use human language, those crushed beneath the advancing cleats of the bulldozer?

Readers will have to decide for themselves. In ancient Israel and subsequently in cultures influenced by the biblical tradition, prophets hearing God's word challenged their society with new demands or unexpected promises. Court prophets, however, spoke what was in style, while other excitable speakers cried whatever came into their heads. There were no clear marks to help the public distinguish one from another. Each spoke the truth sometimes, and surely the best and most holy was occasionally in error. In a society which tolerates prophecy, the public must listen with discernment so that God's word may come not from, but through, the prophet.

Meanwhile, the bearer of a novel message has every reason to tremble when presenting words that cannot, in any case, be held back. When Jeremiah contemplated his audience he felt both anxious and foolish, yet he found speaking easier than the discomfort of silence:

> You have seduced me, Yahweh, and I have let myself be
>     seduced;
> you have overpowered me: you were the stronger.
> I am a daily laughing-stock,
> everybody's butt.
> Each time I speak the word, I have to howl

and proclaim: "Violence and ruin!" . . .
I used to say, "I will not think about [Yahweh],
I will not speak in [God's] name any more."
Then there seemed to be a fire burning in my heart,
imprisoned in my bones.
The effort to restrain it wearied **me**,
I could not bear it.

(Jeremiah 20:7–9, JB, alt.)

# Part I.

# *Liberation*

A "doctor of the law" told Jesus, "Master, I will follow you wherever you go." Jesus replied, "Foxes have their holes, the birds their roosts; but the Son of Man has nowhere to lay his head" (Matthew 8:19–20, NEB). Here, as so frequently, Jesus identified himself with the dispossessed. He warned this establishment admirer not to expect comfort in his company until things are put right in God's kingdom. Until then, Jesus and those who traveled with him would share the lot of the homeless.

Dispossession and repossession is an important recurring biblical theme, to which modern Christians are becoming sensitive. Those of us who are white, male, affluent Christians have had to notice the struggles for a better share of life by black, brown, red, and yellow peoples, by women, and by poor people within Western borders and in the Third World. Some of these have laid claim to the biblical drama itself in support of their ambition. Blacks identified with the Exodus and claimed the witness of the prophets during American civil rights struggles in the 1960s. In Latin America and the Philippines, which have a Roman Catholic tradition, some religious leaders have joined with poor people to form "base communities" that have shaped "liberation theology" into a potent spiritual, social, and political force. They claim Jesus as companion in their dispossession. Religious women, including many aroused by their experience of discrimination within their Christian community, have also responded with theological sophistication and prophetic vigor.

In biblical history this theme of dispossession and repossession appears primarily in relation to the "promised land" which had been offered by the Lord in return for faithfulness, justice, and compassion. A people who remembered slavery now wanted to live on the land in freedom. They dreamed of "a land flowing with milk and honey" (Exodus 3:8, KJV)—a watered land with grass and flowers where a family could take surplus honey from beehives and graze a small, private flock of sheep or goats for meat and milk. The biblical vision of freedom within a responsible community extended beyond the human family to include the land itself and those creatures, wild and domestic, who shared the land with God's people. It was a vision rooted in the knowledge of oppression and filled with memories of human bondage, abused creatures, and damaged landscapes.

This promise of liberation, discovered in escape from Egypt, shaped a cry that crumbled the walls of oppression surrounding Jericho and other city-states within the promised land. The covenant that created this liberated biblical community embraced not just faithful people but the land itself and the range of created life. Ultimately, God's incarnation in Jesus Christ pledged freedom for all creatures, and thus it bears strongly on the modern environmental crisis.

The Bible's ecological perspective is remarkable, for it brings nature within the community of covenant love and moral responsibility. The Lord tends a landscape which, though often injured by human oppression, yearns to flourish under just treatment and, beyond that, to respond compassionately to human needs. Abused land, like afflicted people, may yet hope for liberation:

> [The Lord] turns rivers into desert
> and springs of water into thirsty ground;
> [God] turns fruitful land into salt waste,
> because the [people] who dwell there are so wicked.
> Desert [the Lord] changes into standing pools,
> and parched land into springs of water.
> There [God] gives the hungry a home,

and they build themselves a city to live in;
they sow fields and plant vineyards
  and reap a fruitful harvest.
[God] blesses them and their numbers increase,
  and [God] does not let their herds lose strength.
Tyrants lose their strength and are brought low
  in the grip of misfortune and sorrow;
[God] brings princes into contempt
  and leaves them wandering in a trackless waste.
But the poor . . . [the Lord] lifts clear of . . . troubles
  and makes families increase like flocks of sheep.

(Psalm 107:33–41, NEB, alt.)

# 3. *Hebrews in the Land*

During the thirteenth century before Christ, the empires that had dominated the world of the ancient Near East entered periods of decline. From Troy to the borders of Persia, a dark age began that would continue for two centuries. In Palestine the dozens of tiny city-states, which had paid tribute to the great powers in return for protection, were now free to pursue savage competition with each other. "With very few exceptions," George Mendenhall writes, "every excavated site from Palestine and Syria to Greece shows the remains of destruction by violence during the period from 1250 to 1150 B.C."[1] As trade declined and warfare increased, the petty tyrants of these towns leaned on their subjects more heavily, extracting taxes and conscripting fighters. Wells, springs, and forests were destroyed and farmland scorched in the tyrants' efforts to terrorize into allegiance those outside the walled towns and to deprive hostile communities of food and fuel.[2]

In Egypt the reigning pharaoh responded to economic decline by increasing the pressure on his forced labor crews, requiring those who made bricks, as the Bible reports, to gather their own materials while maintaining previous levels of production.[3] One band of such workers, led by a gifted organizer, Moses, managed to escape along with their families; aided by favorable winds and tides, this little band eluded a pursuing regiment by crossing the Red Sea and disappearing into the Sinai wilderness. Although some within this group had ancestral roots in Palestine, others were ethnically diverse, "a mixed company of strangers" (Numbers 11:4, NEB). Surely other groups had also fled Egyptian oppression, but this one stood to influence the course of world history.

Moses led the group to meet YHWH, the Lord, the deity introduced to him by his father-in-law Jethro and the One who, he believed, had summoned him to his vocation. Speaking through Moses, the Lord offered this mixed company an extraordinary agreement. If they would vow allegiance to the Lord alone, God would make them "my kingdom of priests, my holy nation" (Exodus 19:5, NEB). In other words, the Lord would set them free from political obligations. They could declare themselves exempt, like priests, from any king's taxation; they would owe loyalty only to the Lord. In return, however, they must obey the Lord radically. Furthermore, the Lord proposed a revolutionary standard of obedience. Instead of receiving capricious demands like those of their former taskmasters in Egypt, the people were issued, through Moses, a set of permanent instructions which everyone could understand—ten words that began with the duty to serve only the Lord and ended with an order not to covet what belonged to another. These commandments would not be easy to follow, but they were clear; and compared to the arbitrary obedience required by earthly rulers, they were a charter of liberty. Once having taken these laws into the heart, a person could do *"that which was* right in his [or her] own eyes" without submission to another human authority (Judges 21:25, KJV, alt.). This was an unprecedented opportunity for freedom. The people responded, "All that the LORD has spoken we will do" (Exodus 19:8, RSV).

Decades of hardship followed as the band wandered in the wilderness, unable to reach a promising place for settlement. During this time, however, a new generation matured, younger people without the servile, passive mentality that many of their parents had carried with them from Egypt. Rebellious and independent, this new group must have seemed like hardened outlaws, although historically they were merely free people who had broken away from the repressive style of late Bronze Age culture.

They were Hebrews. At length the wanderers reached the Transjordan area northeast of Palestine, which was then attracting settlers from various regions. Here, according to a theory first proposed by George Mendenhall, the band began to forge a social compact unprecedented in human history.

This is not the only band of "Hebrews" of whom we have evidence, for a similar name appears in several nonbiblical texts recovered from this age. The word refers to outlaws in general, but sometimes specifically indicates those who have renounced their customary political allegiance. As the power of states to enforce their authority diminished during this era, "Hebrews" became a growing problem; on an Amarna tablet, for example, a provincial administrator complains of them to the king of Egypt.[4]

In Transjordan Moses and his followers apparently persuaded a significant part of the resident population to abandon their allegiances to various city-states and covenant with their group instead. These dissidents withdrew their fields, as well as their persons, from taxation and the other claims of political authority, but they bound themselves to defend one another against attempts by their former princes to reassert control. They became Hebrews together, rejecting in the name of the Lord the predatory powers of the region. Members of this new confederation then settled their claims to lands and fields among themselves, ratifying their understanding before the Lord. These Hebrews eventually organized into the biblical tribes of Reuben and Gad and a portion of the tribe of Manasseh. The Transjordan covenant was Moses' last great achievement before his death; a memory of it survives in Deuteronomy, chapters 29–31, as the second giving of the law.[5]

When Joshua assumed leadership of this enlarged alliance of Hebrews, he extended Moses' strategy with fresh vigor. The consequences were stunning: Hebrews crossed the Jordan into Palestine. There were some pitched battles, but the principal technique was what we now call guerrilla infiltration. The Hebrews' major weapon was a call to freedom in the name of the new Lord, YHWH. Their "spies" were warmly received by some of the underclass who had already heard stories of this god. Some cities crumbled from within, while a number of walled towns were bypassed until later.[6] Joshua's infiltrators concentrated on the countryside and those towns ripe for rebellion. It would be 150 years before Jerusalem, one of the strongest citadels, was overrun by Hebrews under David's leadership. The goal of Joshua's snowballing revolution was not to make war, but to find peace and security in a land where the old order was devouring itself.

At the climax of this process Joshua gathered from throughout Palestine and Transjordan people ready to renounce the jurisdiction of traditional rulers. They met at Shechem for a third solemn covenant ceremony. When Joshua challenged them, "Choose you this day whom ye will serve," they responded, "The LORD our God will we serve, and [God's] voice will we obey" (Joshua 24:15, 24, KJV, alt.). They organized into twelve tribes and became Israel. This confederation was a precarious, unlikely phenomenon. In rebellion against familiar patterns of authority, it renounced all formal leadership and relied for over a century on charismatic "judges" who responded to the Lord's messages in emergencies and whose authority depended on recognition by members of the confederation. A number of Canaanite kings retained control of cities within the area Israel hoped to pacify. A rival confederation, the Philistines, later emerged to create confusion even among Israel's charismatic leaders. The book of Judges reads, in places, like darkest anarchy. Nevertheless, tribal memories of oppression were so acute, the desire for peace and freedom was so strong, and loyalty to the Lord so robust that the confederation of Israel continued to grow until, under David, it fully secured a homeland and briefly enjoyed real peace. Long after King Solomon disemboweled this social experiment, the moral principles upon which it had been based continued to influence the prophetic tradition as well as other streams of Hebrew religious reflection.

I have followed George Mendenhall in this historical reconstruction which contrasts sharply, at points, with the impression created by the biblical record of the period. "In summary," Mendenhall writes, "there was no real conquest of Palestine at all; what happened instead may be termed . . . a peasant's revolt against the network of interlocking Canaanite city states." The grand slaughter over which some biblical accounts gloat, and which has offended some modern sensibilities, was evidently the exaggerated construction of subsequent patriotic editors. Mendenhall concludes,

> The appearance of the small religious community of Israel polarized the existing population all over the land; some joined, others, primarily the kings and their supporters, fought. Since the kings were defeated and forced out, this became the source of the tradition that all the Canaanites and Amorites were either driven out or slain en masse, for the only ones left were the predominant majority in each area—now Israelites.[7]

Twelve tribes did not arrive in Transjordan from Egypt, nor did Israel confederate existing tribes. The twelve tribes were geographical and religious constructions, a theocratic reorganization of people and land fashioned within Palestine to express a new identity. The escape from Egypt and the covenant with the Lord at Sinai, experiences which created this revolutionary identity, in time came to be accepted by all as their heritage. Ancestral memories held by various local communities in Canaan eventually blended together and harmonized with the people's allegiance to the Lord. Many of these memories are preserved in the book of Genesis as the traditions of the Patriarchs.

* * *

This brief description of the formation of Israel brings into focus early Hebrew convictions concerning peace, social equity, and the "holy" land. The Hebrews' revolution was rooted not in a lust for conquest, but in a yearning for security and peace. Those who had been oppressed in Canaan, Transjordan, or Egypt shared a common desire: that they might "sit every man under his vine and under his fig tree;/And none shall make *them* afraid" (Micah 4:4, KJV). Several characteristics of the Hebrew faith were direct responses to this desire. One was the prohibition of blood vengeance—a practice common in simple societies whereby an aggrieved family revenged the death or injury of one of its members by ambushing a member of the family under suspicion. In the ancient "Song of Moses," however, the Lord declared,

> Vengeance is mine, and recompense, . . .
> For the LORD will vindicate [God's] people.
> (Deuteronomy 32:35–36, RSV, alt.)

The frequent repetition of this thought in the Bible has led some to imagine that this God is vengeful and ill-tempered, but in fact, the Lord's claim to vengeance helped maintain peace among the families of Israel. Where human vengeance was permitted, following a formal religious inquiry, it was restricted: "eye for eye, tooth for tooth, hand for hand," nothing more (Exodus 2:24, KJV).

Similarly, only the Lord had authority to call Israel to war. People in Canaan had dreaded conscription, but within the covenant of Israel no civil authority could declare war or require service. Only the Lord, speaking through an inspired judge or tribal assembly, could do so. Since there was no fixed authority and no coercion, any cause had to appeal to the people who had the moral obligation to respond. This was not a pacifist ethic but rather a strategy to discourage gratuitous conflict. The politics of Canaan were based upon the power to coerce obedience. Israel's covenant, by contrast, was grounded in the people's God-given conviction that the instruments of human dominion should be neither feared nor relied upon:

> Some call on chariots, some on horses,
> but we on the name of Yahweh our God.
> (Psalm 20:7, NJB)

The Hebrew covenant community also rejected those elements of political hierarchy and social stratification which had, in their experience, become especially oppressive. The typical functions of a ruler—making war, promulgating laws, establishing religion—were reserved for the Lord alone. Even personal claims to achievement were discouraged because they implied a hierarchy of worth or an obligation from one's beneficiaries:

> Let not the wise man boast of his wisdom
> nor the valiant of his valour . . .

> but if any man would boast, let him boast of this,
> that he understands and knows me.
> For I am the LORD.
>
> (Jeremiah 9:23–24, NEB)

At the bottom of the social hierarchy, slavery was discouraged. Voluntary indenture was permitted, but Israel had no machinery to compel the return of runaways.[8] Although society remained patriarchal in the sense that men retained authority over women and children, the Hebrew religion was not patterned upon authoritarian social hierarchies. The Hebrew covenant vision was profoundly revolutionary and, in the context of its times, relatively egalitarian. As Mendenhall argues, the covenant with the Lord was a commitment to place ethical concerns ahead of status and power. It presented

> a new religious synthesis based upon the subordination of power to ethic and [the subordination of] economic concerns to human relationships. . . . The basis of this religion was the rejection of control of human beings by force, and the proclamation that only God was in control—through the voluntary subjection of all members of the community to those policies of the sovereign stipulated in the Decalogue-Covenant.[9]

The covenant understanding of land is the characteristic of Hebrew faith most important to the quest for a biblical ecology. In Egypt those who became Hebrews had been reduced to forced labor: working the lands, mines, and manufactures owned by the pharaoh. Peasants in Canaan had labored under a feudal system where ownership of land resided in a nearby prince and through him, perhaps, in a distant king; their tenancy had depended on the fortunes of war and politics and was subject to arbitrary redefinition. Individual ownership would not have been an option for the Hebrews, even if they had been able to imagine it, because by rejecting the state they removed the authority which could protect private property. Instead, the Lord's claim to the land prevailed. Like the people themselves at Sinai, the land was declared *holy,* removed from politics to the realm of ethical decision: "for the land belongs to me, and you are only strangers and guests of mine" (Leviticus 25:23, NJB). When the holdings of tribes were formally recognized under the covenant, each family received a share not from a political authority but directly from God. Rights of tenancy became a sacred, religious concern, to be zealously protected from power politics and economic manipulation.

Thus the land was included within the circle of ethical reflection at the heart of the Hebrew covenant. Since the promised land was an object of ethical concern, human obligations to a landscape and to other creatures who lived there could be considered. At the greatest breadth of this reflection, the Hebrews struggled to appreciate what it meant to serve a God who was not a tribal deity tied to a particular landscape: "All the earth is mine, and you shall be to me a kingdom of priests and a holy nation" (Exodus 19:5–6, RSV). At its greatest depth, they tried to appreciate the claims of all animals, domestic and wild, who shared the land with them, as well as the rights of the land itself. All these belonged together within the covenant community.

Meanwhile, living freely as God's people upon holy land gave the Hebrews dignity and hope:

> If you live according to my laws, if you keep my commandments and put them into practice, I shall give you the rain you need at the right time; the soil will yield its produce and the trees of the countryside their fruit . . . .
> I shall give peace in the land, and you will go to sleep with no one to frighten you.
> . . . I shall live among you; I shall be your God and you will be my people, I, Yahweh your God, who brought you out of Egypt so that you should be their slaves no longer, and who broke the bonds of your yoke and made you to walk with head held high.
> (Leviticus 26:3–4, 6, 12–13, NJB)

# 4. *Covenant Promise*

The ancient "Song of Miriam" recalled the people's deliverance at the Red Sea:

> Sing to the [Lord], who has triumphed gloriously;
> the horse and the rider God has thrown into the sea.
> (Exodus 15:21, ILL, alt.[1])

Sung by the Hebrews during their Sinai wanderings, it celebrated the Lord's power over both the political and the natural environments. The sea had been tamed to serve God's purpose, while the horse, part of the technology of oppression, had shared the fate of its rider. Confidence that God could influence nature was important to these Hebrews, for to such an unprepared group, the Sinai wilderness was a worrisome place. The Lord helped by providing both water and food, and responded to the people's anxiety with training in trust and discipline. Although after a generation the Hebrews undoubtedly acquired the skills to live amid this sparse, wild landscape, their growing knowledge of nature does not appear in the biblical records—perhaps because in Canaan, where these accounts were written, the indigenous Baal cults encouraged a superstitious, manipulative approach to nature. The Hebrews needed to secure the ethical foundations of their revolutionary perspective before they could open their eyes to engage the natural world with confidence; as the Lord had decreed, "You must keep all my laws, all my customs, and put them into practice: thus you will not be vomited out by the land where I am taking you to live" (Leviticus 20:22, JB).

In another ancient song from the time of the judges, the prophet Deborah sang of a victory by poorly-armed Hebrews who overran a Canaanite chariot corps because a timely downpour mired the chariot wheels. In ascribing this triumph to the Lord, Deborah emphasized the enthusiasm with which nature responded to God's commands:

> O LORD, at thy setting forth from Seir,
> when thou camest marching out of the plains of Edom,
> earth trembled; heaven quaked;
> the clouds streamed down in torrents.
> Mountains shook in fear before the LORD, the lord of Sinai,
> before the LORD, the God of Israel.
> . . . . . . . . . . . . . . . . . . . . . . . . . .
> The stars fought from heaven,
> the stars in their courses fought against Sisera.
> The Torrent of Kishon swept him away,
> the Torrent barred his flight, the Torrent of Kishon;
> march on in might, my soul!
> (Judges 5:4–5, 20–21, NEB)

Centuries later, when the Hebrews had come to believe that nature itself belonged within the sacred history of which Israel was a part, a psalmist addressed the Red Sea, the Jordan, and the mountains of Israel, speaking to them as fellow participants in a blessed dance of salvation:

> When Israel came out of Egypt,
> Jacob from a people of outlandish speech,
> . . . . . . . . . . . . . . . . . . . . . . . . . . . . . . .
> The sea looked and ran away;
> Jordan turned back.
> The mountains skipped like rams,
> the hills like young sheep.
> What was it, sea? Why did you run?
> Jordan, why did you turn back?
> Why, mountains, did you skip like rams,
> and you, hills, like young sheep?
> Dance, O earth, at the presence of the Lord,
> at the presence of the God of Jacob,

who turned the rock into a pool of water,
the granite cliff into a fountain.
(Psalm 114, NEB)

The Hebrews came to see that the landscape through which they
had traveled, and the promised land in which they lived, were
themselves beneficiaries of the Lord's covenant. In principle,
God's plan of salvation encompassed the whole world of living
things.

\* \* \*

One question which troubled those living in covenant with
the Lord was whether this God, who was so concerned for just
relationships among creatures, would turn in wrath and vent
unrestrained fury upon those who failed to fulfill their covenant
responsibilities. Discipline was expected, but could the Lord be
depended upon not to abandon the enterprise of salvation? The
Hebrews found God's answer to this question in the story of a
great flood. Similar stories were common among peoples of the
ancient Near East, but in the Hebrew version disaster transformed into promise. The focus of the Genesis account, Walter
Brueggemann observes, "is not on the flood but upon the change
wrought in God which makes possible a new beginning for
creation."[2] In fact, the Genesis story is actually two Hebrew versions woven together. One strand, part of a magnificent inte-
gration of ancient stories compiled soon after the reign of David,
scholars call "Yahwist" or "J." The other strand, labeled "Priestly"
or "P," is from a compilation perhaps four hundred years younger,
edited after the Israelites returned from the Babylonian exile,
but also incorporating older material.[3] Each found a distinctive
way to convey reassurance that the Lord, once on the verge of
decisive despair over creation, had resolved instead to assure the
continuation of life so that the work of salvation might begin.

The Yahwist account places the flood at the nadir of
earthly degradation, the result of a long process of decadence: the
disobedience of the first humans and their expulsion from the
garden; the disorientation of agriculture and all human relationships with other species; the spread of jealousy, murder, and

revenge within society; even a collapse of spiritual propriety so
that heavenly beings sought sexual relations with humans. The
Priestly narrative simply states, "God saw that the whole world
was corrupt and full of violence" (Genesis 6:11, NEB). Together
these two mythic descriptions suggest confusion within the created ecosystem. The beauty of the relationships God intended,
within species and between them, had been corrupted. The Yahwist reports the depth of God's anger and disgust: "This race of
men whom I have created, I will wipe them off the face of the
earth—man and beast, reptiles and birds. I am sorry that I ever
made them" (6:8, NEB). Nevertheless, a single just person remained: Noah. In a repentance so typical of God's personality as
portrayed in Scripture, the Lord—furious yet still in love with the
world—accepted this one person as sufficient reason for renewing the commitment to life on earth.

The story of Noah's ark, of the assembled pairs of creatures, of the rising waters and their subsiding, is familiar to all.
My concern here is the status that God gave to nature at the
resolution of that story. The Yahwist narrative concludes—after
Noah, his family, and all the creatures have disembarked to dry
land—with the Lord's reflection. Speaking inwardly, God re-
pealed the curse on the ground, a part of the stern sentence which
had accompanied Adam and Eve's expulsion from Eden, so that
agriculture could again flourish unimpeded. God also resolved
that the regularity of seasons would not again be disrupted by a
catastrophe. Finally, God determined never again to initiate
wholesale destruction of life on earth, despite a recognition that
human wickedness would continue. The text is beautiful:

> Never again will I curse the ground because of [humanity], how-
> ever evil [their] inclinations may be from [their] youth upwards.
> I will never again kill every living creature, as I have just done.
>
> > While the earth lasts
> > seedtime and harvest, cold and heat,
> > summer and winter, day and night,
> > shall never cease.
> >
> > (Genesis 8:21–22, NEB, alt.)

The resolution to the flood in the Priestly narrative, Genesis 9:1–17, is ecologically more complex, and echoes the magnificent day-by-day account of creation at the opening of Genesis. Following the tragic drowning of terrestrial life in the flood, God renewed the instruction given once before to be fruitful, multiply, and fill the earth. This time, however, God was more realistic about the character of relationships among creatures. For the first time, according to this narrative, humans received permission to eat flesh, even though this practice would add to discord in nature: "The fear and dread of you shall fall upon all wild animals on earth, on all birds of heaven, on everything that moves upon the ground and all fish in the sea; they are given into your hands" (9:2, NEB). God also pledged vengeance against anyone, human or animal, who took human life, since humanity had been formed in God's image. As if to balance this augmentation of human dominion, God then announced to Noah a covenant that embraced all living things: "I now make my covenant with you and with your descendants after you, and with every living creature that is with you, all birds and cattle, all the wild animals with you on earth, all that have come out of the ark" (9:9–10, NEB). God promised that "Never again shall the waters become a flood to destroy all living creatures" (9:15, NEB), and sealed the covenant with a sign of profound consequence:

> My bow I set in the cloud,
> sign of the covenant
> between myself and earth.
> When I cloud the sky over the earth,
> the bow shall be seen in the cloud.
>                 (Genesis 9:13–14, NEB)

The Hebrew word that suggests "rainbow" in this context usually means "the bow of war."[4] Bow and arrow were the most advanced weapon during this era. The visible sign meant that God had set aside, or unstrung, the bow of wrath; from this time forth, God's approach to the world would be gracious.

In each of these flood narratives we can see how the Hebrews' covenant experience influenced their perspective on nature. The Yahwist narrative derives from Israel's youth, when her land had been liberated from the crudest forms of political and economic exploitation to become God's own land. The curse of oppressive relationships in agriculture had been ameliorated. With faithful tending, that place could now become "a good and broad land, a land flowing with milk and honey" (Exodus 3:8, RSV). In the new beginning following the flood, this confidence was conveyed through the memory of God's lifting the curse from the ground. A fruitful relationship between humanity and nature was again possible.[5]

The Priestly narrative reflects a longer, more ambiguous historical experience and also a more cosmopolitan perspective. In this account human exploitation of the earth was a persistent reality; other creatures had reason for "fear and dread." Nevertheless God made a commitment to treat the earth and all living things with mercy and grace. By placing roots of the covenant near the beginnings of natural and human history, this narrative implies that the saving history which began with the Hebrew liberation will have worldwide consequences. God's mercy, it suggests, is intended not for Israel alone but for the whole world. Divine love embraces not simply humanity but all life.

As depicted in the Priestly narrative, human roles with respect to nature remain paradoxical. How could a species so highly valued by God be at once an exploiter of the earth and a means for its fulfillment? Did the rainbow promise to all life—the unstringing of the Lord's bow—require limits to human technology as well? Comments from two widely different sources point toward a resolution of this paradox. One draws from modern, ecological understanding of the role of *predation*—one warmblooded species killing and eating members of other warmblooded species—in a healthy ecosystem. The other comment, longer and more complex, is from the prophet Hosea, who imagined a fulfillment of the covenant within which the human bow, as well as the divine, would be unstrung.

According to the Priestly account of creation, God originally limited all warm-blooded creatures to a vegetarian diet. Predators had no place in a fully just ecology—a point of view shared by Isaiah and Ezekiel, two prophets within the Jerusalem

priestly community.[6] After the flood, God allowed humans to eat
flesh as a compromise with the corrupted reality of earthly life.
The modern ecological analysis of predation, however, pioneered
by Aldo Leopold, has made available a new moral perspective.
This theory affirms that predation makes a useful contribution to
the complex development of life on earth, benefiting not just the
predators, but also the species preyed upon, and their environment as well.[7] Simple predation, then, need not remain the
ethical issue. Gerhard von Rad points out that in the Genesis
passage describing the earth as "corrupt and full of violence," the
Hebrew word here translated as "violence" carries the connota-
tion of "arbitrary oppression."[8] I believe that human participation in predation does not compromise the justice of created relationships or their beauty—not until we extend our reach, as we
have, with thoughtless oppression of living things.

   Hosea's vision of covenant restoration modified the paradox we observed in the Priestly view of human relationships with
nature. Hosea heard God proclaim that when the people of Israel
finally renounced the seductions of Baal and returned to the
Lord, then God would renew the covenant through both a new
peace with nature and a marriage with Israel.  The Lord's
intended treaty between the Hebrews and their natural environment was an agreement under which Israel would set aside
technologies of oppression so that creatures would need to fear no
longer.  Then God would reunite with Israel in a marriage of
mutual love. These acts would restore the responsive, productive
character of natural life.  Through Hosea the Lord proclaimed,

> On that day she shall call me "My husband"
>    and shall no more call me "My Baal"....
> Then I will make a covenant on behalf of Israel with the wild
> beasts, the birds of the air, and the things that creep on the earth,
> and I will break bow and sword and weapon of war and sweep
> them off the earth, so that all living creatures may lie down
> without fear. I will betroth you to myself for ever, betroth you in
> lawful wedlock with unfailing devotion and love; I will betroth
> you to myself to have and to hold, and you shall know the Lord.
> At that time I will give answer, says the Lord, I will answer for
> the heavens and they will answer for the earth, and the earth will

answer for the corn, the new wine, and the oil . . . . Israel shall be
my new sowing in the land. (Hosea 2:16–23, NEB)

* * *

New Testament authors stressed that covenant renewal
would revitalize nature as well as the human spirit. Luke reported that when Jesus joined Simon Peter, who had fished
through the night in vain, the fish swarmed around the boat and
overburdened the nets.[9] Jesus radiated the vitality of the new
covenant, the restored community of life. He also expressed
God's concern for all creatures: "Can you not buy five sparrows
for two pennies? And yet not one is forgotten in God's sight" (Luke
12:6, JB). Later Paul, convinced that the new covenant was being
born in Christian experience, remembered nature's interest in
liberation. "The whole creation is eagerly waiting for God to
reveal [God's children]. . . , " he affirmed. "Creation still retains
the hope of being freed, like us, from its slavery to decadence, to
enjoy the same freedom and glory as the children of God"
(Romans 8:19–21, JB, alt.).

In the New Testament the attitude toward nature, however, is somewhat ambivalent. The book of Revelation, a vision
recorded by John of Patmos, depicts an unsettling inconsistency.
Early in John's vision the Lamb of God, the Savior, appears before
God's throne and receives praise from the congregation of angelic
beings. Another burst of adulation arises from the host of life on
earth:

> Then I heard all the living things in creation—everything that
> lives in the air, and on the ground, and under the ground, and in
> the sea, crying, "To the One who is sitting on the throne and to the
> Lamb, be all praise, honour, glory and power, for ever and ever."
> (Revelation 5:13, JB)

The fish, birds, plants, trees, wild beasts, cattle, and worms all
join in praising not just their Creator, but now also their Savior.
Joyfully they acknowledge their place in Christ's work. Fifteen
chapters later, though, at the close of John's vision the New
Jerusalem descends from heaven and most of this vast and varied
chorus in the drama of redemption is lost from view. John reports

seeing "a new heaven and a new earth" (21:1, KJV), borrowing the phrase from Isaiah, who had imagined that a lush ecosystem of plants and creatures would flourish along with redeemed humanity at the climax of history.[10] Yet the city John describes lacks an environment and contains only a limited number of faithful men and women, accompanied by a few trees distinct from earthly species. For all its splendor, there is a constrained, fearful quality to John's final vision. The earth has been consumed in fire and all conceivable enemies have been annihilated, but the city still retains high walls. The sea is banished, as are the cycles of day and night. Of the world community only a tiny remnant is redeemed—a handful of humans. What has become of all those creatures who sang the praises of the Lamb? Were they just whistling in ignorance before their own immolation? The earlier vision of God's generous purpose for all of life stands in contrast to John's latter vision of redemption, which lacks the breadth and vitality of God's original creation.[11]

# 5. *Jesus' Baptism*

Soon after his baptism, speaking to friends in Nazareth, Jesus read with new emphasis words from Isaiah:

> *The spirit of the Lord has been given to me,*
> *for [God] has anointed me.*
> *[God] has sent me to bring the good news to the poor,*
> *to proclaim liberty to captives*
> *and to the blind new sight,*
> *to set the downtrodden free,*
> *to proclaim the Lord's year of favour.*
> (Luke 4:18–19, JB, alt.)[1]

To the attentive congregation Jesus added, "This text is being fulfilled today even as you listen" (4:21, JB). How broadly, though, did Jesus apply this promise? Isaiah himself had included all types of earthly life within his hope for God's favor. Indeed, in a passage where Christians have usually seen Christ foretold, Isaiah anticipated a time when humanity and all of nature would be reconciled to each other:

> Then the wolf shall live with the sheep,
> and the leopard lie down with the kid;
> the calf and the young lion shall grow up together,
> and a little child shall lead them;
> the cow and the bear shall be friends,
> and their young shall lie down together,
> . . . . . . . . . . . . . . . . . . . . . . . . . . . . . . .
> They shall not hurt or destroy in all my holy mountain;
> for as the waters fill the sea,
> so shall the land be filled with the knowledge of the LORD.
> (Isaiah 11:6–9, NEB)

Was Jesus' vision also this comprehensive? Were oppressed

creatures to be set free? Among the downtrodden, might Jesus recognize the land itself? Did the Lord's year of favor apply to nature as well as to humanity? A number of strands suggest a positive answer to these questions.

* * *

Jesus' baptism, to me, symbolizes Christ's engagement with the natural world.[2] From Nazareth Jesus traveled to the Jordan River, whose lower portion served as an approximate boundary between human settlement and the wilderness. Experience in that wilderness had shaped the zealous prophet John the Baptist, and following his own baptism Jesus also went there to come to terms with his vocation.

This John stood in a line of Old Testament prophets— Elijah, Elisha, and Amos—who either had emerged from wilderness to speak God's word to Israel, or had used wilderness as their refuge. Just as the original Hebrew band had been formed by the Lord in Sinai, away from the influence of established cultures, so prophets sometimes heard God's word when they withdrew from civil society, pondered their own deepest yearnings, and listened. The Baptist cultivated such a wilderness identity, wearing rough clothes and remaining at the edge of civilization. He apparently did not visit the towns of Palestine but required the curious to come to him so that, away from their homes and familiar surroundings, they might be open to a new perspective. His message cut through the despair and passivity typical in a nation under foreign rule. "Repent," John said, "for the kingdom of Heaven is upon you!" (Matthew 3:2, NEB); he urged his hearers to return to the standards of the Lord so they might participate in changes about to occur. For those who wished to reform, John provided a symbolic act, a simple immersion in the Jordan to represent their commitment to begin again, clean, as God's people. With his revolutionary message and its accompanying baptism, John echoed the ancient Hebrew covenant themes—renunciation of corrupt allegiances, withdrawal to the wilderness, and commitment to the law and promises of the Lord.

At his own baptism Jesus heard God's call to speak with divine authority and to begin the formation of the new covenant

community. He became filled with that spirit, perhaps even overwhelmed, and he needed to discover from within himself how to
answer this call. Alone in the wilderness for forty days, he fasted
to sharpen his self-awareness and then wrestled with questions
of integrity and strategy. Matthew and Luke report this wrestling as three temptations. First Jesus rejected the temptation to
reach for political leadership, preferring to stand with that most
ancient part of the Hebrew tradition which clearly separated
God's kingdom from power politics. He also rejected the materi-
alistic temptation of feeding people in order to render them
dependent and grateful; such manipulation would patronize the
poor whom Jesus loved, enslaving them to a new provider.
Finally he rejected the temptation to gather a following by means
of spectacular miracles, for addicts of religious extravaganza are
distracted from the task of forming themselves in faith and
obedience to the living God. Jesus chose instead a Hebrew
strategy of liberation: he called the wicked to cast off the chains
of sin, and he called the oppressed to trust life and act as though
they were free, in the faith that with God's power they could join
together to renew their world.[3]

I would like to know more about Jesus' experience with the
wilderness itself. When he ended his fast did he live off the land
like John the Baptist, eating locusts and wild honey? Or, like the
American wilderness explorer John Muir, had he set forth with
a bag of bread crumbs over his shoulder? The latter seems more
likely, unless Jesus had spent time before in the wild. Living from
a wild landscape requires concentration; it is not a skill to learn
when one is preoccupied with other questions. From the Gospels
we might surmise that "temptations" came because Jesus was
hungry, but that theory demeans his struggle. Jesus' temptations arose from the strength of his baptismal call —that divine
inrush of spirit amid which God said, "You are my Son, the
Beloved; my favour rests on you" (Mark 1:11, JB). Matthew wrote
that when the temptations of Jesus were resolved, "angels appeared and looked after him" (4:11, JB), a detail required by the
etiquette of biblical memory, because angels had ministered to
Elijah during another famous wilderness ordeal. Elijah, how-

ever, had been in a deep depression and longed for death;[4] Jesus
was bursting with energy to sort out a strategy for new life, and
was not likely to need special angelic sustenance. More to the
point, Mark noted simply that "He was with the wild beasts"
(1:13, JB). Here at the dawning of a new age, God's creatures
shared some type of fellowship, however wary, with the new
Adam. Isaiah would have felt gratified.

* * *

During the following three years Jesus met some people
whose response to his message was to exalt the messenger but
overlook the practical implications of his teaching. Jesus himself
avoided traditional titles, and though his presence was arresting,
his personal style was to serve rather than command. Precisely
for this reason his embodiment as the Lord of the Hebrews
became ever more transparent. Schooled to subservience and
conditioned to wait for a deliverer to rescue them without effort
on their part, some persisted in exalting Jesus with praise rather
than following him in obedience. Just before his final trip to
Jerusalem, Jesus spoke directly to such followers with an image
of exaltation they might appreciate. He told of his return in
judgment when he would gather the nations before him and
separate the righteous from the wicked, as a shepherd separates
sheep from goats. The corral of the redeemed, he implied, would
hold not those who bleated the loudest, but those who had worked
usefully. This story was more than a bit of information about the
end of the world; it was Jesus' effort to instruct those who loved
him how they might meet him after he was gone. In the dialogue
that followed, Jesus spoke even more specifically:

> "For when I was hungry, you gave me food; when thirsty, you
> gave me drink; when I was a stranger you took me into your
> home, when naked you clothed me; when I was ill you came to my
> help, when in prison you visited me." . . .
> "Lord, when was it that we saw you hungry and fed you, or
> thirsty and gave you drink? . . . When did we see you ill or in
> prison, and come to visit you?" . . .
> "I tell you this: anything you did for one of my [sisters and]
> brothers here, however humble, you did for me."
>
> (Matthew 25:35–40, NEB, alt.)

The words *hungry, thirsty, estranged, naked, ill,* and *imprisoned* can also describe the parts of God's creation that are eroded, polluted, endangered, or valued only for their usefulness to humanity. Christ stands with the vulnerable, with those who are weak, threatened, or abused. I believe that we serve Christ when we assist creatures, landscapes, species, and ecosystems, for all of these are cherished by the God who fashioned them. They stand within the embrace of the covenant.[5]

\* \* \*

Why did Jesus go to the Jordan River to be baptized by John? The traditional answer is *identification*. Jesus Christ, God's particular child, was identifying himself with those who needed their wickedness washed away, thus taking the first step in the mighty journey of redemption which culminated with Jesus' death on a cross and resurrection from the tomb. Jesus was also identifying himself with those who wished to stand apart from the despair and compromises of occupied Palestine and reclaim God's moral purpose. He announced a new kingdom; for that, as much as anything else, he was killed. Furthermore, Jesus identified with John the Baptist. Though he would come to distinguish himself from John—for he was not a rigorous ascetic[6]—he acknowledged the prophetic moral tradition from which John spoke; and although Jesus would go from town to town in Palestine, he retained the spirit of John's stance at the margin of society. Jesus, like John, challenged his hearers to break the confines of the culture they knew, to imaginatively construct a society of just and merciful relationships, and to live according to this new vision. These, we imagine, were some of the motives which led Jesus to submit to John's baptism.

However, the Jordan River to which Jesus came also needed him. For nine hundred years, since King Solomon of Israel and King Hiram of Tyre had begun intensive logging of the cedars of Lebanon, the Jordan watershed had been deteriorating. Farming without respite, brushcutting, and overgrazing had further reduced the capacity of the watershed to hold moisture and retain its thin topsoil.[7] When the rains came the Jordan and its tributaries now flooded more quickly; in the long, dry summer the flow was more sluggish than before. Beyond the Jordan, the whole Fertile Crescent—that cradle of civilization spanning the Mediterranean coast to the valleys of the Tigris and Euphrates —was declining. Palestine was now governed by agents of Rome concerned only for production and taxes, and there were increasing pressures on people and land. The promised land was in pain. Like the pilgrims who visited John, the waters themselves cried once again for liberation.

Within Israel's memory the Red Sea had parted for Moses, and the waters of the Jordan also had "turned back" before Joshua and the Hebrews when they first carried the ark of God's covenant across into Canaan.[8] But there was no reason for the waters to retreat from the presence of the new Adam and the power of God's spirit. Jesus entered the water, felt its warmth, and was submerged:

> And when he came up out of the water, immediately he saw the heavens opened and the Spirit descending upon him like a dove; and a voice came from heaven, "Thou art my beloved Son; with thee I am well pleased." (Mark 1:10–11, RSV)

At the moment when Jesus received God's highest commendation, he stood in the river that flowed through the Lord's chosen land. That baptism was both a liberation and a promise, and it represented Jesus' identification with *all* the needy and oppressed—including the yearning landscape of the earth.

# Part II.

## *Creativity*

Although Christian theologians have traditionally discussed nature within a "doctrine of creation," and Christian ethicists have discussed nature under "stewardship," I find both categories inadequate. Creativity, the category I prefer, is more than God's creative acts to establish the earth we know; more, indeed, than God's continuing sustenance of that world. Creativity is something God has shared with the earth, not just by being creative, but by supporting adaptive ecosystems within which other beings may also live creatively. The ethics of stewardship are likewise too narrow a context for nature, because the natural world is much more than something for humans to take care of. Our earth is a congregation of lives called by God to nourish each other and challenged to respond to God's will.

This perspective on creativity modifies the emphasis on God's controlling providence which is characteristic of the Calvinist tradition within which I learned theology. When we appreciate the beautiful, self-giving character of God's creativity, we can see that the "image of God" which we bear is not so much a license to dominate as it is a commission to know and tend the earth. The biblical understanding of God clearly emphasizes the Lord's moral authority as distinguished from arbitrary dominion. However, the social application of this insight within the Hebrew community was often compromised by political pres-

sures and undermined by patterns of patriarchal control. Biblical understanding is also unique in distinguishing God's creativity from reproductive sexuality. The Hebrew struggle to protect
this distinction, however, generated sexual anxiety that persists
in our religious tradition and inhibits self-understanding in
Christian culture.

Biblical writers stressed, furthermore, that no creative act
is complete without rest, reflection, and celebration. The sabbath
tradition gave form to this insight. Within this tradition all
creatures are summoned to worship, while God's people are
charged to reflect on just social practices and responsible relationships with land and living creatures.

# 6. *God Creating*

In the Bible the two formal accounts of God creating life are the story of the seven days, which has been incorporated into the Priestly narrative, and the Yahwist story of Eden. Significant meditations on God's creativity are recorded in the Psalms, the book of Job, and the Gospel of John as well. The Yahwist narrative, usually considered the most ancient, chiseled a Hebrew perspective on God's creativity to contrast with the fertility cults of the Baal, a competing faith that continued to attract farming people in Canaan up through the reigning kingdoms of Israel and Judah. Since Hebrew interpretations of the Lord's creativity contained reactions to popular worship of the Baal, I offer Gerhard von Rad's description of this folk religion:

> [Each of the] Baal was the owner . . . of a mountain, or an oasis, or some other place. . . . He is the mythical generative power that fructifies the earth by means of the sperm of the rain. Human beings share in his fertilising power by entering this mystery and imitating it. Cultic prostitution was therefore an essential characteristic of this worship: sacred prostitutes lived at the sanctuaries. . . . Alongside Baal stood Astarte, who was patently the goddess of fertility.[1]

Behind the local Baal stood the great Baal, the creator and "Lord of Heaven," who also bestowed fertility through rain.

The Yahwist narrative suggests that the Lord formed life from the soil without intercourse with the sky: "Yahweh God had not sent rain on the earth . . . . Instead, water flowed out of the ground" (Genesis 2:5–6, NJB). God shaped the human being from damp earth and breathed life into the human's nostrils. A Lord who worked so intimately with the earth, and yet whose engagement was not sexual, could not be confused with the Baal. Then

God established a garden in Eden with rivers for irrigation—another departure from rain-fertility—and within the garden God planted trees and also fashioned animals from the ground. The intimate charm of creation in this narrative expresses the quality of God's love as the Hebrews had experienced it.

The Priestly creation story of the seven days (Genesis 1:1 —2:4) may be equally ancient and may reflect Egyptian influence even more than Babylonian.[2] It opens with a vision of watery emptiness: "the earth was a formless void, there was darkness over the deep, with a divine wind sweeping over the waters" (Genesis 1:2, NJB). The Lord had no competitor and met no resistance from the elements. God inaugurated creation decisively, using powerful words: "And God said, Let there be light: and there was light. And God saw the light, that *it was* good" (1:3–4, KJV). Again and again, day by day, God spoke and it happened, God fashioned and it stood. No he-god sired, no she-god gave birth. While sexual distinction was a vital characteristic of many created species, it was not cast back upon the Creator. God "said" and God "made"; creation involved word and deed, speaking and fabricating. Very soon—on the third day—the newly formed earth began to express itself in response to God's creative intention:

> God said, "Let the earth produce vegetation." . . . And so it was. The earth produced vegetation: the various kinds of seed-bearing plants and the fruit trees with seed inside, each corresponding to its own species. God saw that it was good.
> (Genesis 1:11–12, NJB)

In this creative relationship there was no jealousy or tension between God and the earth. Regularly God surveyed the work and saw how good it was. God was self-giving, and creation was beautiful.

As one day unfolded after another, God felt increasing delight in how many things came to life. On the fifth day God created multitudes of birds to "fly above the earth across the vault of heaven," as well as fish and sea creatures to "swarm in the waters" (1:20, 21, NEB). God addressed them directly; in this account God's first commandment is a word of blessing and encouragement spoken to fish and birds: "Be fruitful and increase, fill the waters of the seas; and let the birds increase on land" (1:22, NEB). This text, like others in the Bible, presumes that God could communicate with all creatures and they could answer. The relationships between God and living creatures were not mechanical and manipulative, but intimate and responsive. Though humanity would later receive important rights and duties in relation to other forms of life, it was God who held a truly intimate relationship with both plants and animals.

This intimacy is reflected in the book of Job, the magnificent drama that probes the Lord's moral character. The tragic hero finally receives some comfort not only because God is willing to speak to him directly, and also because God affirms closeness with all creatures. God asks Job,

> Do you hunt game for the lioness
> and feed her ravenous cubs,
> when they crouch in their den, impatient,
> or lie in ambush in the thicket?
> Who finds her prey at nightfall,
> when her cubs are aching with hunger?
>
> Do you tell the antelope to calve
> or ease her when she is in labor?
> Do you count the months of her fullness
> and know when her time has come?
> She kneels; she tightens her womb;
> she pants, she presses, gives birth.
> Her little ones grow up;
> they leave and never return.
>
> Who unties the wild ass
> and lets him wander at will?
> He ranges the open prairie
> and roams across the saltlands.
> He is far from the tumult of cities;
> he laughs at the driver's whip.
> He scours the hills for food,
> in search of anything green.
>                    (Job 38:39–39:6, Mitchell)[3]

\* \* \*

The *biblical ecology* which I seek is a moral understanding, not a technical one—the latter is a modern phenomenon. To the scientist, *ecological understanding* is knowledge of how a variety of species, using materials found in their environment and energy derived from the sun's radiation, support and nourish one another, while they also feed upon each other in systems that tend to evolve toward greater complexity and diversity. Despite a century of research and reflection since the pioneering work of Charles Darwin, our knowledge of these systems remains tentative and incomplete. In Hebrew thought the Lord's providence substituted for ecological understanding. Where we see predation and adaptation in an ecosystem of mutual support, the Hebrew poet saw the Lord directly feeding the lion and the raven, and acting as midwife for the successful birth of a fawn. This perspective need not embarrass modern Christians. We can appreciate how environmental systems are expressive of God's beauty in that the Lord not only creates but also bestows creativity upon the earth. Because earthly life is creative, with inner resources as well as interdependence, it can respond to God. Yet modern men and women need God's words to Job to remind us that the Lord is an active participant in the life of the world. Neither passive nor remote, the Lord cares about the antelope in labor and feels the pain and joy of all who live.

God's delight in natural diversity shines through the stately repetitions of the Priestly creation narrative: "God made wild animals in their own species, and cattle in theirs, and every creature that crawls along the earth in its own species. God saw that it was good" (Genesis 1:25, NJB). We may infer this same delight from the Yahwist narrative, in which God proudly paraded before the human being "all the wild animals and all the birds of heaven" so this first person could identify them with human names (2:19, NEB). These creatures were not automatons programmed to a narrow track of life, nor were they puppets dangling from God's fingers. God instilled in them the breath of life, the capacity to live from within themselves, however critical their dependence upon the environment. God proudly "unties the wild ass and lets him wander at will" (Job 39:5, Mitchell). And yet the Lord cares; God follows all the creatures with love.

Sometimes theologians—ignorant of ecology and unwittingly captive to authoritarian or mechanical perspectives—have inverted the ethics of this biblical pre-ecology to suggest that God directly supervised every natural relationship and that the only legitimate posture for any creature, whether human or beast, was supine dependence with blind obedience. Some have called authoritarian rule over dependent creatures "providence," imagining that an earth so lacking in vitality and creativity would give glory to God. However, as we will see over and over again, biblical writers insisted that moral responsibility was the essential quality of the relationship between every creature and the Lord. Each landscape and each creature had the capacity—and with it the obligation—to respond to God and to respond appropriately to others. The initiative that biblical writers imputed to all of these beings is striking, for our modern culture has trained us to regard lands and creatures as mere things which we may manipulate with impunity. We need the biblical perspective as an antidote to our arrogance. God's beauty inherently gives forth. The ecosystems of this earth, which we are beginning to understand, reflect that beauty. Only a freely giving God would have made an earth so vital, so alive, so self-sustaining.

John the Evangelist, opening his Gospel with a meditation on the Word of God, identified Christ with the creative process which resulted in such a lively world. What John wrote in Greek may be translated "all that came to be was alive with his life" or "no single created thing came into being without him" (John 1:3, NEB, text and footnote). Both of these renderings show that John associated Christ with the creation of all things, including all species. The personality of Jesus resonated with the creative process, giving life and even creativity to others. Jesus would endure humiliation and submit to death in order to renew the lives of others. This divine love is consistently self-giving.

This Lord is wholly different from what gods are supposed to be like. God did not fashion a spectacular display of objects to confirm the prowess of their Creator, nor a merely decorative backdrop for the human drama. This God created an earth, lively

and life-giving, overflowing with diverse creatures. Although the
Bible contains no theoretical understanding of ecology as such, it
abounds with celebrations of creatures which are unique and yet
dependent upon other creatures as well as upon their changing
environment and their God. The Psalms praise God as the
sustainer of what we now call the earthly ecosystem:

> Thou dost make springs break out in the gullies,
>    so that their water runs between the hills.
> The wild beasts all drink from them,
>    the wild asses quench their thirst;
>    the birds of the air nest on their banks
>    and sing among the leaves.
>
> From thy high pavilion thou dost water the hills;
>    the earth is enriched by thy provision.
> Thou makest grass grow for the cattle
>       and green things for those who toil for [people],
>    bringing bread out of the earth
>    and wine to gladden [people's] hearts,
>    oil to make their faces shine
>    and bread to sustain their strength.
>       The trees of the LORD are green and leafy,
>          the cedars of Lebanon which [God] planted;
>    the birds build their nests in them,
>    the stork makes her home in their tops.
> High hills are the haunt of the mountain-goat,
>    and boulders a refuge for the rock-badger.
>
> Thou hast made the moon to measure the year
>    and taught the sun where to set.
> When thou makest darkness and it is night,
> all the beasts of the forest come forth;
>    the young lions roar for prey,
>    seeking their food from God.
> When thou makest the sun rise, they slink away
>       and go to rest in their lairs;
>    but [people come] out to [their] work
>       and to [their] labours until evening.
> Countless are the things thou hast made, O LORD.
> Thou has made all by thy wisdom;
>    and the earth is full of thy creatures,
>    beasts great and small.
>                (Psalm 104:10–25, NEB, alt.)

# 7. *Image of God*

A biblical ecology differs from the popular, modern environmental movement in two ways. First, it includes a sense of God's purpose, since the Bible portrays nature not as an autonomous system but as a moral one, whose health and integrity stem from an intimate relationship with God. Second, in the Bible the moral engagement between nature and humanity is critical to both parties. Nature's vulnerability to human influence is not an accident of evolutionary history; rather, it has been God's intention from the beginning, because despite the grave risks, mutual vulnerability opens potential benefits to all.

Since human impact upon earthly life has become so pervasive, modern society has begun to understand the necessity of limiting that impact so that natural systems are not destroyed. The environmental movement has urged nations to screen some areas, such as parks and wildernesses, from human degradation, and to control pollution of the basic environmental systems, such as air, rivers, and lakes, that touch all life. Many environmentalists assume that while humanity could not survive without healthy natural systems, the rest of nature could get along quite well without humanity. The environmental movement has perceptively identified where we must disengage from nature and pull back, but it has had more difficulty developing positive visions of desirable relationships between human culture and nature. I believe that biblical ecology's most significant contribution is a moral vision of human engagement with nature. Such a vision can help us reach an ethical sensitivity in our personal, institutional, and cultural relationships with life on this earth. So the primitive, evocative Yahwist narrative in Genesis 2 suggests that God formed humanity to be caretaker for the earth, while the more sophisticated Priestly narrative in Genesis 1 suggests a human vocation to bear the "image of God" to nature.

* * *

As we have seen, the Yahwist narrative begins with an empty landscape, barren for two reasons: "There was neither shrub nor plant growing wild upon the earth [Hebrew, *adamah*] because the LORD God had sent no rain on the earth; nor was there any [person, (Hebrew, *adam*)] to till the ground" (Genesis 2:5, NEB, alt.). To support life the ground needed water from God and also someone to tend it, an "earth creature," *adam*, whom God would form from the soil itself. *Adam* was not yet a proper name for the first human, and as Phyllis Trible shows in her brilliant analysis of this passage, the word should not be translated "man," as there was no sexual distinction until the second person was created. Only after that were these people identified as woman (Hebrew, *ishshah*) and man (*ish*).[1] Sexual division would both separate woman from man and also attract the two to each other. Prior to that, however, the Yahwist tells how the human was separated from the earth in order to be attracted to it again and to discover the human vocation through working with the landscape. The human was formed from earth and filled with breath from God. Although humanity would not be complete without sexuality, human relationships to God and to the earth came before the claims of sexual desire.

After forming the human, the Lord planted a garden with rivers for irrigation. Then "Yahweh God . . . settled the [person] in the garden of Eden to cultivate and take care of it" (2:15, JB, alt.). The garden stimulated the human because it was both aesthetic and useful, "pleasant to look at and good for food" (2:9, NEB). Since the human and the landscape needed each other— the human needed food, the garden needed tending—mutual benefit resulted. Such personal engagement with a landscape, Phyllis Trible notes, is expressive and satisfying:

> The two infinitives, *to till* and *to keep*, connote not plunder and rape but care and attention. They enhance the delight of the

> garden. By the same token, they give to the earth creature the joy of work. This work changes human life from passivity to participation. . . . Work fulfills both creature and environment, providing dignity and integrity. It testifies to the oneness of humanity and soil at the same time that it establishes the responsibility of the earth creature for the earth.

The narrative's emphasis on work before the human was divided sexually suggests to Trible that working with natural life and materials is basic to human identity, regardless of whether one is female or male.[2]

Working with the earth continues to challenge human creativity. Even in Eden creativity was necessary, not because securing a harvest was difficult—nourishment could be plucked with ease—but because God's charge to "cultivate and take care of" this landscape was morally complex. This command was not a set of pragmatic instructions in the technology of gardening—you must plant if you want to harvest; you must prune if you want fruit. Instead the charge was an ethical constraint: you must tend the needs of the plants if you are to deserve their fruit. The plants had purpose beyond any human need for them; some, indeed, served no human purpose at all. Also, the human creature was given limits: "You may freely eat of every tree of the garden; but of the tree of the knowledge of good and evil you shall not eat, for in the day that you eat of it you shall die" (2:17–18, RSV). This prohibition reminded the human that God had moral authority to define relationships among creatures. Additionally, as Trible observes, it "witnesses to the integrity of nature apart from its use by the earth creature."[3] Within this context of nourishment, delight, freedom, responsibility, and limits, the human was challenged to work and live creatively—to beautify the garden.

Animals appear in this narrative as companions: "It is not good for the [human] to be alone. I will provide a partner" (2:18, NEB, alt.). This is a play on our expectations, for like the ancient listeners to this familiar story, we know that a beautiful sexual climax is near. But the mention of animals is much more than a rhetorical tease. Living creatures, domesticated and wild, were companions who shared with humanity a common origin, both having been fashioned from the soil by God. Their association with human beings was meant to extend beyond exploitative roles as domestic workers or wild prey. A just relationship had to begin with *recognition*: "Whatever the [human] called each living creature, that was its name. Thus the [human] gave names to all cattle, to the birds of heaven, and to every wild animal" (2:19–20, NEB, alt.). Recognition suggests a profound human responsibility. We influence creatures by how we identify them, and therefore we have an obligation to discern them with care.

The narrative then comes to its happy conclusion. God created sexual distinction not by returning to the ground, but by reaching like a surgeon into the human, removing a part, and fashioning another person. There were now two who differed from each other, woman and man; but they delighted each other and were drawn together. Again, relationship began in recognition:

> "Now this, at last—
> bone from my bones,
> flesh from my flesh!"
> (Genesis 2:23, NEB)

Man and woman joined together without shame. The Yahwist narrative celebrates human sexuality as the epitome of God's creative blessings, skillfully separating sexuality from potentially abusive contexts. Sex was a delightful desire within human relationships, husband with wife; it was not part of the human relationship to God or of human relationships to animals and crops. The Lord's creative scheme of life, unlike the fertility-centered worship of Baal, did not exalt sex as the key to existence.

\* \* \*

In the Priestly narrative (Genesis 1), man and woman received life together on the sixth day, at the highest pitch of God's creative activity. All the creatures of the land were also created that day, "cattle, reptiles, and wild animals, all according to their kind" (1:24, NEB), and God admired them. After man and woman were created and given their commission, God once more surveyed everything made from the beginning, "and, behold, *it was* very good" (1:31, KJV). God's charge to man and woman in this narrative is complex and somewhat ambiguous:

> God said, "Let us make humankind in our image, after our likeness; and let them have dominion over the fish of the sea, and over the birds of the air, and over the cattle, and over all the earth, and over every creeping thing that creeps upon the earth." So God created humankind in God's own image, in the image of God was the human being created; male and female God created them. And God blessed them, and God said to them, "Be fruitful and multiply, and fill the earth and subdue it; and have dominion over the fish of the sea and over the birds of the air and over every living thing that moves upon the earth."
>
> (Genesis 1:26–28, ILL[4])

The Priestly account refers to "image" and also to "likeness" in other places. Genesis 5:1–3 implies that the human likeness to God is analogous to Seth's likeness to his father Adam, suggesting what we might call "a family resemblance." In Genesis 9:6 the "image" serves as a sign or warning not to kill a human being, like the protective "mark" which, in the Yahwist narrative, God put on Cain (4:15).

Hebrew religion was acutely sensitive to the word *image*. When the word appeared in the second commandment, it carried threatening connotations:

> You shall not make yourself a carved image or any likeness of anything in heaven or on earth beneath or in the waters under the earth; you shall not bow down to them or serve them. For I, Yahweh your God, am a jealous God. (Exodus 20:4–5, JB)

This warning not to worship created things, nor objects made to represent them, became a central tenet of Hebrew faith. Worshiping human beings or images of people was also prohibited by this commandment.[5] The psalm that later celebrated the Genesis commission shows this same caution about human pride and self-worship, reminding hearers that humans do not deserve their exalted role:

> [W]hat are human beings that you are mindful of them,
>     and mortals that you care for them?

> Yet you have made them little less than God,
>   and crowned them with glory and honor.
> You have given them dominion over the works of your hands.
>                               (Psalm 8:4–6, ILL[6])

In the Priestly creation narrative, the words *image* and *likeness* are closely associated with God's charge to establish "dominion" over life on the earth. An image was something to be seen by other creatures, a symbol of the divine authority behind human administration of nature. Gerhard von Rad explains this association in the light of an ancient practice:

> Just as powerful earthly kings, to indicate their claim to domin-
> ion, erect an image of themselves in the provinces of their empire
> where they do not personally appear, so man is placed upon earth
> in God's image as God's sovereign emblem. He is really only
> God's representative, summoned to maintain and enforce God's
> claim to dominion over the earth. The decisive thing about man's
> similarity to God, therefore, is his function in the nonhuman
> world.[7]

The commission to humanity was expressed in imperial language to signify that no creature, seeing men and women, could doubt that they bore authority from God. It would be foolish, however, for these field representatives of God's dominion to imagine that their power was their own. They would be secure in their position so long as they did God's will. Provincial administrators who followed their own desires and exploited or abused their subjects without imperial authorization would be considered corrupt stewards and would be dismissed. As soon as the man and woman received their commission and its accompanying blessing, God followed with field instructions. They were to eat only plants; indeed, these plants were the food for all the multitude of animals God had formed.[8] The dominion that humans were instructed to establish was God's; they received no authority to exhaust the earth's life for exclusively human ends.

It is easy to see how, in the long history of Christian culture, some people may have read this commission as divine authorization to exploit the earth without thought for the welfare of other creatures or the landscape. Whenever biblical writers took images derived from kingship and applied them to God—as many did—they opened a possible misunderstanding. The Lord claimed sovereignty as absolute as any king's, but the Lord did not behave like a typical ruler. Rather than exploiting dominions, the Lord tended them and cared for them; the Lord was self-giving, as Jesus would reveal, even unto death. Uzziah, remembered in Judah as a good king, typified such generous dominion: "He ... dug many cisterns, for he had large herds of cattle both in the Shephelah and in the plain. He also had farmers and vine-dressers in the hill-country and in the fertile lands, for he loved the soil" (2 Chronicles 26:10, NEB).

\* \* \*

Christian theology has generally followed the lead of Paul, who affirmed that Christ, the new Adam, manifested the image of God fully, and that believers would exhibit that image as they conformed to Christ's character.[9] When we recognize the image of God in Christ, who "emptied himself, taking the form of a servant" (Philippians 2:7, RSV), it is easier to separate the core of truth from the imperial language chosen by the Priestly writer. Jesus' concern for nature had more in common with the Yahwist's emphasis on delight, recognition, and caretaking than it did with the Priestly narrative's concern for dominion. Jesus urged that we interrupt our habit of fretful exploitation to notice our surroundings:

> I bid you put away anxious thoughts about food and drink to keep you alive, and clothes to cover your body. Surely life is more than food, the body more than clothes. Look at the birds of the air.... Consider how the lilies grow in the fields; they do not work, they do not spin; and yet, I tell you, even Solomon in all his splendour was not attired like one of these. But if that is how God clothes the grass in the fields, which is there today, and tomorrow is thrown on the stove, will [God] not all the more clothe you? How little faith you have! ... Set your mind on God's kingdom and [God's] justice before everything else, and all the rest will come to you as well. So do not be anxious.
>
> (Matthew 6:25–34, NEB, alt.)

If we have faith in God's covenant, we will notice the world around us, love it, and take care of it. A loving effort and just regard for the needs of other life will bring us nourishment and, in addition, will provide more satisfaction than anxious strivings, because God knows what we need and has fashioned a world within which our needs can be met.

The image of God is not something closeted inside us, for that would contradict God's own expressive, self-giving character. Instead, it is something we exhibit to the world beyond ourselves—most particularly to the living world beyond the human. We need this emphasis on other life, which has not been prominent in Christian history, to realize the human vocation. Men and women have been created to play a critical role in the ecosystem; we are called to represent God to the "mighty throng" (Genesis 2:1, NEB) of created life. This does not imply that communication between God and nature is limited to the human channel. Indeed, God knows the creatures more intimately than we do, and all creatures are summoned to praise God with their own voices. Yet men and women live at the moral center of earthly life, for we and our descendants will determine whether the world can remain a just, caring, and healthy place for all creation. God has given us the responsibility of dominion to maintain and to enhance the quality of life. The test of our dominion will be whether creatures, from their contact with us, gain experience of the loving character of God.

At worst, the sad Priestly warning following the flood will continue to represent nature's perception of humanity, and because of human abuse nature's knowledge of God will dim as well:

> The fear of you and dread of you shall fall upon all wild animals on earth, on all birds of heaven, on everything that moves upon the ground and all fish in the sea; they are given into your hands.
> (Genesis 9:2, NEB)

Alternatively, as Isaiah hopefully prophesied, perhaps "the wolf shall live with the sheep . . . and a little child shall lead them; . . . so shall the land be filled with the knowledge of the LORD" (Isaiah 11:6–9, NEB).

Humanity stands in a crucial and sobering position. We are not alone—for we can draw upon God's guidance and assistance—but we cannot avoid the consequences of our commission. Modern Christians, watching the world teeter on the brink of environmental disaster, may wish that God had chosen a more prudent course. Nevertheless, we bear responsibility for life; God has given it to us, and God still expects us to discharge our duty.

# 8. *Moral Creativity*

Genesis introduces human sexuality side by side with the image of God: "In the image of God was the human being created; male and female" (Genesis 1:27, ILL[1]). This verse suggests that *eros* may be an additional aspect of God's image, even though the Priestly writers of this creation narrative understood that their God was not a sexual being. God urged the man and woman, as well as all the animals, to "be fruitful and multiply" (1:28, ILL), but the Priestly account specifies sexual differentiation only for the human creatures. Human sexuality merited special mention.

This concern for sexuality goes to the heart of a subtle biblical insight that has revolutionized religious understanding. An important facet of biblical faith was God's asexual nature, even though the Bible employs a wide range of images—both masculine and feminine—to convey the character of God's creativity. The Lord guided the faithful to form a society less exploitative than the Canaanite kingdoms and challenged them to display *moral creativity*—not just sexual productivity—in response to God's own self-giving.

As the Priestly creation narrative hints, human creativity is rooted in our human sexuality, which is different from that of animal species. Nearly all animals experience "heat"—a physical desire for coupling—during specific, limited periods; human desire, however, is a continuous possibility except during the periods of relaxation following intercourse. This desire tends to infuse all our aspirations and is responsible for our level of psychic energy, commonly called *eros*, a Greek word for self-expressive love. *Eros*, or "the self come vividly to life,"[2] has more in common with self-giving *agape* (another Greek word for love) than most Christian thinkers have acknowledged, for self-giving love depends upon a healthy capacity for self-expression. Whole human beings, both men and women, enjoy creating.

The Hebrew word *bará*, characteristically employed in the Bible to describe God's creativity, was not used for human sexuality or for natural productivity.[3] Although not sexual, God's creating is clearly self-expressive as well as self-giving. God's love manifests *eros* while humans, in turn, are challenged to emulate God's covenant-love (Hebrew, *hésedh*) and self-giving love (Greek, *agape*). Like their Lord, humans are capable of creativity that transcends the simple fulfillment of needs—though our creativity rarely runs contrary to our needs. Since God invites humans to express our vitality in ways which support the life and creativity of others, it seems appropriate to relate human *eros* to the image of God.

Modern culture's attention to human sexuality, and modern efforts to achieve social equality among women and men, raise in religious minds questions about divine gender that are quite different from the questions faced by ancient Hebrews. Looking back at biblical history from a new perspective may help us hear freshly God's word.

\* \* \*

When we compare biblical accounts of the Lord's creativity with competing myths about Baal, we see the importance of the biblical understanding that the Lord was not a sexual being. According to tablets discovered at Ugarit amid the remains of a temple to Baal and translated by Norman Habel,[4] Baal won his pre-eminent position through bloody contest with other gods. When his victory was achieved, his consort, Anat, reveled beside him:

> Her heart is full with joy,
> The liver of Anat with victory!
> For she plunges her knees in the blood of warriors
> Her loins in the gore of heroes.

Anat shared in Baal's tending of the world. When as god of the

storm Baal prepared to water the earth, he invited Anat to join
him in the fields for lovemaking:

> "Meet me in the turbulent earth,
> "Diffuse love across the land,
> "Pour out peace in the midst of earth
> "That I may increase love amidst the fields."

When these winter rains were completed and the dry season approached, Baal began to lose strength. Yet before he was drawn
to the underworld realm of death, he insured the fertility of cattle
by impregnating a heifer:

> Baal the Victor hears,
> He loves a heifer in the pasture,
> A cow in the field . . . ,
> He lies with her seven and seventy times,
> Yea eight and eighty times,
> And she conceives and bears a male.

The underworld to which the dying Baal descended was the
realm of the death-god Mot, who was also the god of grain, since
in folk-understanding the germination of a new plant resulted
from the "death" of a seed planted from the previous harvest. At
harvest time Baal was rescued by Anat. "With vengeful enthusiasm," writes Habel, "she reaps Mot who now becomes the bread
of life, just as Baal had been the water of life":

> She seizes Mot, son of El,
> With a blade she slashes him,
> With a flail she winnows him,
> With fire she parches him,
> With millstones she grinds him,
> In the field she strews him.

After Baal revived, the winter rains returned to begin a new
annual cycle.

   The worshipers of Baal participated in these mythological
events, employing human sexuality and personal violence to manipulate agricultural productivity. The Bible reports that when

Solomon's son, Rehoboam, permitted the revival of pagan practices in Judah,

> They erected hill-shrines, sacred pillars, and sacred poles, on every high hill and under every spreading tree. Worse still, all over the country there were male prostitutes attached to the shrines, and the people adopted all the abominable practices of the nations whom the LORD had dispossessed in favour of Israel.
>
> (I Kings 14:23–24, NEB)

A later king of Judah, Manasseh, even incorporated occult practices and child sacrifice into worship at the Jerusalem temple: "He built altars to the whole array of heaven in the two courts of the Temple of Yahweh. He caused his son to pass through the fire of sacrifice, he also practised soothsaying and divination and set up mediums and spirit guides" (2 Kings 21:5–6, NJB). When the prophet Amos protested such practices, he noted that economic oppression and sexual exploitation went hand in hand with apostasy. He lamented,

> they trample on the heads of ordinary people
> and push the poor out of their path,
> ... father and son have both resorted to the same girl,
> profaning my holy name,
> ... they stretch themselves out by the side of every altar
> on clothes acquired as pledges,
> and drink the wine of the people they have fined
> in the house of their god.
>
> (Amos 2:7–8, JB)

Strategies of an entirely different kind, however, were required to assure blessings from the Lord of the Hebrews. The Lord insisted upon a moral ecology, including faithfulness to God, justice among people, and care for the promised land:

> If you listen to these laws and are careful to observe them, then the LORD your God will observe the sworn covenant . . . and will keep faith with you. [The Lord] will love you, bless you and cause you to increase. [God] will bless the fruit of your body and the fruit of your land, your corn and new wine and oil, the offspring of your herds, and of your lambing flocks.
>
> (Deuteronomy 7:12–13, NEB, alt.)

The prohibition of idolatry was at the heart of this Hebrew understanding. Created life could not represent God, nor could human desires manipulate the all-powerful Lord. God had no form, not even the human figure, and the Lord's favor could not be claimed through sexual ecstasy. Although God blessed human sexuality within its appropriate, moral context, sex could not be used to approach the divine or to stimulate agriculture. Instead God must be engaged through moral insight and responsible action. Crops were not to be raised by fornication; but they could be nurtured when humans understood the name and needs of each species and appreciated the place of all within the covenant of God's concern.

* * *

Since Hebrew society was patriarchal, its writings depicted God more often with masculine characteristics than with feminine ones. As modern times replace patriarchy with equality, Christians are reexamining sexist elements in our religious tradition. It is particularly important for us to recognize that the biblical Lord was not a male, sexual being. The Lord had no consort. In no sense did God inseminate as did Baal or give birth as did Anat. The patriarchal character of Hebrew society, where women were subsumed beneath men in family order, was reflected in their language. As in English, the word *man* could stand for *person*, and references to God primarily took the male gender. Yet in Hebrew the divine "Wisdom" and the "Spirit" of God usually were not masculine; whether they were considered feminine or merely abstract is a matter of scholarly disagreement.

Even while using masculine constructions to refer to God, the writers of the Old Testament differentiated the Lord from the explicitly sexual gods, male and female, whose worship surrounded the Hebrews. I believe it is fortunate that these writers did not resort to abstract language, devoid of emotion, to protect their characterizations of God from misunderstanding. Instead of hiding in abstractions, they proclaimed a vital Lord, attacking the spurious sexuality of other gods and ridiculing them as impotent, however the sexual parts on their idols might be exaggerated. The prophets appropriated the full range of human sexual imagery, masculine and feminine, to express the Lord's vigorous personality. They were determined that the Lord be understood as more alive, not less, than competing deities. In the book of Job, for example, the author has God claim responsibility for creation with confident androgyny:

> Has the rain a father?
> Who sired the drops of dew?
> Whose womb gave birth to the ice,
> and who was the mother of the frost from heaven?
> (Job 38:28–29, NEB)

Free from anxiety about inviting literal rather than metaphorical interpretation, this poet expresses the Lord's creativity through both fatherly and motherly images.

Although masculine references predominate, Hebrew imagery for God is often androgynous. However, a reader cannot recognize a feminine image in biblical writings if the translation has not preserved the feminine nuance, and more often than not, male translators have veiled such connotations. Let us note, therefore, that in Isaiah God is like a consoling mother ["As a mother comforts a child, / so I shall comfort you" (Isaiah 66:13, NJB)]; to Hosea God seemed like a vengeful female bear ["I will meet them like a she-bear robbed of her cubs / and tear their ribs apart" (Hosea 13:8, NEB)]; and the "Song of Moses" depicts God as a mother eagle:

> As an eagle stirreth up her nest, fluttereth over her young,
> Spreadeth abroad her wings, taketh them,
> Beareth them on her wings:
> *So* the LORD alone did lead [Israel],
> And *there was* no strange god.
> (Deuteronomy 32:11–12, KJV, alt.)

A few verses later the Lord is androgynous. Moses rebukes the Hebrews for straying from their father-mother God:

> You were unmindful of the Rock that begot you,
> and you forgot the God who gave you birth. (vs. 18, RSV)

Biblical scholar Phyllis Trible has suggested that the Hebrews' understanding of God's compassion is kin to their awareness of a mother's "womb-love." The King James Version contains frequent allusions to God's "bowels of compassion," a phrase which, according to Trible, should be translated "womb of compassion" to clarify the meaning of the metaphor. Characterizing a deeply loving Lord, Isaiah invokes the image of a mother with her newborn child:

> Does a woman forget her baby at the breast,
> or fail to cherish the son of her womb?
> Yet even if these forget,
> I will never forget you.
> (Isaiah 49:15, JB)

Trible translates another divine oracle from the writings of Jeremiah this way:

> Is Ephraim my dear son? my darling child?
> For the more I speak of him,
>    the more I do remember him.
> Therefore, my womb trembles for him;
> I will truly show motherly-compassion upon him.
> Oracle of Yahweh.
> (Jeremiah 32:20)

And when Isaiah cries out for God's mercy, he also addresses a powerful mother:

> Where are thy zeal and thy might,
>    the trembling of thy womb and thy compassion?
> (Isaiah 63:15, Trible)

This image of a woman caring for the child she has borne was especially appropriate to show the Lord's love for a people carried from Egypt and nurtured by God through their history. Such images taught the Hebrews that the moral creativity of their Lord extended beyond productivity and fertility to include compassion for the new life brought forth.[5]

Because Jesus rejected the notions of social hierarchy that formed the basis for patriarchal language, his words have particular relevance to the question of sexual imagery. Jesus preached social reversal in the kingdom of God—"the last will be first, and the first last" (Matthew 20:16, RSV)—as a judgment upon hierarchical pretensions. He transformed the regal Hebrew image of the Messiah by living as a servant and by giving his life rather than claiming power. Rosemary Radford Ruether, a Roman Catholic feminist theologian, points out that even Jesus' invitation to call God "Father" represents a departure from patriarchal tradition:

> Jesus revises God-language by using the familiar *Abba* [father] for God. He speaks of the Messiah as servant rather than king to visualize new relations between the divine and the human. Relation to God no longer becomes a model for dominant-subordinate relations between social groups, leaders, and the led. Rather, relation to God means we are to call no man "Father, Teacher or Master" (Matt. 23:1–12). Relation to God liberates us from hierarchical relations and makes us all brothers-sisters of each other. Those who would be leaders must become servants of all. . . . Jesus as the Christ, the representative of liberated humanity and the liberating Word of God, manifests the *kenosis* [emptying] *of patriarchy*, the announcement of the new humanity through a lifestyle that discards hierarchical caste privilege and speaks on behalf of the lowly.[6]

Like his predecessors, Jesus understood that it was not appropriate to ascribe sexual distinction to God or to the "angels in heaven" who manifest God (Matthew 22:30, RSV). Jesus recommended calling God "Father" to facilitate intimacy, not to suggest sexuality or to reinforce patriarchy. His image of God's fatherhood was not authoritarian, but warm and indulgent:

> Ask, and you will receive; seek, and you will find; knock, and the door will be opened. . . . Is there a man among you who will offer his son a stone when he asks for bread, or a snake when he asks for fish? If you, then, bad as you are, know how to give your children what is good for them, how much more will your heavenly Father give good things to those who ask him!
> (Matthew 7:7–11, NEB)

\* \* \*

A range of vital masculine and feminine images can be used to describe God's personality if they are clearly metaphors pointing to a God who is beyond the polarity of sex. The problem today, however, is that most people conclude from biblical language and Christian imagery that God is masculine. This fundamental misunderstanding blunts the power of the biblical word to convey the character of the Lord. Worse yet, our language may contribute to a false image of God—a modern idol as dangerous to true faith as was the golden bull borrowed from the worship of Baal. Once upon a time, when women accepted a subordinate position in a patriarchal system, they might also have accepted the patriarchal pattern of speech in which masculine references supposedly included themselves. But today, with the dismantling of patriarchal practices, equally archaic speech patterns no longer suffice. As patriarchal assumptions collapse, Christian churches will find that masculine language, masculine images for God, and exclusively masculine clergy are inadequate to portray the living God. Too many persons will be unable to hear what the church attempts to say. Indeed, when masculine imagery seems to convey that God is male, or that men stand closer to God than women do, then such imagery has become a false god, an idol.

During this period of cultural and linguistic transition, perhaps no style of expression is wholly adequate. Old usages are being discarded, but a fully-developed inclusive language has not yet arisen to take its place. I have risked awkwardness to avoid using pronouns with reference to God, whether masculine or feminine, for fear that any pronoun might be misleading. The word *Lord*, however, despite its masculine antecedents, is a useful and recognized English equivalent for the Hebrew *Yahweh*, the name of God. I find it important to retain a term that refers not just to "god," but to this distinctive Divine Personality. The biblical connotations of *Lord* so dominate any other usage of the word (in American culture, if not in British) that I believe it can continue to be a useful word while we clarify our understanding of the Deity.[7]

* * *

The Bible shows us a God of unique moral creativity, far removed from the manipulations that characterized the competing deities of pagans. The Lord has no sexuality, does not need to struggle, and does not delight in violence. This also differs from the imperial creativity which some Christians—in my Calvinist heritage and in other traditions—have ascribed to God. The Lord breathes life into the world, calling other creative lives into being. Humans, animals, plants, and landscape are interdependent, and they each, as well, need God; yet none of these is a puppet creature ruled by a divine tyrant. Relationships are far more complex since the Lord who is so demanding is also self-giving, and obedience to this Lord includes initiative, attentiveness to others, and moral responsibility. The world is so lively because it reflects the character of the creative, attentive Lord:

> Thou visitest the earth and waterest it,
>     thou greatly enrichest it;
> the river of God is full of water;
>     thou providest their grain,
>     for so thou hast prepared it.
> Thou waterest its furrows abundantly,
>     settling its ridges,
> softening it with showers,
>     and blessing its growth.
> Thou crownest the year with thy bounty;
>     the tracks of thy chariot drip with fatness.
> The pastures of the wilderness drip,
>     the hills gird themselves with joy,
> the meadows clothe themselves with flocks,
>     the valleys deck themselves with grain,
>     they shout and sing together for joy.
>                     (Psalm 65:9–13, RSV)

# 9. *Sexual Anxiety*

The Bible depicts human sexuality as a fusion of desire, love, and justice—a beautiful relationship in which a man and woman help fulfill each other while contributing creatively to the society that sustains them. Biblical examples show this moral vision to be both broad and flexible: Jacob's delight in Rachel existed within an ambitious, property-centered polygamy; Ruth's love for Boaz was rooted in her even deeper devotion to her mother-in-law Naomi; David's exuberant desire for women progressed through temptation to repentance, and his friendship with Jonathan was "more wonderful than the love of a woman" (2 Samuel 1:26, JB). The Hebrew faith demythologized human sexuality, liberating sex from idolatrous pretensions and trying to rescue it from the manipulative pragmatism that led to bad politics and worse agriculture.

God intends sex to be enjoyed, not used. Within its energy a man and woman can mingle their flesh in delight, truly communicate, and feel "no shame in front of each other" (Genesis 2:25, JB). This biblical ideal was sufficiently clear for Hosea to risk making marriage an analogy for the Lord's relation to Israel, while the Apostle Paul reversed the analogy and took Christ's relation to the church as a symbol for marriage.[1] Nevertheless, biblical images of sexuality are often repressive, and a strong current of sexual anxiety runs through the Scriptures.

Anxiety, defined by psychologists as "blocked excitement,"[2] often accompanies sexuality in the real world where desires can be unsuitable, and suitable desires can be unreachable. While occasional anxiety may be beneficial, continual anxiety is neither healthy nor inevitable. In Hebrew society two characteristics encouraged pervasive sexual anxiety. One was the patriarchal social structure which Hebrews shared with their neighbors and, indeed, with most human cultures. The other was centuries of defensive reaction to the Baal cults that had myth-ologized human sexuality as the key both to contact with the di-vine and to agricultural productivity.

* * *

When the kingdom of Israel broke in two after the oppres-sive reign of King Solomon, Jeroboam sought to shore up his political authority in the northern kingdom and stem the tide of pilgrims to the Jerusalem temple in the south by erecting golden bull calves at Dan and Bethel, where they would serve as bearers of *Yahweh's* presence.[3] This introduction of sexual fertility im-agery into the worship of the Lord was such a flagrant violation of the Ten Commandments that it seemed to require a response from Moses himself, though the great law-giver had died three centuries before. Several scholars believe that the familiar Exo-dus story of Moses' discovering a golden calf was a response to the religious crisis created by Jeroboam.[4]

During Moses' long absence on Sinai, the story began, anxious Hebrews pleaded with Aaron, "Come, make us gods to go ahead of us. As for this fellow Moses, who brought us up from Egypt, we do not know what has become of him" (Exodus 32:1, NEB). So Aaron gathered jewelry, melted it, and cast a bull calf; afterward the Hebrews "sat down to eat and drink and then gave themselves up to revelry" (vs. 6), including, presumably, sexual orgies. The story's point was not that the people were seeking to worship a different god, but that they were adopting patterns of worship common to the time in hopes of feeling close to the Lord again. Just at this time, of course, Moses reappeared, carrying the tablets of God's law designed to structure a relationship with the Hebrews that was ethical rather than sexual. As he neared the camp, "Moses saw the bull-calf and the dancing, and he was angry; he flung the tablets down, and they were shattered to pieces at the foot of the mountain" (vs. 19). In rage Moses ground the bull to dust, mixed the dust with water, and made the people drink the sobering liquid. The people's act of contrition, however, was followed by a shocking act of repression. A group of Levites —who in Canaan became minor priests and militant defenders of the temple cult—moved through the camp in indiscriminate slaughter to restore Moses' authority. The story, therefore, authorized priestly vengeance in the name of Moses upon inappropriate worship and upon sexual expression within worship.

Sexual anxiety is even more clearly the focus of the story of the Baal of Peor, also set in the time of Moses, which told how human lust led both to apostasy and to a plague:

> When the Israelites were in Shittim, the people began to have intercourse with Moabite women, who invited them to the sacrifices offered to their gods; and they ate the sacrificial food and prostrated themselves before the gods of Moab. The Israelites joined in the worship of the Baal of Peor, and the LORD was angry with them. . . . So Moses said to the judges of Israel, "Put to death, each one of you, those of his tribe who have joined in the worship of the Baal of Peor."
>
> One of the Israelites brought a Midianite woman into his family in open defiance of Moses. . . . Phinehas son of Eleazar, son of Aaron the priest, saw him. He stepped out from the crowd and took up a spear, and he went into the inner room after the Israelite and transfixed the two of them, the Israelite and the woman, pinning them together. Thus the plague which had attacked the Israelites was brought to a stop; but twenty-four thousand had already died. (Numbers 25:1–9, NEB)

This ancient story is well told, polished from many repetitions in Hebrew villages and around young shepherds' campfires. The moral is clear: control your desires and stay away from strange women and pagan shrines, or your lusts will be your undoing. Sex is a fearful power which sometimes can be restrained only by violent measures.

This sexual anxiety is a problem endemic in patriarchy, the social organization most typical of human culture, though in Hebrew society it was aggravated by competition with the Baal cult. Because we in the twentieth century have begun to criticize patriarchy and to imagine more just and loving alternatives, we are struck by biblical incidents that previous generations passed

over or took for granted. Abraham, the first mythic patriarch, illustrates the anxieties and personal abuse fostered by this social
order—as surely as he also models its virtues of faith and hospitality. Owning a wife as beautiful as Sarah made Abraham
nervous; he feared that a stronger king might slay him to obtain
her. In two accounts, probably variants of the same story, he even
passed Sarah off as his sister, prostituting her to a king whose
protective favor he sought. The patriarch's need for a son and
heir created further tensions, and Sarah, unable to conceive,
urged Abraham to sleep with her servant Hagar. However, the
subsequent birth of Hagar's son Ishmael led to jealous competition between the women for Abraham's attention. After Sarah
miraculously bore Isaac, she persuaded Abraham to drive off
Hagar and Ishmael into the wilderness, with scant provisions,
and cast them upon God's mercy. This story also shows, though,
that Hebrew patriarchy took second place to obedience to the
Lord. After Abraham banished Hagar and her son, the Lord
challenged him to risk all his hope and to make preparations to
slay Sarah's son Isaac in order to confirm that his loyalty to God
claimed precedence over his interest in an heir.[5]

The practice of male circumcision is a tragic symbol of the
sexual anxiety that permeated Hebrew culture. Only today are
we beginning to understand the enduring consequences of inflict-
ing this sexual trauma upon a newborn child.[6] Circumcision,
which may have originated as a puberty rite, apparently served
as a ritual of initiation into the Hebrew covenant. Eventually
infant male circumcision became common practice. Although the
Old Testament presents circumcision positively, as a sign of
God's blessing, the physical trauma associated with the act
surely had psychological impact. Particularly when adminis-
tered to infants, who suffered the trauma but could not interpret
it, this painful act was likely to reinforce a cultural pattern of
diffuse sexual anxiety. Many texts indicate that circumcision
supported an attitude of racial superiority over "the uncircumcised."[7] Nevertheless, in one of the most beautiful passages of
Scripture, circumcision transforms from a badge of anxious,
cultic isolation into a spiritual image designed to temper the

arrogance of the chosen people and inspire them to love the aliens in their midst. The writer of Deuteronomy placed these words on Moses' lips:

> What then, O Israel, does the LORD your God ask of you? Only to fear the LORD your God, to conform to all [God's] ways, to love [God] and to serve [God] with all your heart and soul. This you will do by keeping the commandments of the LORD... which I give you this day for your good. To the LORD your God belong heaven itself, the highest heaven, the earth and everything in it; yet the LORD cared for your fore[parents]... and chose their descendants after them. Out of all nations you were [God's] chosen people as you are this day. So now you must circumcise the foreskin of your hearts and not be stubborn any more, for the LORD your God is God of gods and Lord of lords, the great, mighty, and terrible God. [The Lord] is no respecter of persons and is not to be bribed; [God] secures justice for widows and orphans, and loves the alien[s] who [live] among you, giving [them] food and clothing. You too must love the alien, for you once lived as aliens in Egypt.
>
> (Deuteronomy 10:12–19, NEB, alt.)

* * *

In the modern world, while reexamining traditional assumptions about gender and sexual expression, we have a fresh opportunity to fashion a moral sexuality. Anxious repression will not make sex moral, but a moral context may make sex beautiful. Such a context includes a sense of justice, respect for the other, eagerness to know and give to the other, sensual openness, and of course the ineffable thrill of excitement that springs up between two loving persons. Moral desire is neither arrogant nor apprehensive; it chooses to risk mistakes rather than hesitate in fear, but it accepts responsibility. It forgives and asks forgiveness, from God and from another person who may be hurt, and thus it grows and learns. Beautiful sex requires not lists of regulations, but moral sensitivity.

Certainly, traditional anxieties and inhibitions threaten the realization of beautiful sexuality, but an even greater threat occurs when a person deflects sexual expression onto an inappropriate object, as the Baal cult illustrated. Human sexuality makes a poor religion and is no help to agriculture. Yet twentieth-century worship of "Gross National Product" is, in a way, a sophisticated replay of the Baal practices, for as George Mendenhall observes, "The fertility cult is the deification of the process of production."[8]

Modern faith in productivity and consumption has become a religion based upon deflection of real human desires and aspirations to commercial objects. This popular religion exploits our dissatisfactions, pandering commercial substitutes for personal relationships. Advertising does not explain how a product meets our needs, but instead exploits our fantasies of sex and power and reinforces our anxieties about self-worth. We are encouraged to alleviate desires by buying products rather than to satisfy our needs through meaningful activities and relationships. Meanwhile, technologies designed to achieve "productivity" tighten control over both human workers and natural materials, discarding the living qualities of each. Often the products lack craftsmanship: they do not exhibit creative human engagement with materials, nor do they please the consumer for long. We learn not to value beautiful things but to use up cheap things, and then to discard and replace them. As we produce more and consume more, we enjoy ourselves less. This wasteful style of living aggravates human impact upon the natural environment. When modern society replaced craftsmanship with productivity and substituted consumption for satisfaction, we started down a path that leads to the destruction of the earth. Two strong influences—the sexual repression so often characteristic of the biblical and Christian tradition, and the sexual deflection that joins consumerism to the practices of Baal worship—help to push us further along this tragic route.

The world needs an expressive ethic more liberating than the false god of modern exploitative technology. If Christians are willing to take risks, we can respond to the modern crisis by calling for *satisfaction*:

> Come, all who are thirsty, come, fetch water;
> come, you who have no food, buy corn and eat;
> come and buy, not for money, not for a price.
> Why spend money and get what is not bread,

> why give the price of your labour and go unsatisfied?
> Only listen to me and you will have good food to eat,
>     and you will enjoy the fat of the land.
> Come to me and listen to my words,
>     hear me, and you shall have life:
> I will make a covenant with you, this time for ever,
> to love you faithfully as I loved David.
>
>                                  (Isaiah 55:1–3, NEB)

Affirming satisfaction implies trusting the Lord enough to set aside our fear of sensuousness, so we may open our eyes to see, our ears to hear, our mouths to taste, and our fingers to touch. In this way we can expand our love for each other. We will also learn to love and enjoy the earth, and will respond to the challenge of creating with nature rather than anxiously exploiting the world. The earth has a chance to survive the impact of its many people if humanity can learn to take satisfaction—in life, love, nature, and our Lord—and to turn away from compensatory exploitations that fail to satisfy. Rescuing the earth from destruction, while meeting human needs and aspirations, will require a creativity that stretches all human capacities beyond old limits.

Although sexual anxiety may give us pause, we need not let our fears block our deepest yearnings and hold us captive to misguided repression. Jesus assures us that with God's help we can let our feelings emerge and can learn to express them beautifully. When we uncover our desire to love and our need to receive love, as well as our capacity for hope, we will also discover plenty of energy to create what is good. We can fashion growing lives of moral integrity.

The biblical Song of Songs is a stirring charter of Christian sexual rights. It is the word of God and, despite centuries of neglect, it deserves to be taken seriously by the church. In this book of the Bible we can hear God's affirmation of erotic desire when man or woman comes together joyfully with a suitable partner. Although the images in the Song of Songs are archaic, the feelings are timeless, for they are desires that every person—including every Christian—may own. The verses celebrate experiences that every person—including every Christian—has a right to share. We are created in the image of God, male and female, and the Lord calls us to be sexual people:

*Bride*
>Like an apricot-tree among the trees of the wood,
>so is my beloved among boys.
>To sit in its shadow was my delight,
>and its fruit was sweet to my taste.
>He took me into the wine-garden
>and gave me loving glances.
>He refreshed me with raisins, he revived me with apricots;
>>for I was faint with love.
>His left arm was under my head, his right arm was round me.
>>>>(Song of Songs 2:3–6, NEB)

*Bridegroom*
>You are stately as a palm-tree,
>and your breasts are the clusters of dates.
>I said, "I will climb up into the palm
>to grasp its fronds."
>May I find your breasts like clusters of grapes on the vine,
>the scent of your breath like apricots,
>and your whispers like spiced wine
>flowing smoothly to welcome my caresses,
>gliding down through lips and teeth.

*Bride*
>I am my beloved's, his longing is all for me.
>Come, my beloved, let us go out into the fields
>to lie among the henna-bushes;
>let us go early to the vineyards
>and see if the vine has budded or its blossom opened,
>if the pomegranates are in flower.
>There will I give you my love,
>when the mandrakes give their perfume,
>and all rare fruits are ready at our door,
>fruits new and old
>which I have in store for you, my love.
>>>>(Song of Songs 7:7–13, NEB)

# 10. *Seventh Day Delight*

Creativity is completed in rest, which includes satisfaction, reflection, and celebration. This final act of the creative process is essential because it distinguishes creativity from mere productivity, the endless manufacture of things. At rest, the creator receives impressions and learns; in rest, relationships between the creator and the created are acknowledged. Although modern biologists, physicists, and astronomers have now led us to a much fuller comprehension of biological and astrophysical creative processes than that which was available to the Priestly narrators who wrote the opening of Genesis, the biblical account still offers invaluable moral insights. Among these are the information that God rested, and the suggestion that God ordained cycles of rest to insure the possibility of continuing creativity within the life of the earth:

> God saw everything that God had made, and indeed it was very good. Evening came, and morning came, a sixth day. Thus heaven and earth were completed with all their mighty throng. On the sixth day God completed all the work, and on the seventh day God rested from all the work. God blessed the seventh day and made it holy, because on that day God had rested after all the work of creating. (Genesis 1:31—2:3, author, adapting NEB and JB)

Exodus 31:17 suggests further, according to Jürgen Moltmann, that after the six days of creative work God "drew a breath of relief."[1]  A deep exhalation completes the discharge of creative energy and says, "It is done." It is our signal to rest. Without such acknowledgment we might not stop working, and unless we stop, the creative experience is incomplete.

Nearly all the earth's cycles of life include periods of rest. Most creatures respond to the daily alternation of light and dark, some taking rest in the night, others hiding away in the heat of the day. Many plants, too, respond to the daily cycle, though we are more likely to notice their response to the cycle of seasons. In temperate zones the productivity of the summer depends upon the dormancy of the winter. Rest is not a total lack of activity, for a great deal may happen during periods of natural rest, just as much happens during human sleep. The passivity of rest prepares plants, animals, and people for renewed energetic interaction with their environments. If we consider these cycles at the level of the species rather than the individual, we can also see how death complements rest to assist the continuous renewal of life on earth. Death of the tired and weak makes room for the vitality of the energetic without overcrowding a species' niche in its ecosystem. A death in one species nearly always feeds members of other species, nourishing more life. While a system without death would commit all species to stability, death helps to make change, growth, evolution, and creativity possible.

Among conscious human beings, deliberate rest makes an important contribution to creativity. If we choose to rest, we usually bring a task to completion or to a point where we can let go of it; we take the deep breath; conscious of resting, we open ourselves to the benefits of this state. The fourth commandment, "Remember the sabbath day, to keep it holy" (Exodus 20:8, KJV), gives us a chance to choose rest, trains us to make this choice regularly, and requires us to offer the same opportunity to others.

With rest—after we have taken the deep breath and had time to recover from exhaustion—comes reflection. If life is filled with unsatisfying work and meaningless production, we may wish to avoid reflection by taking a stiff drink before we unwind and by turning on the television quickly; thus we take nominal rest but still stay on the treadmill. But if we have been creative, reflection can be a happy time. We look back and admire what we have accomplished, just as "God saw everything that God had made, and indeed it was very good." Feeling gratified is a crucial part of the creative process. Without such satisfaction we do not realize ourselves as creative beings and we are less likely to attempt creativity again.

Satisfaction, binding the creator to what is created, is essential to craftsmanship, for a craftsperson works the materials until satisfied with the result. Creative satisfaction need not be uncritical; indeed, when we are happy with a good effort we may still acknowledge defects in the product since we recognize, realistically, limitations in ourselves. But when the creative cycle is completed by satisfaction, we are much more likely to attempt another cycle, perhaps with greater vigor, with sharper discernment, or in response to a more difficult challenge.

Some religious people are afraid to acknowledge satisfaction, believing that they must always conclude a task as with the confession "We are merely servants: we have done no more than our duty" (Luke 17:10, JB). This may be an appropriate response when someone is obeying a supervisor or fulfilling routine responsibilities. When we step forward to be creative, however, fulfilling some aspect of God's image within us, it is good to take satisfaction. Rather than cringing to beg approval or boasting to force it, a mature believer may find satisfaction inwardly with a spirit of peace. This peaceful reflection in turn leads to evaluation, a morally creative process stimulated more by satisfaction than by fear. If we fear the judgment of another, we will simply apply to our work a projection of what that judgment might be; cheating ourselves of insight and growth we will remain, at best, productive servants. But if we are at peace we may evaluate our work more astutely, combining our understanding of the desires and standards of others with insights from our own creative experience. Furthermore, our judgment will likely deepen as our efforts improve.

Rest and reflection open the creator to the created in new ways. When we cease our shaping efforts, we are more receptive to the influence of what we have made. We stand on the receiving side of love and can revel in the continuing claim that a created object makes upon its creator. The two are bound together. Moltmann illustrates this connection when he describes how God's rest enhances the quality of relationship between God and the earth:

> By "resting" from his creative and formative activity, he allows the beings he has created, each in its own way, to act on him. He receives the form and quality their lives take, and accepts the effects these lives have. By standing aside from his creative influence, he makes himself wholly receptive for the happiness, the suffering and the praise of his creatures. . . . The God who rests in face of his creation does not dominate the world on this day: he "feels" the world; he allows himself to be affected, to be touched by each of his creatures.[2]

Peaceful reflection also deepens our ability to remember so that our creative interactions can permeate the fiber of our being and become part of who we are. We grow. Like the remarkable wilderness explorer John Muir, we can progress through physical and spiritual intensity to a deep, restful enjoyment at the end of a day's discoveries. In relaxation Muir articulated memories that nourished his prophetic determination to speak for the wild landscapes that he so loved:

> These beautiful days must enrich all my life. They do not exist as mere pictures—maps hung upon the walls of memory to brighten at times when touched by association or will, only to sink again like a landscape in the dark; but they saturate themselves into every part of the body and live always.[3]

* * *

Celebration is the corporate aspect of rest, a group expression equivalent to one's personal release, reflection, satisfaction, and evaluation. To these responses celebration adds joy, the acknowledgment of delight among the celebrants. Although Genesis mentions no celebration on the seventh day of creation, those who preserved this account—the priests of the Jerusalem temple —followed a vocation of celebration. Along with the ethics of sabbath rest which we will consider in subsequent chapters, the celebratory practices of the Hebrews reveal the genius of their religion. Their worship incorporated nature's celebration as well as human praise.

Since they lived in tension with Baal cults, which made

nature an object of worship, Hebrews were tempted to respect only the relationships between humanity and God. Within the sacrificial tradition, animals and crops were regarded as human commodities, a portion of which should be offered at the temple. This reinforced an *anthropocentric* perspective in which appreciation for nature emphasized its usefulness to people. This attitude came under severe criticism by prophets and animal sacrifices proved to be an ethically unsatisfactory method of worship.

Another relationship to nature, however, appears in the book of Psalms, the hymnal of the Jerusalem temple. Many psalms recognize nature's participation in the worship of the Lord, a role derived from the covenant understanding. No doubt well aware of the land's longstanding connection with the chosen people, the psalmist imaginatively expanded this election to embrace the whole living fabric of earth. For the Hebrew New Year's festival, which reenacted the Lord's establishment of sovereignty over the earth, a typical psalm proclaimed:

> Let the heavens rejoice and the earth exult,
>   let the sea roar and all the creatures in it,
>   let the fields exult and all that is in them;
>   then let all the trees of the forest shout for joy
>   before the LORD when [God] comes to judge the earth.
>   [The LORD] will judge the earth with righteousness
>     and the peoples in good faith.
>                                    (Psalm 96:11–13, NEB, alt.)

Here judgment did not refer to the end of time but to the ongoing covenant relationship, within which God comes "triumphantly into situations of injustice and makes them right," as Walter Brueggemann interprets this text.[4] God was coming not only for God's people, but for the fields and forests, who therefore had reason to rejoice in God's promise to defend the weak and the vulnerable.

Although the Jerusalem temple was not designed with an aviary, an intrusion of birds was apparently acceptable, since they were beloved of the Lord and since their songs added to congregational praise. In one psalm of pilgrimage toward Jerusalem, expectant worshipers sang:

> I pine, I faint with longing
>   for the courts of the LORD's temple;
> my whole being cries out with joy
>   to the living God.
> Even the sparrow finds a home,
>   and the swallow has her nest,
> where she rears her brood beside thy altars,
>   O LORD of Hosts, my [ruler] and my God.
> Happy are those who dwell in thy house;
>   they never cease from praising thee.
>                     (Psalm 84:2–4, NEB, alt.)

Creatures who could not be present within the temple were also invited to join the praise:

> Bless the LORD, all created things,
>   in every place where [God] has dominion.
>                     (Psalm 103:22, NEB, alt.)

Finally, in Psalm 148, a hymn transcending the boundaries of the temple cult raised a chorus of praise appropriate to the seventh day of creation. In a vision of the cosmos as a worshiping community, the poet imagined the full congregation of creation praising God:

> O praise the LORD.
>
> Praise the LORD out of heaven;
>   praise [God] in the heights.
> Praise [God], all ... angels;
>   praise [God], all ... host.
> Praise [God], sun and moon;
>   praise [God], all you shining stars;
> praise [God], heaven of heavens,
>   and you waters above the heavens.
> Let them all praise the name of the LORD,
> for [God] spoke the word and they were created;
> [God] established them for ever and ever
> by an ordinance which shall never pass away.
> Praise the LORD from the earth,
>   you water-spouts and ocean depths;
> fire and hail, snow and ice,
>   gales of wind obeying [God's] voice;
> all mountains and hills;
>   all fruit-trees and all cedars;

> wild beasts and cattle,
>    creeping things and winged birds;
> kings and all earthly rulers,
>    princes and judges over the whole earth;
> young men and maidens,
>    old men and young together.
> Let all praise the name of the LORD.
>                                    (vs. 1–13, NEB, alt.)

Although this inclusive theme recurs in the Revelation of John,[5] the Christian church has not maintained a consciousness of nature's participation in the congregation of faith. There are exceptions: an early Irish monastic tradition, for example, seems to have celebrated such awareness, and Francis of Assisi certainly did so with radiant clarity. Accepting all creatures as brothers and sisters, Francis found it natural to worship with them and to invite beasts and birds to join him in God's praise. In a splendid study of Francis's religious perspective on nature, Edward Armstrong observes that

> we envisage him with friendly birds and beasts around him; but his attitude was always that of an unworthy guest and immensely privileged participant amid the miracles of beauty by means of which God is constantly manifesting Himself. . . . He sang, not to charm Creation, but because he was charmed by it.[6]

Francis lived with nature in wonder and delight, reaching out to form peaceful relationships with plants, birds, and animals, and thus exhibiting the image of God.

* * *

When we rest from our work and reflect upon it, we may wish to draw our creativity into harmony with our Lord's. We may decide to serve the earth more and exploit it less; to know it more deeply while treading upon it less heavily. We may also wish to reflect the image of God, tending and keeping the Lord's cherished earth, showing other species a peaceful face and an attitude of respect. To this end we must set aside times of rest during which we worship side by side with nature. Since worship forms the center of corporate Christian experience, new theology

will have little impact until, growing beyond humanocentric worship, we fashion celebrations which express our solidarity with
all the life God loves.

The Lord, while continuing to work creatively in this
world, also pauses in reflection, open to the world's response. We
can best meet the resting, listening Lord not as special pleaders
asking to be rescued from a crumbling world, but as members of
a universe of praise. With the full natural environment, we can
sing the hymn written by Francis of Assisi:

> Most High, Omnipotent Lord,
>   Praise, glory and honour be given to Thee with one accord!
>
> To Thee alone, Most High, does praise belong,
>   Yet none is worthy to make of Thee his song.
>
> Be praised, my Lord, with all Thy works whate'er they be,
>   Our noble Brother Sun especially,
>   Whose brightness makes the light by which we see,
>   And he is fair and radiant, splendid and free,
>   A likeness and a type, Most High of Thee.
>
> Be praised, my Lord, [by] Sister Moon and every Star
>   That Thou hast formed to shine so clear from heaven afar.
>
> Be praised, my Lord, [by] Brother Wind and Air,
>   Breezes and clouds and weather foul or fair —
>   To every one that breathes Thou givest a share.
>
> Be praised, my Lord, [by] Sister water, sure
>   None is so useful, lowly, chaste and pure.
>
> Be praised, my Lord, [by] Brother Fire, whose light
>   Thou madest to illuminate the night,
>   And he is fair and jolly and strong and bright.
>
> Be praised, my Lord, [by] Sister Earth, our Mother,
>   Who nourishes and gives us food and fodder,
>   And the green grass and flowers of every colour.[7]

# Part III.

# *Sabbath Ecology*

Ethics—regard for the moral beauty in relationships—are central to the biblical vision. Faith in the Lord sets up a priority in which power and productivity are indisputably subordinate to moral relationships between God and humanity. Repeatedly the Bible affirms this same priority in relationships between God and nature, and between people and nature as well.

In the Old Testament there are two distinct currents in the stream of legal interpretation that flowed from the Ten Commandments. One amplified the commandments with additional lists of prohibitions and with often severe penalties; this current could be quite repressive. Another current, however, developed ethical reflection from the fourth commandment, "Remember the sabbath day, to keep it holy" (Exodus 20:8, KJV), resulting in positive injunctions similar to modern affirmations of civil rights. Indeed, the Hebrew injunctions reached more broadly than modern civil codes, conferring rights upon the whole covenant landscape and the various plants and creatures within it, not just upon its human citizens. Through sabbath reflection Hebrews discovered design in the relations between the Lord, humanity, and nature which became an inspired architecture for justice—a biblical ecology.

Biblical ethics emerged from the experiences of life; they did not derive from a detached, rational analysis. The Hebrews' interaction with the promised land, within which they lived and worked, profoundly influenced their sense of human identity and their awareness of a calling to be a distinctive, ethical community. As this landscape was recognized within the covenant community, the sabbath framework helped the Hebrews articulate rights and responsibilities for the land itself and for various forms of life upon it. The rights of jubilee, a visionary reform program to recreate just social and environmental relationships, emerged from this sabbath reflection. Jubilee rights expressed the Hebrew desire to apply ethics within history, among real people, in their relationships to a specific landscape. Many years later Jesus incorporated this understanding of jubilee rights in his liberating proclamation of the kingdom of God, a new beginning for earthly life.

The Hebrews learned from the Lord that earthly community of land, plants, animals, and people is nourished not only by rain but even more by righteousness:

> Rain righteousness, you heavens,
> let the skies above pour down;
>   let the earth open to receive it,
>   that it may bear the fruit of salvation
> with righteousness in blossom at its side.
> All this I, the LORD, have created.
>                         (Isaiah 45:8, NEB)

# 11. *The Land*

While the Hebrews wandered the Sinai wilderness, they yearned for agricultural lands where they might earn their livelihood and manage their destiny; failing that, some longed to return to Egypt where slavemasters could be depended upon to provide regular, if meager, provisions. They feared the wilderness environment which they could not control, and they also feared trusting the Lord, so ethical and intangible, for their future. Yet the Lord kept the Hebrews in the wilderness until a new generation could be taught moral relationships that depended neither on control nor on subservience. In his provocative study of Israel's involvement with land, Walter Brueggemann suggests:

> Israel had misread wilderness and had miscalculated about Yahweh and so had yearned for managed land. The wilderness is not managed land. This is what makes it wilderness. But it is gifted land, and surprising meat and bread and sabbath do come there. Always Israel is in gifted land yearning for managed land, but characteristically Israel learned that *gifted land* gives life and *managed land* does not.[1]

When these Hebrews entered Canaan to topple oppressive political structures, they formed a holy people liberating a land that was also to be dedicated to the Lord. Political victories were followed by centuries of moral wrestling with the implications of God's claim upon both people and land. On the one hand it must have been exhilarating to sing over and again,

> The earth is the LORD's and all that is in it,
> the world and those who dwell therein.
> (Psalm 24:1, NEB)

On the other hand anxious Hebrew farmers, and priests who lived off farmers' sacrifices, took a long time to accept the consequence that God refused to be influenced by ritual offerings:

> I need take no young bull from your house,
>    no he-goat from your folds;
> for all the beasts of the forest are mine
>    and the cattle in thousands on my hills.
> I know every bird on those hills,
> the teeming life of the fields is my care.
> If I were hungry, I would not tell you,
> for the world and all that is in it are mine.
>                               (Psalm 50:9–12, NEB)

The book of Deuteronomy contrasts the Lord's approach to farming with conditions remembered from Egypt where human effort—planting seed and carrying water from the Nile to the rich delta soil—controlled the outcome. Canaan was a more complex environment where many plants and creatures interacted and where the rain came from heaven at God's discretion. Therefore the Lord would act as head gardener, and the chosen people as God's associates. The most difficult part of farming in Canaan was not the physical labor but obedience to God and moral sensitivity to intricate natural relationships:

> You shall love the LORD your God and keep for all time the charge [God] laid upon you, the statutes, the laws, and the commandments. This day you know the discipline of the LORD.... The land which you are entering to occupy is not like the land of Egypt from which you have come, where, after sowing your seed, you irrigated it by foot like a vegetable garden. But the land into which you are crossing to occupy is a land of mountains and valleys watered by the rain of heaven. It is a land which the LORD your God tends and on which [God's] eye rests from year's end to year's end. If you pay heed to the commandments which I give you this day, and love the LORD your God and serve [God] with all your heart and soul, then I will send rain for your land in season, both autumn and spring rains, and you will gather your corn and new wine and oil, and I will provide pasture in the fields for your cattle: you shall eat your fill.
>                               (Deuteronomy 11:1–2, 10–15, NEB, alt.)

Since land was a part of the covenant community, it could not be treated as a commodity to be exchanged at one's convenience. The covenant distribution of lands among tribes and families was seen as the assignment of responsibilities as well as rights; farming rights, along with the duty to care for the land and the family heritage, passed to one's children. An unfortunate farmer might fall into debt and lose his holding, but even this alienation was considered temporary. King Ahab was one who stumbled over this understanding of landed relationships. Eager to become a sophisticated ruler, Ahab married a daughter of the king of Sidon and welcomed the prophets of Baal who came to his court in Jezebel's retinue. He wished to trade some land to improve the efficiency of his kitchen garden:

> One day Ahab made a proposal to Naboth: "Your vineyard is close to my palace; let me have it for a garden; I will give you a better vineyard in exchange for it or, if you prefer, its value in silver." But Naboth answered, "The LORD forbid it that I should let you have land which has always been in my family."
>
> (1 Kings 21:2–3, NEB)

Naboth conveyed not only his own reluctance but also his conviction that the Lord would not approve such a transfer. Jezebel, raised in a Canaanite court, could not understand why a king could not buy what he wished or simply appropriate what he desired. Therefore, after lecturing her husband she gave him a lesson in efficient rule by arranging a murderous conspiracy to eliminate Naboth. This aroused Elijah the prophet to pronounce the Lord's condemnation of Ahab's reign, and a bitter struggle began among these stubborn personalities, continuing until Ahab died in battle.

The covenant understanding of landholding also met with other threats, subtle and perhaps more subversive than the behavior of Jezebel. Forgetfulness and anxiety were especially insidious. In good times shepherds and farmers were tempted to credit success to their own management skills rather than to their obedience and ethical sensitivity, thereby denigrating the

landscape's covenant participation in environmental health and
production. As Brueggemann aptly observes, "Security dulls the
memory."[2]   Consequently, one of Moses' warnings was often
repeated:

> Take care not to forget the LORD your God and do not fail to keep
> [God's] commandments.... When you have plenty to eat and live
> in fine houses of your own building, when your herds and flocks
> increase, and your silver and gold and all your possessions
> increase too, do not become proud and forget the LORD your God
> who brought you out of Egypt, out of the land of slavery.... Nor
> must you say to yourselves, "My own strength and energy have
> gained me this wealth," but remember the LORD your God; it is
> [God] that gives you strength to become prosperous.
>
> (Deuteronomy 8:11–18, NEB, alt.)

The landscape's covenant character was also compromised by
anxious farmers who hoarded their crop beyond the reach of wild
animals and needy neighbors. Later Jesus preached to such
farmers, telling the story of one who responded to a bumper
harvest by tearing down his barns to build larger ones. When
these were completed, the farmer felt secure: " 'Soul, you have
ample goods laid up.' . . . But God said to him, 'Fool! This night
your soul is required of you.' " As an antidote to such temptations,
Jesus urged his hearers to notice how birds thrive without stored
surpluses and how lilies grow so beautifully in healthy fields. "I
tell you, do not be anxious about your life," he counseled. "Sell
your possessions and give alms" (Luke 12:13–34, RSV). In other
words, build relationships of compassion with the life around
you, fashioning a moral ecology; that is where security lies.

Those who sang Psalm 37 rehearsed these landholding
ethics. Quiet dependence upon God, rather than aggressive
competition, led to satisfaction on covenant lands:

> Do not strive to outdo the evildoers
> or to emulate those who do wrong.
> For like grass they soon wither,
> and fade like the green of spring.
> Trust in the LORD and do good;
> settle in the land and find safe pasture.

> Depend upon the LORD,
> and [God] will grant you your heart's desire.
> (vs. 1–4, NEB, alt.)

Recalling the uprising which created the Hebrew covenant community—and also anticipating Jesus' beatitude—this psalm affirms that the Lord will cast out the wicked and the strong so that the "meek" or the "humble" may "possess the land" (vs. 11, RSV, NEB). The core of the Hebrew agricultural strategy was "Turn from evil and do good,/ and live at peace" (vs. 27, NEB). Within this perspective, domestic animals were more important than lifeless possessions. Valuable in themselves, animals created relationships and responsibilities more significant than wealth, and also more enduring. Flocks and herds would respond in kind to those who cared well for them—unlike goods, which lacked vital sensibilities. A biblical proverb, both practical and beautiful, gives these relevant instructions:

> Know your flocks' condition well,
>   take good care of your herds;
> since riches do not last for ever,
>   wealth is not handed down from age to age.
> The grass once gone, the aftergrowth appearing,
>   the hay gathered in from the mountains,
> you should have lambs to clothe you,
>   goats to pay for your fields,
> goat's milk sufficient to feed you,
>   and to provide for your serving girls.
> (Proverbs 27:23–27, JB)

Such agricultural ethics evoked a loving relationship with the landscape. Farmers, shepherds, and vinedressers touched the land with feeling, remaining sensitive to its character while cultivating it for their needs. Though all agriculture manifests human dominion, Hebrew ethics warned against dispassionate and cruel manipulation, enjoining instead a respectful, open approach that sought peace with nature. Mythologizing the environment through "nature religion," and manipulating it through sympathetic magic, were both rejected. Hebrews employed the tools and methods of the age, but they warned each other against trusting technology. Maintaining a moral relationship with nature required instead a patient receptivity rooted in trust of the Lord.

The Hebrews, of course, were not the only people to love the land. This sentiment may be found in nearly every culture, beautifully expressed in many languages. But the Hebrews were unusual, for they integrated this love into a comprehensive moral framework that encouraged human creativity while it affirmed the integrity of other species and the landscape itself. The vocations of farmer, vinedresser, and shepherd became moral human identities linking men and women to their world. Because Hebrews remembered the oppression of slavery, they tried to control their own temptations to exploit people, animals, or land. They also tried to rescue farming from its characteristic grinding monotony by insisting upon rest and celebration and by cultivating affection for the plants and animals under the farmer's care. When freed from false religious mythology and infused with ethics, the human vocation of farming gained dignity that lent respect to both livestock and landscape. Within this context of moral beauty, the "good shepherd" became a metaphor for God's Messiah, and "the lamb" became a symbol for the Christ as well.

When we read Deuteronomy's lavish descriptions of Canaan, the promised land, we may be reminded of the enthusiasm of travel brochures that entice potential tourists with romantic exaggeration. However, the words appear to reflect long experience, for the scroll of Deuteronomy was discovered in the Jerusalem temple during the reign of Josiah, when Hebrews had lived in Canaan more than five hundred years. They had fallen in love with the place. These words, attributed to the authoritative mouth of Moses, voice the feelings of Hebrew people who had farmed that landscape longer than descendants of European settlers have farmed Virginia or New England:

> The LORD your God is bringing you to a rich land, a land of streams, of springs and underground waters gushing out in hill and valley, a land of wheat and barley, of vines, fig-trees, and pomegranates, a land of olives, oil, and honey. It is a land where

you will never live in poverty nor want for anything, a land whose
stones are iron-ore and from whose hills you will dig copper. You
will have plenty to eat and will bless the LORD your God for the
rich land that [God] has given you. (Deuteronomy 8:7–9, NEB)

Nevertheless there were seasons of drought and years of famine,
and at such times the more sensitive Hebrews reexamined their
moral relationships. Drought suggested God's displeasure, not to
be appeased by burnt offerings. This Lord insisted upon righteousness:

Yahweh indicts the inhabitants of the country:
there is no fidelity, no tenderness,
no knowledge of God in the country,
only perjury and lies, slaughter, theft,
adultery and violence, murder after murder.
This is why the country is in mourning, and all who live in it
   pine away,
even the wild animals and the birds of heaven;
the fish of the sea themselves are perishing. (Hosea 4:1–3, JB)

Such a moral perspective, however, created its own temptations
to manipulate the system or to relax in self-satisfaction. Some
people imagined that by observing the commandments they
might force God to bless them with prosperity. Others, already
prosperous, imagined that good fortune confirmed their virtue.
The story of Job, a righteous man surrounded by pious friends
who blamed him for his own affliction, protested such moralisms.
Job asked pointedly,

Why do the wicked enjoy long life,
hale in old age, and great and powerful?
. . . . . . . . . . . . . . . . . . . . . . . . . . . . . . . .
Their bull mounts and fails not of its purpose;
their cow calves and does not miscarry.
             (Job 21:7–10, NEB)

In his affliction Job was painfully aware that the relationship between virtue and prosperity was not automatic. Proud
that he had cared for his land with discernment and treated his

workers with integrity, Job nevertheless rejected the simplistic equation of morality with productivity. Farmers could not use piety to manipulate the fertility of their fields, nor could they appraise their own virtue from the size of their crop. No technique can bypass simple trust in the Lord, and no indicator for righteousness can replace active compassion and fairness. Moral beauty lies in expression, not calculation. Although suffering often accompanies joy, and death inevitably follows life, those who trust God enough to give themselves to the world feel no disappointment.

# 12. *Rights for Life*

Directly following the Ten Commandments is a second ancient code of laws in the book of Exodus, chapters 21 through 23. Biblical scholars, who have called this the "Covenant Code," believe it to be one of the oldest collections of law from the Hebrew settlement of Canaan.[1] Several verses in this collection spell out implications of daily and yearly sabbath cycles for both social and environmental relationships:

> For six years you may sow your land and gather its produce; but in the seventh year you shall let it lie fallow and leave it alone. It shall provide food for the poor of your people, and what they leave the wild animals may eat. You shall do likewise with your vineyard and your olive-grove.
>
> For six days you may do your work, but on the seventh day you shall abstain from work, so that your ox and your ass may rest, and your home-born slave and the alien may refresh themselves.
>
> (Exodus 23:10–12, NEB)

This brief passage is remarkable for its breadth of moral concern. Sabbath law forestalled the vice most characteristic of agriculture: the temptation to turn work into perpetual drudgery. It gave rights to servants, children, and strangers, and it provided rest for domestic animals. The law afforded the land itself a fallow time for renewal, and it gave the landless poor access to food. It even upheld a place for wild animals within the agricultural domain.

I do not for a moment suppose that Old Testament law was adequate to achieve all these purposes. Since the Hebrew community was suspicious of state authority, enforcement was usually informal, depending upon the consensus of elders sitting at a village gate. Law came to life in tradition, group consciousness, and personal conscience; it grew through local deliberation under pressure from new circumstances. Although some of the laws were rarely enforced, they nevertheless remained important to Hebrew ethical reflection, for they cited rights to which members of the covenant community could aspire. The weak could share the dignity of claims on the collective conscience; prophets could employ moving oratory to cajole compliance in the name of the Lord—and the strong, if they were anxious, might be uneasy about these things. Covenant ethics formed the core of Hebrew identity: when Hebrews acted like God's holy people, they knew who they were.

Modern Western traditions of law, ethics, and rights reflect the influence of these ancient Hebrew laws. Although biblical precepts merged with Roman laws and other traditions in the evolution of Western law, the Christian church has, in addition, kept the Bible alive alongside this civic tradition as an independent ethical check. At times of reformation or revolution, some people have made fresh use of biblical standards of justice. Many modern laws, the fruit of this long evolution, seem to be morally superior to biblical laws: I am glad that American law supports free speech and does not, for example, prescribe the death penalty for those who curse their parents, as does the Covenant Code.[2] But in other areas biblical law manifests ethical sensitivity not equalled in modern law; in these areas it may still inspire moral reflection and stimulate reforms. One such concern is the application of what we call "civil rights"—the legal recognition of a claim upon the community—to the full ecosystem of animals, plants, and landscape.

* * *

The first purpose of sabbath was to stop work and insure regular rest, a practical benefit to those who worked for others. This commandment, however, was also for the moral benefit of those who governed homes, possessed lands, and imagined they were in control. God instructed such patriarchs to interrupt work, to reflect, to recognize the needs of others, and to have

enough faith to leave the ripe crop in the field one more day.
Landholders, who were called to be righteous, could respond
morally only when trust overcame anxiety, when consideration
tempered their desire to manage, and when they acknowledged
their community and the surrounding environment rather than
imagining that they alone were the center of life. Brueggemann
observes that those who manage land "are tempted to create a
*sabbathless* society in which land is never rested, debts are never
canceled, slaves are never released . . . and all of life can be
reduced to a smoothly functioning machine."[3] The powerful must
resist this temptation, stop managing, and relax in openness to
their community; then concerns for equity, justice, and mercy
may come to the fore.

As far back as we can see, Hebrews recognized a sabbath
cycle of seven years as well as the cycle of seven days. Their
conviction of the moral necessity to rest from productive work
was matched by a moral concern about other practices that
created injustice when continued for long periods of time. The
Covenant Code specifies, for example, that Hebrew men acquired
as slaves be set free in the seventh year of their service, while
Deuteronomy prescribes a general forgiveness of debts each
sabbatical year.[4]

A concern for timeliness, combined with the sabbath desire to limit the rights of the powerful, appeared in other aspects
of Hebrew moral reflection as well. Hebrews recognized that
personal duties and opportunities might take precedence over
the common good. There were private joys which the community
should not disturb, and individual weaknesses which the community must respect. Illustrative of these beliefs, a military
manual in Deuteronomy requires that new conscripts be addressed as follows:

> "Is there any man here who has built a new house and not yet
> dedicated it? Let him go home lest he die in battle and another
> perform the dedication.
> "Is there any man here who has planted a vineyard and not yet
> enjoyed its fruit? Let him go home lest he die in battle and
> another enjoy its fruit.

> "Is there any man here who has betrothed a wife and not yet taken her? Let him go home lest he die in battle and another take her. . . .
> "Is there any man here who is fearful and faint of heart? Let him go home lest he make his fellows lose heart too."
>
> (Deuteronomy 20:5–9, JB)

Whether such an announcement was ever made to Hebrew troops, we do not know. Only a society that placed more confidence in God than in military power, sought righteousness rather than victory, and respected individual needs and fears, would have proposed such a military code.

The Lord owned covenant lands, but landholding was under human jurisdiction. A tension existed, therefore, between God's requirements for justice and the practical consequences of varied human skills and unequal human fortunes. Since there were always people without land, access to land and its fruits were prominent concerns. Hebrew law set up a variety of communal rights and landholders' duties to assure some access for all. Deuteronomy, for example, grants anyone permission to snack in another's field:

> When you go into another man's vineyard, you may eat as many grapes as you wish to satisfy your hunger, but you may not put any into your basket.
> When you go into another man's standing corn, you may pluck ears to rub in your hands, but you may not put a sickle to his standing corn. (Deuteronomy 23:24–25, NEB)

The poor and the alien were allowed to glean after harvest, gathering what the landholder or his crew had missed. Landholders, in turn, were instructed by Hebrew law to leave generous gleanings. They were to leave the edges of a grainfield uncut, and not to pick up ears that fell from the harvest baskets. They should not harvest all the grapes from their vines, nor pick up grapes that had fallen to the ground. They were to beat their trees for olives only once. The law proclaimed, "What is left shall be for the alien, the orphan, and the widow. Remember that you were slaves in Egypt; that is why I command you to do this" (24:21–22, NEB).[5] The biblical story of Ruth, spinning a charming romance between a generous landholder and a virtuous gleaner, celebrates the superiority of Hebrew culture and ethics.[6]

Laws collected in the book of Leviticus required a land-holder to support, in his own home, a brother who fell on hard times: but it is not clear whether "brother" in this context meant any fellow Hebrew, a blood brother, or specifically a farming partner who could no longer work.[7] The poor, along with wild beasts, were entitled to glean all that grew during the sabbatical year when the landholder neither planted nor harvested, and since orchards and vines would continue to bear abundantly this was a significant right. Surely it was a right often hard to claim. Proverbs notes ruefully,

> Untilled land might yield food enough for the poor,
> but even that may be lost through injustice.
> (Proverbs 13:23, NEB)

Next to the land itself, domestic animals were the most important agricultural resource. When Jesus taught "Love your enemies, do good to those who hate you" (Luke 6:27, RSV), he generalized from an ancient provision of the Covenant Code concerning such animals and their owners:

> When you come upon your enemy's ox or ass straying, you shall take it back to him. When you see the ass of someone who hates you lying helpless under its load, however unwilling you may be to help it, you must give him a hand with it. (Exodus 23:4–5, NEB)

Was this an obligation to help the animal because of its covenant status, or to help even one's enemy because livestock was so vital to human welfare? I believe that both of these moral concerns joined to create an imperative strong enough to transcend the anger in a personal dispute. Domestic animals certainly had covenant rights, such as their right to sabbath rest. Anyone who has mowed with workhorses knows that a work animal's practice of nibbling is annoying to the farmer, but Deuteronomy gives the animal that right: "You shall not muzzle an ox when it treads out the grain" (25:4, RSV). The same book forbids yoking an ox and an ass together to the plow; such a cruel mismatch would overwork the one and frustrate them both.[8]

Since modern genetic engineering is rapidly perfecting

techniques to alter species and even mix them, we may wish to ponder the biblical insistence upon the integrity of species:

> You shall keep my rules. You shall not allow two different kinds of beast to mate together. You shall not plant your field with two kinds of seed. You shall not put on a garment woven with two kinds of yarn. (Leviticus 19:19, NEB)

This verse shows a fundamental respect for each separate species, along with its seed or its fruit, even though such separation is not always biologically functional. Hebrew concern for "holiness" occasionally deteriorated into a generalized anxiety about mixing people or things together. Stories of the patriarch Jacob suggest that Hebrew shepherds were proud of their ability to improve herds through selective breeding, though they abhorred mixing and mismatching.[9] The right of species to propagate themselves with integrity is still a valid concern.

No doubt Hebrew farmers tried to keep wild animals away from their standing crops, but nevertheless wild creatures held an acknowledged right to glean agricultural leavings. Other laws, too, recognized rights for natural species within cultivated regions. Specific regulations, for example, limited the harvesting of birds; intuitively, Hebrews came to associate protection of birds with maintenance of a productive agricultural environment. One law decreed,

> When you come across a bird's nest by the road, in a tree or on the ground, with fledglings or eggs in it and the mother-bird on the nest, do not take both mother and young. Let the mother-bird go free, and take only the young; then you will prosper and live long. (Deuteronomy 22:6–7, NEB)

Fruit trees received special recognition and protection, for each fruit or olive tree was an important addition to the Hebrew agricultural community. A law from Leviticus required that trees were to be brought into the covenant fellowship ceremoniously, much as children or converts were. For three years after planting, any early fruit should not be eaten. Fruit from the fourth year should be removed (in explicit analogy with circumcision) and offered to the Lord "in a feast of praise" (19:24, JB). Then, in the

fifth year, the fruit from this new member of the community
might be enjoyed. Fruit trees outside the covenant community,
whether wild or cultivated, also merited protection. In this instance it is Deuteronomy which anticipates Jesus' commandment to love one's enemies:

> If, when attacking a town, you have to besiege it for a long time
> before you capture it, you must not destroy its trees by taking an
> axe to them: eat their fruit but do not cut them down. Is the tree
> in the fields human that you should besiege it too? Any trees,
> however, which you know are not fruit trees, you may mutilate
> and cut down and use to build siege-works against the hostile
> town until it falls. (Deuteronomy 20:19–20, JB)

This commandment, ascribed to Moses, limited warfare's impact
upon nature. In the light of biblical strictures' conscientious
preservation of the natural world, our modern battle technique of
"scorched earth"—Sherman's march from Atlanta to the sea, or
the napalm bombing of Vietnam, to say nothing of atomic warfare
—is shocking, unjustifiable anathema.

* * *

The sabbatical granted rights to the land itself, affirming
its covenant status. These rights, the centerpiece of the Hebrew
moral ecology, were surely the most difficult test of faith for
landholders:

> When you enter the land which I give you, the land shall keep
> sabbaths to the LORD. For six years you may sow your fields and
> for six years prune your vineyards and gather the harvest, but in
> the seventh year the land shall keep a sabbath of sacred rest, a
> sabbath to the LORD. You shall not sow your field nor prune your
> vineyard. You shall not harvest the crop that grows from fallen
> grain, nor gather in the grapes from the unpruned vines. It shall
> be a year of sacred rest for the land. (Leviticus 25:2–5, NEB)

This version, from the "Holiness Code," carries the same implica-
tion as the more ancient version from the "Covenant Code" cited
at the opening of this chapter: fruit from the fallow sabbatical
land would be available as gleanings for the poor, aliens, and wild
beasts. A later modification, however, which allowed the landholder and his family to join the gleaning, was added in the

Holiness Code.[10] Such competition for the gleanings is evidence
that sabbatical law was more than a legal fantasy; Hebrews,
struggling to live with this difficult requirement, debated the
details. The charming stories about Joseph, the wise Hebrew
ancestor who guided the pharaoh of Egypt to store grain during
prosperous years so the family of Israel might be fed during lean
years, may have been attempts to train people for the sabbatical
cycle.[11] When Hebrews returned to Jerusalem after the Babylonian captivity, Nehemiah led them in a covenant renewal ceremony that included this pledge: "We will not buy . . . on the
sabbath or on any holy day. We will forgo the crops of the seventh
year and release every person still held as a pledge for debt"
(Nehemiah 10:31, NEB).

The main purpose of the sabbatical year was not to test the
faith of landholders, nor to provide a special opportunity for the
poor, but to show respect to the land itself as a covenant partner.
"This 'sabbath year of the land' makes it clear that the sabbath
is not merely a feast for human beings," Jürgen Moltmann explains. "It is the feast of the whole creation. In the seventh year
*the land* celebrates."[12] Johannes Pedersen, examining the culture of Israel, argues that in Hebrew understanding, "earth itself
is alive":

> The relation between the earth and its owner is not that the
> earth, like a dead mass, makes part of his psychic whole—an
> impossible thought. It is a covenant-relation, a psychic commu-
> nity, and the owner does not solely prevail in the relation. The
> earth has its nature, which makes itself felt, and demands
> respect. The important thing is to deal with it accordingly and
> not to ill-treat it. . . .
> This forbearance was consequently observed. Every seventh
> year the owner must refrain from all encroachments upon the life
> of the earth. . . . The idea is that the earth is for a time to be free,
> so as not to be subjected to the will of man, but left to its own
> nature.[13]

The "holy land" thus drawn into God's saving covenant obtained
rights it had not known under Canaanite oppression. Along with
its wild animals, its trees, birds, and grasses—as well as domestic

livestock, landholders, and the poor—the land participated in a
community designed to achieve abundance through righteousness, honoring the Lord and respecting the needs of each participant. This was a moral ecology. Life was not to be trusted to
technology, power, or human control, though each of these had its
place. Nor was life enhanced by endless work, either compulsive
or exploitative; both the weekly sabbath and the sabbatical year
gave Hebrews time to meditate on this truth. Powerful bribes,
manipulation of gods, and sympathetic magic were all ineffective
protectors, for the only surety of life was sensitive and just action.
The landscape, with all its members, claimed justice, and in the
covenant community only justice guaranteed abundance and
satisfaction.

The conclusion of the Holiness Code in Leviticus warns the
Hebrews about the consequences of ignoring the law. One of these
warnings describes the fate of the land, and though it speaks
predictively from the time of Moses, it can be read as an ecological
reflection on the greatest trauma of Old Testament history, the
fall of Jerusalem in 587 B.C., when most of the prominent landholders in Judah were forcefully moved to Babylon. God spoke to
the Hebrew landholders:

> I will scatter you among the heathen, and I will pursue you with
> the naked sword; your land shall be desolate and your cities
> heaps of rubble. Then, all the time that it lies desolate, while you
> are in exile in the land of your enemies, your land shall enjoy its
> sabbaths to the full. All the time of its desolation it shall have the
> sabbath rest which it did not have when you lived there.
> (Leviticus 26:33–35, NEB)

The standard of justice to which God held the chosen people
embraced the landscape's environmental integrity. These biblical instructions on caring for the earth were meant to be taken
seriously, for the Lord who promised to vindicate the faithful,
and to protect the poor and helpless against maltreatment, also
intended to vindicate the land if anyone should abuse it.

# 13. *Jubilee*

The law of jubilee, the crown of Hebrew sabbath ethics, lies within the "Holiness Code" of Leviticus, chapters 19 through 26, from which I have already quoted extensively. This code was named by scholars after its characteristic refrain, "Ye shall be holy: for I the LORD your God *am* holy" (Leviticus 19:2, KJV). In these chapters from the Priestly tradition we find a profoundly moral interpretation of the relations between holy people and the covenant lands. The Lord was the acknowledged landholder, as opposed to the covenant people who were merely visitors upon the landscape. Therefore human property rights were provisional, subject to the requirements of justice:

> Land must not be sold in perpetuity, for the land belongs to me, and to me you are only strangers and guests. You will allow a right of redemption on all your landed property.
> (Leviticus 25:23–24, JB)

This "right of redemption" protected the vulnerable from sudden action by creditors. It gave a victim's relatives the right to redeem, for the family, property foreclosed by a lender; also, it assured a person selling a town house the right to repurchase his home within a year if he was able.[1]

When such recourse was exhausted, dispossessed Hebrews hoped for the restoration of their covenant rights at the "year of jubilee," when relations among people, and with the landscape, would be restored to ancient equity. On every seventh day, all people and livestock had a right to rest; in every seventh year, the landscape itself was freed to grow wild, slaves were given freedom, and debts were cancelled; whenever seven cycles of seven years were completed, the whole of society was called to reorganize and to reestablish justice. In this jubilee year the trumpet that had once brought down the walls of Canaanite oppression sounded again so that the Hebrews could reconstitute their liberation:

> You shall count seven sabbaths of years, that is seven times seven years, forty-nine years, and in the seventh month on the tenth day of the month, on the Day of Atonement, you shall send the ram's horn round. You shall send it through all your land to sound a blast, and so you shall hallow the fiftieth year and proclaim liberation in the land for all its inhabitants. You shall make this your year of jubilee. Every man of you shall return to his patrimony, every man to his family.
>
> (Leviticus 25:8–10, NEB)[2]

Both the oppressed and the improvident received a new start, while the strong and the skillful relinquished their acquired lands for the good of the community. Thus a grandchild's lot in life was not bound to the relative fortune, rectitude, or ability of parents and grandparents. At jubilee each farmer would return to the lands allotted to his ancestors and start afresh. Just as land reform had been integral to the formation of the Hebrew covenant, so it was central to the renewal of just relationships within Israel.

Hebrew history furnishes ample evidence for jubilee's vitality as a moral idea, but evidence of its successful implementation is scarce. Although the Holiness Code was probably assembled shortly before the Babylonian exile, or perhaps soon after the Jews' return, the radical reform strategy of jubilee preserves a conviction from the early Hebrew experience in Canaan. The name *jubilee* itself derives from a word for "ram's horn" that had fallen from use by the time the Holiness Code reached its present form. Jubilee regulations themselves show evidence of development over a long period of time. It is noteworthy that the Holiness Code applied the requirement for jubilee redemption to property held in unwalled towns, but exempted property held within the walled cities. Perhaps this merely exempts urban real estate from regulations more appropriate to agricultural lands. More probably it suggests that jubilee rights developed during

the earliest centuries of Hebrew landholding and were waived for
certain towns brought into the confederation later.[3] At first I
imagined that jubilee was a late addition to sabbath reflection,
resulting from the evolution of social criticism in Israel, but now
I believe that jubilee—like the sabbatical year—was an early,
integral part of the sabbatarian moral construct that related a
liberated people to a holy land within God's covenant.

We can infer the Hebrews' expectation of jubilee from the
common biblical injunction "Do not move your neighbour's boundary stone, fixed by the men of former times" (Deuteronomy 19:
14, NEB). Beyond warning one landholder not to cheat another,
this statute protected evidence of historic boundaries that would
be critical guidelines during a jubilee redistribution. God's interest in the boundary stones of the weak became proverbial:

> The LORD pulls down the proud man's home
> but fixes the widow's boundary-stones.
>                          (Proverbs 15:25, NEB)

> Do not move the ancient boundary-stone
> or encroach on the land of orphans:
> they have a powerful guardian
> who will take up their cause against you.
>                          (Proverbs 23:10–11, NEB)

The prophet Micah, who emerged from the countryside to
preach in the capitals of both the northern and southern kingdoms before their fall, was particularly furious at exploitation of
the farming population. Implicit in the jubilee concept was the
notion that, when necessary, ancestral lands would be reas-
signed among landless descendants by means of a lottery. Micah
evidently proposes that those notorious for expropriating land
from the weak should themselves be pauperized by exclusion
from the jubilee redistribution:

> Disaster for those who plot evil,
> who lie in bed planning mischief!
> No sooner is it dawn than they do it,
> since they have the power to do so.
> Seizing the fields that they covet,
> they take over houses as well,

owner and house they seize alike,
the man himself as well as his inheritance.
So Yahweh says this:
Look, I am now plotting
a disaster for this breed
from which you will not extricate your necks;
you will not hold your heads up then. . . .

Because of this, you will have no one
to measure out a share
in Yahweh's community.

(Micah 2:1–5, NJB)[4]

If jubilee had been implemented systematically, however,
we should see more evidence of periodic social upheaval than is
apparent. One ancient case at law produced a verdict, ascribed
to Moses, allowing the tribe of Manasseh to prevent intermar-
riage with another Hebrew tribe lest such marriage compromise
claims to recover patrimony at the jubilee.[5] Effective implementation of jubilee would have produced many more laws to deal
with such unforeseen consequences. Undoubtedly it would also
have generated stories of restoration and psalms of praise for this
admirable achievement.

When the armies of Babylon besieged Judah, King Zedekiah initiated social reform in a desperate attempt to secure
God's favor and postpone disaster. Renewing the covenant together with the people, he invoked a sabbatical year and proclaimed freedom for all Hebrew slaves. His reform implies that,
while the moral claim of the sabbatical was recognized, it had in
fact fallen into disuse. Furthermore, during this time of siege
when food was already scarce, there was no resolve to grant the
land itself a year of rest. It may be that Zedekiah's proclamation
included jubilee land reform, without which the freeing of slaves
would have been an empty gesture. However it was done, the act
of liberation did not last; greed and hunger, aggravated by the
pressures of war, led to renewed enslavements. The failure of
this emancipation prompted the prophet Jeremiah to proclaim
the Lord's condemnation of Judah.[6]

A century and a half later Nehemiah, a pious Jew serving

in the court of the Persian emperor Artaxerxes, secured an appointment as governor of the province of Judah, along with permission to rebuild Jerusalem. When he returned to this impoverished land and established his authority in Jerusalem, he launched a jubilee reform to halt oppression of the rural people. Nehemiah recorded the event in his memoirs:

> There came a time when the common people, both men and women, raised a great outcry against their fellow-Jews. Some complained that they were giving their sons and daughters as pledges for food to keep themselves alive; others that they were mortgaging their fields, vineyards, and houses to buy corn in the famine; others again that they were borrowing money on their fields and vineyards to pay the king's tax. "But," they said, "our bodily needs are the same as other people's, our children are as good as theirs; yet here we are, forcing our sons and daughters to become slaves. Some of our daughters are already enslaved, and there is nothing we can do, because our fields and vineyards now belong to others." I was very angry when I heard their outcry and the story they told. I mastered my feelings and reasoned with the nobles and the magistrates. I said to them, "You are holding your fellow-Jews as pledges for debt." I rebuked them severely and said, "As far as we have been able, we have bought back our fellow-Jews who had been sold to other nations; but you are now selling your own fellow-countrymen, and they will have to be bought back by us!" They were silent and had not a word to say. I went on, "What you are doing is wrong. You ought to live so much in the fear of God that you are above reproach in the eyes of the nations who are our enemies. Speaking for myself, I and my kinsmen and the men under me are advancing them money and corn. Let us give up this taking of persons as pledges for debt. Give back today to your debtors their fields and vineyards, their olive-groves and houses, as well as the income in money, and in corn, new wine, and oil." "We will give them back," they promised, "and exact nothing more. We will do what you say." So, summoning the priests, I put the offenders on oath to do as they had promised. Then I shook out the fold of my robe and said, "So may God shake out from his house and from his property every man who does not fulfil this promise. May he be shaken out like this and emptied!" And all the assembled people said "Amen" and praised the LORD. And they did as they had promised.
>
> (Nehemiah 5:1–13, NEB)

Both compassionate and skillful, Nehemiah held the landholders

to their word by suspending collection of the taxes due to him as
long as they behaved properly. After repairs to Jerusalem were
completed, Nehemiah held a great ceremony to renew the covenant of Moses. The law was read aloud to the people and they
pledged, among other things, to respect the sabbath and to give
to the land its sabbatical rest.[7]

* * *

The jubilee conveyed the character of the Hebrew social
ethics derived from ancient experience of liberation. These ethics
did not protect stability without righteousness, but required periodic social reorganization to restore justice and compassion to
all people. Sabbath ethics, of which jubilee formed a part, were relevant to the historical process because they did not require static
perfection but mandated, instead, periodic reform to correct
abuses. They were not perfectionist. Rather than suppressing
freedom for an ideal order, they addressed freedom's unavoidable
inequities with regular correction. Sabbath ethics were not, however, "realistic" in the sense of accommodating the desires of the
powerful. Nor were they escapist, avoiding the moral evaluation
of daily life in favor of some resolution beyond historical expectation. The sabbath, the sabbatical, and the jubilee reminded with
rhythmic, prophetic insistence that the claims of justice and the
needs of life must be dealt with *now*.

If the gathering of the Hebrew people was indeed an act of
liberation, then the right to jubilee was an apt means to institu-
tionalize this liberating spirit. Hebrews distrusted formal gov-
ernments that, if strong, would be more likely to protect the
mighty than enforce the rights of the weak, and so they preferred
to rely directly upon moral authority. The prophets articulated
moral claims upon social behavior. When those who were corrupted by power resisted the message, prophets took this as con-
firmation of the integrity of their protest, and they redoubled
their efforts. Even though land reform was not achieved at regular intervals, the anticipation of jubilee destabilized routine
property transactions. Jubilee carried the authority of Moses, to
whom all fundamental laws were attributed, and it exemplified
the ethical core of the people's covenant with the Lord. Every

land transaction was shadowed by the Holiness Code, which discounted the speculative value of real estate:

> In buying from your fellow-countryman, you will take account of the number of years since the jubilee; the sale-price he fixes for you will depend on the number of productive years still to run. The greater the number of years, the higher the price you will ask for it; the fewer the number of years, the greater the reduction; for what he is selling you is a certain number of harvests. So you will not exploit one another, but fear your God, for I am Yahweh your God. (Leviticus 25:15–17, NJB)

In a close-knit community where most people felt uncomfortable about openly violating the moral consensus of elders at the gate, jubilee ethics had considerable impact. Landgrabbing, though not prevented, was undermined. The anxiety surrounding speculation increased when prophets warned that the land itself would refuse to nourish those who possessed it unjustly:

> Woe to those who add house to house
> and join field to field
> until everywhere belongs to them
> and they are the sole inhabitants of the land.
> Yahweh Sabaoth has sworn this in my hearing,
> "Many houses shall be brought to ruin,
> great and fine, but left untenanted;
> ten acres of vineyard will yield only one barrel,
> ten bushel of seed will yield only one bushel."
> (Isaiah 5:8–10, JB)

When the majority felt defrauded of access to land, they remembered their jubilee rights, and they knew the Lord was committed to their cause. If jubilee was delayed until the count of years was lost, did not the poor still listen for the liberating tones of the ram's horn sounding across the land, calling them to repossess the farms of their ancestors? Such specific hopes made systematic oppression more difficult. Furthermore, the Holiness Code insisted there could be no security in Israel without justice:

> You must not victimize one another, but you shall fear your God, because I am the LORD your God. Observe my statutes, keep my judgements and carry them out; and you shall live in the land in security. (Leviticus 25:17–18, NEB)

Nature also had an interest in jubilee, but it was more subtle. Just as domestic animals benefited from sabbath rest, and agricultural lands were refreshed by sabbatical freedom to grow wild, so jubilee served two natural ends: it promoted the health of the landscape by restoring it to loving care, and it allowed the covenant lands to achieve their moral purpose.

In Hebrew experience a tended landscape was a healthy landscape. Wholesome relationships between people and nature were conveyed by familiar images—shepherds guarding their hillside flocks, and farmers dwelling each "under his own vine, under his own fig-tree, undisturbed" (Micah 4:4, NEB). The prolific covenant lands, where human attention encouraged the flowering of natural life, stood in strong contrast to the comparatively unproductive wilderness lands and to estates of the powerful, where the land was worked by slaves. Oppressed lands, like enslaved people, yielded grudgingly. Farming demanded more than technique; it required love, attention, and presence. Agriculture involved a participating relationship among living beings in a moral context, expressive of the "image of God" to which humans were appointed at creation. Therefore jubilee, by reuniting the earth with people who cared for it, freed lands as well as people.

The covenant landscape also had an obligation to exemplify God's justice and to support God's people, particularly the poor and unfortunate. During the sabbatical, fallow lands and unpruned vines discharged their obligation by continuing to bear grains and fruits for needy gleaners and to provide forage for wild animals. When sabbatical and jubilee were ignored, however, the landscape lost its responsiveness:

> The earth dries up and withers,
> the whole world withers and grows sick . . .
> because they have broken the laws, disobeyed the statutes
> and violated the eternal covenant.
>
> (Isaiah 24:4–5, NEB)

Covenant lands, like people, needed the year of jubilee; reunion with the poor and needy helped them fulfill their intended purpose and contributed to the general revitalization of nature that was such an important part of covenant renewal.

In some ways the messianic tradition within Hebrew faith
contrasted with the covenant and sabbath traditions. Derived
from memories of King David, messianism anticipated a strong
leader to reestablish God's justice among dispirited people.
However, a disciple of Isaiah integrated messianism with the
sabbath tradition when he heard the Messiah announce a jubilee
year—a time to liberate the afflicted, to repossess the land, to
rebuild the culture, and to begin earthly life again with integrity:

> The Spirit of the Lord GOD *is* upon me;
> Because the LORD hath anointed me
> To preach good tidings unto the meek;
> [God has] sent me to bind up the broken-hearted,
> To proclaim liberty to the captives,
> And the opening of the prison to *them that are* bound;
> To proclaim the acceptable year of the LORD,
> And the day of vengeance of our God;
> To comfort all that mourn;
> To appoint unto them that mourn in Zion,
> To give unto them beauty for ashes,
> The oil of joy for mourning,
> The garment of praise for the spirit of heaviness;
> That they might be called Trees of righteousness,
> The planting of the LORD, that [God] might be glorified.
> And they shall build the old wastes,
> They shall raise up the former desolations,
> And they shall repair the waste cities,
> The desolations of many generations.
>                                   (Isaiah 61:1–4, KJV, alt.)

Many years later, while Roman garrisons occupied Palestine,
these words would be heard again as a call to jubilee.

# 14. *Jesus' Kingdom*

Luke writes that after baptism and retreat to the wilderness Jesus "returned in the power of the Spirit into Galilee" (Luke 4:14, KJV), where his teaching in the village synagogues spread his fame. In Nazareth, after reading the passage from Isaiah which combines the messianic and jubilee traditions, Jesus excited his hometown congregation by announcing, "This day is this Scripture fulfilled in your ears" (4:21, KJV). Jürgen Moltmann observes that "Jesus' public ministry began with his proclamation of the messianic sabbath in Nazareth."[1] A most provocative analysis of this point appears in *The Politics of Jesus*, by John Howard Yoder, a Mennonite theologian and president of Goshen Biblical Seminary. Yoder argues that when Jesus proclaimed the fulfillment of Isaiah's prophecy, his hearers understood him to announce "the jubilee year, the time when the inequities accumulated through the years are to be crossed off and all God's people will begin again at the same point."[2] Jesus did not preach the end of history, then, but rather the renewal of history in the tradition of Joshua, for whom he had been named.[3] He had read,

> *The spirit of the Lord has been given to me,*
> *for [God] has anointed me.*
> *[God] has sent me to bring the good news to the poor,*
> *to proclaim liberty to captives*
> *and to the blind new sight,*
> *to set the downtrodden free,*
> *to proclaim the Lord's year of favour.*
> (Luke 4:18–19, JB, alt.)

About eight days later, according to Luke's narrative, Jesus astonished Simon Peter by attracting so many fish to his boat that the nets were overloaded. Here was a sign of the covenant renewal of nature; and seeing it, Simon and his companions abandoned fishing and joined Jesus' pilgrimage.[4] As they traveled together declaring liberation, the group also claimed their rights to the fruit of the land, making a special point to associate this claim with the sabbath tradition:

> On a sabbath, while he was going through the grainfields, his disciples plucked and ate some ears of grain, rubbing them in their hands. But some of the Pharisees said, "Why are you doing what is not lawful to do on the sabbath?" ... And he said to them, "The Son of man is lord of the sabbath." (Luke 6:1–2, 5, RSV)[5]

Shortly afterward, as Luke describes, Jesus appointed the twelve disciples whom he would use to speed the announcement of the kingdom throughout Palestine—a symbolic act recalling Joshua's covenant at Shechem that claimed the holy land for the Lord and organized the twelve tribes of Israel as an alternative to Canaanite tyranny.[6] Jesus taught his disciples a litany to characterize the new kingdom:

> How blessed are you who are poor: the kingdom of God is yours.
> Blessed are you who are hungry now: you shall have your fill.
> Blessed are you who are weeping now: you shall laugh. . . .
>
> But alas for you who are rich: you are having your consolation now.
> Alas for you who have plenty to eat now: you shall go hungry.
> Alas for you who are laughing now: you shall mourn and weep.
> (Luke 6:20–21, 24–25, JB)

These words make fresh sense if read in the context of jubilee. Jesus was not pointing to a final judgment but to the immediate pleasures and pains that would follow a radical, long-overdue redistribution of land and wealth. When he taught his disciples a prayer, Jesus stressed realizing God's kingdom on this earth and trusting God for material provision. He also linked God's forgiveness to the sabbatical practice of debt cancellation:

> Our Father in heaven,
> may your name be held holy,
> your kingdom come,

> your will be done,
> on earth as in heaven.
> Give us today our daily bread.
> And forgive us our debts,
> as we have forgiven those who are in debt to us.
> (Matthew 6:9–12, NJB)

Jesus urged the weak not to attempt force, but to demonstrate the arrival of the new kingdom by their gentle behavior:

> Love your enemies, do good to those who hate you.... To anyone who slaps you on one cheek, present the other cheek as well.... Treat others as you would like people to treat you.
> (Luke 6:27–31, NJB)

Correspondingly he urged the rich to be generous, not anxious, even though debts might soon be canceled: "[L]end without any hope of return" (Luke 6:35, NJB). To find a place in the new kingdom the rich would have to reach out to the poor, whom they now needed for their salvation. In the new covenant community life would depend not on possessions, but on just and compassionate relationships.[7]

Jesus' strategy for renewing the Hebrew covenant appears to parallel the strategy employed first by Moses, then by Joshua, in the formation of the Hebrew nation. It was not so much a frontal attack upon the established political and economic powers as a call to common people to stand forth, to disregard these powers, and to reorganize their lives with strength from God, from each other, and from within. Much of the social content of this renewal was drawn from the sabbath, sabbatical, and jubilee traditions. This explains why Jesus' critics were continually arguing with him about the sabbath. Jesus affirmed the liberating sabbath traditions while he rejected legalistic interpretations that made the sabbath a tool of repression or an instrument for social control by the powerful.

The new kingdom was a covenant community, open to those willing to abide by its spirit. Moses and Joshua had made Hebrews out of anyone willing to stand forth, confess the Lord, and risk separation from the established powers. John the Baptist cried in anger that, if necessary, "God can make children for Abraham out of these stones here" (Luke 3:8, NEB). Jesus directed his disciples to the people of Israel, but he also was flexible about who might respond. The new covenant embraced all those willing to respond, regardless of their ethnic heritage or economic background. God's holy land would be taken away from the power-hungry and given to those willing to tend it in the image of God. In Jerusalem Jesus made this clear when he told a parable of prophetic history to a crowd that included some who wished to arrest him:

> A man planted a vineyard; he fenced it round, dug out a trough for the winepress and built a tower; then he leased it to tenants and went abroad. When the time came, he sent a servant to the tenants to collect from them his share of the produce from the vineyard. But they seized the man, thrashed him and sent him away empty-handed. Next he sent another servant to them; him they beat about the head and treated shamefully. And he sent another and him they killed; then a number of others, and they thrashed some and killed the rest. He had still someone left: his beloved son. He sent him to them last of all. "They will respect my son" he said. But those tenants said to each other, "This is the heir. Come on, let us kill him, and the inheritance will be ours." So they seized him and killed him and threw him out of the vineyard. Now what will the owner of the vineyard do? He will come and make an end of the tenants and give the vineyard to others. (Mark 12:1–9, JB)

Joshua had first formed Israel by uniting the outcasts of crumbling feudal oppression when the world's great powers were weak. King Josiah had attempted sabbatical reform, and Nehemiah had achieved it, at times of acute social instability. Jesus, however, faced a strong Roman occupation with which the civil and religious leaders of Palestine had made a profitable peace. By refusing to countenance violence against political leaders or economic oppressors, Jesus distinguished himself from the zealots and other revolutionaries of the period. Yet his adaptation of the ancient Hebrew strategy—gathering people to live as though a new order already existed—was profoundly subversive. Jesus' circumstances differed from Joshua's: he wisely chose not to employ weapons which he and his followers did not possess.

Instead, he summoned the revolutionary potential of collective self-determination, which he so strikingly manifested and which his followers reflected as they gained faith in him and confidence in the kingdom he announced. "Jesus' proclamation of the kingdom was unacceptable to most of his listeners," Yoder reminds us, *"not* because they thought it could not happen but because they feared it might."[8] For this reason religious and political leadership joined to execute the leader and suppress the movement.

* * *

This hebraic covenant strategy of collective self-determination has been adopted by subsequent groups seeking freedom and justice in the face of apparently overwhelming power. Any listing of such movements is subjective, but among noteworthy modern efforts are Gandhi's struggle for independence in India, Martin Luther King's leadership of the civil rights conflict in America, and the 1980 Solidarity uprising in Poland. After reading in translation one of the theorists of the Solidarity movement, Adam Michnik, and seeing how creatively the hebraic strategy is being adapted to modern conditions, I understood Jesus' kingdom more vividly.

Since Poland is a small country held tightly between the paws of the Russian bear, resistance to oppression during the 1970s appeared futile. Only the popular Catholic Church, by refusing to submit to state control, had preserved an exceptional island in the totalitarian sea of Communist power. Some Polish intellectuals, however, believed that while armed uprising would surely be suicidal, more imaginative resistance might create room for itself. Introducing Michnik's book, Jonathan Schell reports:

> Abandoning, for the time being, all hope of a jailbreak, the members of the Polish opposition began to examine more closely the cell in which, it appeared, it was the country's fate to live for an indefinite period; that is, realizing that there was no salvation for Poland in our time in the movements of armies, they began to scrutinize the minutiae of their local environment. Soviet troops, it was plain, could not be driven out of Poland; but what if ten people gathered in someone's apartment and listened to an

uncensored lecture on Polish history? The Communist party could perhaps not be dislodged from its "leading role" in affairs of state; but what if a group of workers began to publish a newsletter in which factory conditions were truthfully described? And what if millions of people, casting off fear, began to take local action of this sort all over the country? The new ferment, in the words of Irena Grudzinska-Gross ... would be "an effort to overstep the limits of the political horizon while remaining inside the same geographical borders."[9]

These intellectuals planned to speak out in spite of the government. In 1976, four years before the Solidarity uprising, Adam Michnik wrote,

> I believe ... that a program for evolution ought to be addressed to an independent public, not to totalitarian power. Such a program should give directives to the people on how to behave, not to the powers on how to reform themselves. Nothing instructs the authorities better than pressure from below.[10]

That same year, these dissident intellectuals formed the Workers' Defense Committee, known as KOR for its Polish initials, a group which would be folded into the Solidarity organization five years later. The policies they adopted were striking: Schell summarizes them as "openness, truthfulness, autonomy of action, and trust."[11] The founders of KOR not only signed their names to their declaration of purpose, but also added addresses and telephone numbers—actions unprecedented in the face of Polish state security. "Openness," Michnik explains, "was a way of fortifying collective courage, of widening the 'gray area' between the censor's scissors and the criminal code, of breaking down the barrier of inertia and fear. The chances for success lay in openness, not in conspiracy."[12] To introduce truthfulness into a society dominated by propaganda, KOR was meticulous concerning the factual accuracy of its publications. In contrast to the discipline practiced by Communist cells, KOR affirmed autonomy of action. Jósef Lipski, one of the founders, records,

> There was no question of ordering someone by command of the organization to do something he did not want to do. There was a principle that if what they wanted to do was not contrary to the

principles of KOR they should be allowed to pursue their own ideas. And this is why everything that was done was done by people motivated by their own initiative and enthusiasm, and thus produced the best results.[13]

Along with openness, KOR's policy "to trust everyone within the bounds of common sense" was a resourceful strategy to cope with paranoia stimulated by the certainty of infiltration.[14] Deliberately hiding nothing and judging participants by their visible actions, KOR disarmed the power of secret police to disrupt their efforts. The government would have to respond openly. Michnik summarizes the social impact of this strategy:

Radicals . . . typically delude themselves that dictatorships are based exclusively on coercion. This is not true. Long-lived dictatorships engender their own characteristic subculture and their own peculiar normalcy. They create a type of man unused to freedom and truth, ignorant of dignity and autonomy. Rebels are a tiny minority in such dictatorships; they are seen as a handful of desperate men who live like a band of heretics. For every dictatorship, the critical moment arrives with the reappearance of human autonomy and the emergence of social bonds that do not enjoy official sanction. As a rule, such moments are short.[15]

In Poland that moment arrived with the Gdansk shipyard strike of August 1980; and the Solidarity union spread rapidly across Poland to form in a few months a vital alternative society within the boundaries of the Communist state. The government was so disoriented by this movement that it was forced, initially, to make a treaty with it. Sixteen months later, however, under heavy pressure from their Russian supervisors, the Polish military suppressed the visible movement by arresting thousands of its leaders.[16] Nevertheless, Solidarity has been the most successful assertion of human freedom within a modern Communist state. Of the techniques developed to cultivate resistance to modern totalitarianism, the Solidarity strategy appears to be among the most promising, and it may yet prevail in Poland or elsewhere. Writing from prison in 1982, Michnik—like his companions—continued to theorize and to organize on behalf of the now underground movement:

Underground Solidarity's basic goals are obvious: to create an authentic society, a free Poland, and individual freedom in Poland. No political miracle will help the Poles if they do not help themselves. A Polish democratic state will never be born if democratic structures do not exist beforehand in Polish society. And independent of the institutional success of the underground, a base for Polish democracy *is* being created today. It lies in the moral sphere.[17]

* * *

Jesus' kingdom, likewise, did not achieve tangible, political success in its initial stage. Following Jesus' death, in the face of continued suppression, the movement's proclamation of a jubilee to be achieved by popular moral enthusiasm transformed into hope that Jesus might quickly return with heavenly power sufficient to establish righteousness by force. Jesus' spirit continued to infuse his followers, however, and the movement remained surprisingly contagious, spreading quickly among the towns along the trading routes of the Roman Empire. Many were attracted to a community of justice and compassion where people could start living again in the image of God, for "in that image," declared Paul, "there is no room for distinction between Greek and Jew, between the circumcised and uncircumcised, or between barbarian and Scythian, slave and free" (Colossians 3:11, NJB). Convinced that Jesus was alive with them, these Christians were confident that the power of Rome would fade and the future would be theirs—so confident, in fact, that persecution only made them more determined to cling to their ways. And they were right, though by the time Rome officially converted to Christianity early in the fourth century A.D., many worldly aspects of kingdom justice had faded. The church was then far away from the "holy land" milieu where people had once understood the agricultural and environmental dimensions of sabbath ethics. Nevertheless, the emergence of the Christian movement demonstrated a power which Michnik describes as "the reappearance of human autonomy and the emergence of social bonds that do not enjoy official sanction."

This brief examination of Jesus' kingdom in the context of a biblical ecology suggests several conclusions which modify conventional understanding. I present these along with this comment to those who are not well-read in the Gospels and familiar with biblical scholarship: there is much important material I have not covered and there are significant theories of Jesus' ministry which differ from mine, which I have not mentioned.

When we see how Jesus' proclamation stood within the sabbath and jubilee tradition, we can understand his kingdom as a recurring reform within history rather than an ultimate state of static righteousness. In Hebrew history the times of forgiveness and reform did not arrive with rhythmic regularity, and the periods between were often long indeed. But the moral potential remained as long as the weekly sabbath was observed and the law was read and heard—and as long as God called prophets to respond to this word. Seeing Jesus' kingdom as a new beginning, rather than as a final end, makes a profound difference. Jesus did not expect that within his community of covenant renewal all problems would cease and all moral choices would become obvious and effortless. Simon Peter's panic and denial during Jesus' trial, for instance, pained Jesus but did not surprise him.[18] Like jubilee reform, the new covenant was an occasion for people to rebuild the fabric of a righteous community and begin life again, freed from the burdens of oppression and the consequences of former sins. In time new struggles, new mistakes, new sins, and new oppressions would inevitably surface; prophets would again have to blow the ram's horn and call for renewal. Some scholars think that Jesus expected God to complete the kingdom quickly and forcefully, while many Christians believe that the kingdom lies in another realm for which we must wait with patience. I suggest, however, that Jesus' perception of his kingdom, proclaimed in Galilee, fits the subsequent erratic history of the Christian movement. The kingdom comes as we respond with courage to God's moral beauty.

Jesus' kingdom is a moral and practical alternative to power politics, not an escape from this world. Jesus stood firmly in the tradition of Moses and Joshua. He did not propose avoiding the burdens of earthly life, nor did he recommend waiting passively for divine deliverance. Instead he attempted a feasible but high-risk strategy to create a new community of justice and compassion within the geography of Roman oppression, one which eventually might even convert the oppressors. Jesus summoned Israel to awaken to her heritage, to begin acting like people guided by God's law in its most radical aspect—jubilee reforms—so that Hebrews might again experience their identity and come alive. Although Jesus intended immediate and specific changes in the holding of land and wealth, as in sabbatical and jubilee redistribution, he did not preach "class struggle" of the poor against the rich. His strategy required the voluntary, indeed enthusiastic, participation of landholders. The benefit for the "rich young ruler" and others of his type was an opportunity to abandon hypocrisy and recover a sense of moral identity, to join with one's people rather than with their oppressors.[19] In Jesus' preaching the contrast was not rich versus poor, but physical security versus moral identity. Step free from oppressive relationships, Jesus urged both the poor and the prosperous. Become Hebrews again. Do not trust your barns filled with grain and your fine clothing. Rebuild a community of righteousness alongside your fellow Hebrews and experience freedom, life, and joy once more. This message aimed at a people deadened by alien occupation—people who, deep within them, yearned for life. Perhaps they would take real risks to regain it.

The kingdom did not come then, and many subsequent efforts to achieve it have also failed. However, those who patly conclude that Jesus' kingdom is not relevant to this world avoid what that kingdom demands: admitting our mistakes, learning from our failures, rethinking our strategy in the light of current conditions, reorganizing, and trying again.

Jesus' kingdom integrated means with ends. The greatest danger of mobilizing hatred and violence to accomplish change is that if the revolution succeeds, original goals may perish as a new, institutionalized viciousness takes over. In Jesus' process of becoming, the strategy matched the objective, so that those who participated in the struggle for change could taste the new life for which they worked. "Every means was an end," Jonathan Schell notes concerning the KOR policies. "To reform the adversary might take some time, but in the sphere of one's own actions the just society could be established right away."[20]

Additionally, Jesus' kingdom integrated death with life, giving moral meaning to both. Those who trust physical security wonder whether they are happy; they fear death because it may abort their futile search for life. But Jesus endured suffering and risked death in an effort to bring life to his community, and he inspired his followers to do the same. This has nothing whatever to do with the pious glorification of pain which some priests and ministers advertise, hoping that the afflicted will accept misery without question. The risks which become meaningful within the kingdom are those assumed with open eyes for the sake of life; and life lies not in an anxious search for pleasure but in creative expression and righteous relationships. Jesus promised:

> Whoever cares for [one's] own safety is lost; but if a [person] will let himself [or herself] be lost for my sake and for the Gospel, that [person] is safe. What does a [person] gain by winning the whole world at the cost of . . . true self? (Mark 8:35–36, NEB, alt.)

Anxiety about security and personal welfare can paralyze life. Jesus called his followers to know themselves and to act for what they believed; for some, that commitment may mean suffering and even death. Such courage to live is a powerful witness which may draw others, willing to abandon anxious submission to their fate and thus to create meaning in their lives. Furthermore, integrating death with life disarms those who can do no worse than kill. When I was leading the effort to abolish strip mining for coal in West Virginia, I tried to avoid driving between two coal trucks on mountain roads, for fear the drivers would recognize me and stage an accident. I kept on driving, however, until we won some justice for the land.

Since the kingdom of Jesus is relevant to this world, then nature and the earth remain relevant to Christianity. I find it reasonable to imagine that if Jesus' initial proclamation of a new kingdom had been overwhelmingly successful, redistribution of land and wealth would have ensued in Palestine. Moral and practical attention would have been given to the quality of the relationships between the revived Hebrews and God's holy, living landscape. Of Jesus' recorded words, few point clearly to this goal. The Gospel of Mark suggests that Jesus' final wish was for his disciples to return to Galilee and continue reform efforts there; however, either the disciples did not go or the efforts were fruitless.[21] Instead, the Christian community took root first in Jerusalem and then in other urban areas, spreading through the seaports and market towns of the Roman Empire, where Hebrew land ethics had little apparent relevance. Those who repeated and recorded Jesus' words in these places treasured what was useful to them. The texture of the Galilee landscape and Jesus' compassion for nature survived in his parables, but his ethical intentions for the land were largely forgotten.

The Bible proclaims—and human experience, observation, and reason confirm—that the health of nature and the welfare of human society are interdependent. It also tells us something we might not otherwise grasp: that this interdependence is primarily moral and only secondarily technological. Today the complex interrelationships between human culture and the earth are in crisis; this environmental crisis in turn aggravates the general moral dilemma facing human society as we approach the end of the twentieth century. Responsible efforts to renew righteousness on this earth—to achieve freedom, justice, and compassion—need to embrace all life as well as all people. Therefore, those who work for the renewal of God's covenant and the building of Jesus' kingdom must engage with the landed, the landless, and also the landscape.

# Part IV.

## *The Fall*

The prophet Amos believed that when the ecology of righteousness was shattered, the earth itself trembled. Injustice threatened both the human community and the natural order:

> Listen to this, you who crush the needy
> and reduce the oppressed to nothing,
> you who say, 'When will New Moon be over
> so that we can sell our corn,
> and Sabbath, so that we can market our wheat?
> Then, we can make the bushel-measure smaller
> and the shekel-weight bigger
> by fraudulently tampering with the scales.
> We can buy up the weak for silver
> and the poor for a pair of sandals,
> and even get a price for the sweepings of the wheat. . . .
>
> Will not the earth tremble for this
> and all who live on it lament . . . ?
>
> (Amos 8:4–8, NJB)

Biblical ecology includes an interpretation of the causes and consequences of wickedness within the human community and beyond it. My particular concern is to understand the relationships between human sin and the degradation of the natural world and, conversely, the relationships between human justice and natural vitality. The Bible presumes what modern experience has confirmed: the health of all species depends significantly upon the moral health of the human species.

Since I wish to emphasize that this interdependence is tangible—not simply mythological—I begin my consideration of wickedness with Israel's political fulfillment under King David and its fall into state-sponsored oppression under King Solomon. David typified the Hebrew ideal of a beautiful, moral personality, and yet he yielded to temptations of power. Solomon greedily exploited both his subjects and the natural landscape, undermining the moral distinctiveness of the holy people and the holy land.

The myths of the fall in Genesis, which form the basis for Christian theology of sin and evil, were collected in biblical form during this period. These myths explore the broken relationships among God, humanity, and nature; they evaluate the potential of human technology as well as its inherent dangers. Although biblical myths stimulate our insight, I do not believe that modern Christians can use them to avoid making our own evaluation of these complex relationships. We are also helped by Hebrew prophets, who understood environmental pollution to be nature's experience of human oppression. Jeremiah went further to convey the pathos in God's empathy for the wounded earth.

# 15. *Beautiful David*

I love David. He was not a perfect person, but he was a complete personality. Exemplifying the Hebrew vision of human nature, David was expressive, creative, and—most importantly—capable of moral action. He passionately related to God and his contribution to biblical faith, reflected in the Psalms, remains at the heart of Western religious experience. Modern Christians would benefit from giving David the serious theological attention which Christians in other ages have given, for example, to the Apostle Paul. We need to understand the human calling to be a moral agent. The biblical records preserve David well, warts and all. We might consider him the Bible's historical "Adam" who expresses much of the glory and tragedy of human nature.

There are three accounts of the discovery of David, each of which highlights a particular side of his personality. According to one, the mercurial King Saul needed a musician to quiet his fits of distemper. A servant told Saul, "I have seen one of the sons of Jesse the Bethlehemite: he is a skilled player, a brave man and a fighter, well spoken, good-looking and Yahweh is with him" (1 Samuel 16:18, NJB). David was therefore summoned to serve as Saul's armor-bearer, and "whenever the evil spirit from God was upon Saul, David took the lyre and played it with his hand; so Saul was refreshed, and was well, and the evil spirit departed from him" (16:23, RSV). David's poetic and musical gifts eventually inspired the Hebrew psalm tradition, though most of the specific psalms attributed to David were probably composed by subsequent generations of worshipers.

Another story holds that David first appeared in Saul's camp voluntarily, bringing food for three brothers who fought

against the Philistines. The Hebrew troops were paralyzed by a
challenge to one-on-one combat from the huge Philistine cham-
pion, Goliath; David, however, was dismayed at their timidity.
Volunteering for the challenge, David told Saul,

> Sir, I am my father's shepherd; when a lion or bear comes and
> carries off a sheep from the flock, I go after it and attack it and
> rescue the victim from its jaws. Then if it turns on me, I seize it
> by the beard and batter it to death. Lions I have killed and bears,
> and this uncircumcised Philistine will fare no better than they;
> he has defied the army of the living God. The LORD who saved me
> from the lion and the bear will save me from this Philistine.
>                                                 (1 Samuel 17:34–37, NEB)

Refusing armor, David advanced on the heavily clad Goliath, who
"looked David up and down and had nothing but contempt for this
handsome lad with his ruddy cheeks and bright eyes" (vs. 42,
NEB). David stunned Goliath with a stone from his slingshot, then
dispatched him with his own sword. This fearlessness—combining self-confidence with trust in God—along with his dramatic
flair and strategic skills, later made David a great commander
whose troops followed him eagerly.

In a third story the prophet Samuel was guided by God's
spirit to discover David. A few years previously, when the covenant tribes were nearly subdued by the Philistines, Samuel had
reluctantly consented to abandon the traditional style of spontaneous, spirit-filled leadership, and had anointed Saul to be Israel's first king. Saul proved to be an effective military leader,
but he angered Samuel by ignoring covenant traditions, and he
grew increasingly unstable. Looking for a replacement, Samuel
felt led to the family of Jesse in Bethlehem where he examined
eight sons. The youngest had a remarkable vitality:

> He was handsome, with ruddy cheeks and bright eyes. The LORD
> said, "Rise and anoint him: this is the man." Samuel took the
> horn of oil and anointed him in the presence of his brothers. Then
> the spirit of the LORD came upon David and was with him from
> that day onwards. (1 Samuel 16:12–13, NEB)

Of the three accounts this may be the least historical, yet the
most true. The election that creates a close bond between God and

a particular person is mysterious. We do not know for certain how their bond began, but clearly David and the Lord loved and delighted each other. God's patience with David, and David's confidence in God's forgiveness and protection, were extraordinary.

Whatever means brought David to Saul's entourage, his behavior there was unusual. He had little taste for the intrigues that developed in even that rustic court; instead, he followed his heart. He formed his deepest relationship with Jonathan, Saul's admiring son: "Jonathan had given his heart to David and had grown to love him as himself. So Jonathan and David made a solemn compact because each loved the other as dearly as himself" (1 Samuel 18:1–3, NEB). This friendship saved David's life more than once, for Saul grew paranoid as David achieved continued military success and gained popular adulation. Once, in a black mood, Saul threw his spear at David while he played the lyre. At other times he plotted David's death, but Jonathan interceded for David and also warned his friend of dangers. Finally Jonathan persuaded David to flee his father's court. Parting reluctantly, the young men "kissed one another and shed tears together, until David's grief was even greater than Jonathan's" (1 Samuel 20:41, NEB).

Having fled suddenly and without provisions, David sought out Ahimelech and charmed the priest into giving him the sacred bread, "the Bread of the Presence" (1 Samuel 21:6, NEB), and Goliath's sword as well, which was on display beside the altar. Saul's subsequent vengeful slaughter of this priestly family assured that their survivors would be loyal to David forever. When David retreated into the wilderness, he was joined first by his brothers, then by a growing band: "All the oppressed, those in distress, all those in debt, anyone who had a grievance, gathered round him and he became their leader. There were about four hundred men with him" (1 Samuel 22:2, JB). Saul, with an army of conscripts, pursued David.

David was now a Hebrew like the renegades of old. His wilderness band made itself useful by guarding remote herds and attacking enemies of the Hebrew settlers. Like a modern guerrilla band, in return for their services David's men requested provisions from the people among whom they moved. The success of such a guerrilla strategy depended not only upon the valor of the dissidents, but also upon their character and restraint. In these traits David was outstanding.

Hebrew ethics, as we have seen, prohibited vengeance within the covenant community. David's self-control, which contrasted sharply with Saul's erratic disposition, won him widening respect. One story shows David's struggle to master this virtue. Some of his men asked provisions from Nabal, a wealthy herdsman whose region they patrolled. He replied scornfully, "Who is David? . . . In these days every slave who breaks away from his master sets himself up as a chief" (1 Samuel 25:10, NEB). After the men left empty-handed, however, Nabal's shepherds conferred with his wife Abigail and told her of their shame and fear. David's men, they reported, "have been very good to us . . . good as a wall round us, night and day, while we were minding the flocks. Think carefully what you had better do" (vs. 15–17). Abigail quickly assembled provisions and took them to David's hideout to seek his pardon. David had indeed vowed vengeance for Nabal's insulting words, but when he received Abigail he relented gratefully:

> Blessed is the LORD the God of Israel who has sent you today to meet me. A blessing on your good sense, a blessing on you because you have saved me today from the guilt of bloodshed and from giving way to my anger. (vs. 32–33)

In a fitting end to a good morality tale, Nabal soon died of a seizure, and David invited Abigail to be his wife.

David also refused to challenge Saul, and the tales of his grace made Saul's attempts at revenge appear ludicrous. According to one story, David was hiding in a cave when the pursuing Saul entered to relieve himself. Unseen, David crept forward and cut Saul's cloak; and once outside, he called after the departing king:

> "Look, my dear lord, look at this piece of your cloak in my hand. I cut it off, but I did not kill you. . . . I will never lift my hand against you." . . . Saul said, "Is that you, David my son?", and he

wept. Then he said, "The right is on your side, not mine ... so may the LORD reward you well for what you have done for me today!"

(1 Samuel 24:11–19, NEB)

Nevertheless Saul continued pursuit until David made an agreement with Achish of Gath to enter Philistine territory. This nearly compromised David's integrity, but fortunately the Philistine commanders distrusted him and did not let him fight with them against Saul's forces.

When Philistines at last overwhelmed the army of Israel and dispatched both Saul and Jonathan on the field of battle, David felt the full agony of the power politics in which he was implicated. His lament was from the heart:

Tell it not in Gath,
proclaim it not in the streets of Ashkelon,
  lest the Philistine women rejoice,
  lest the daughters of the uncircumcised exult.
. . . . . . . . . . . . . . . . . . . . . . . . . . . . . . . . . . . .
How are the men of war fallen, fallen on the field!
O Jonathan, laid low in death!
I grieve for you, Jonathan my brother;
  dear and delightful you were to me;
your love for me was wonderful,
  surpassing the love of women.

(2 Samuel 1:20, 25–26, NEB)

Despite his grief, David ignored Saul's surviving son Ishbosheth and moved quickly to arrange his own anointing as king of Judah, the southern portion of the Hebrew confederation. From Hebron where he ruled, David gained strength year by year, while Ishbosheth's grip on the northern tribes weakened. At last two of Ishbosheth's courtiers assassinated their lord and carried his head to Hebron. David, always indignant at intrigue, had them executed. Now all the tribes joined to anoint him King of Israel. His reign, first in Hebron and then in Jerusalem, which he conquered for his capital, extended forty years. David overwhelmed all of Israel's enemies and built an empire beyond the territory of the twelve tribes, bringing the Hebrew people their first generation of peace and security.

* * *

The stories about David emphasize the beauty of "this handsome lad with his ruddy cheeks and bright eyes" (1 Samuel 17:42, NEB). This was not just a beauty of form, like that which the Greeks celebrated with statues of Adonis, but an excitement created by the emergence of inner vitality. It was a beauty of interaction, shining from the bright eyes of one who was "a skilled player, a brave man . . . , well spoken," and filled with the spirit of God (16:18, NJB). David expressed himself from the heart—a moral quality which Jesus would recommend—without duplicity or subterfuge. He could be very wrong, yet he remained fully engaged with the people around him and with the Lord he loved. He did not project a false image to others, and—what is most remarkable—he deceived himself only rarely. David's unrestrained exuberance has not always been commended by religious authorities, but such expressiveness is a better foundation for both faith and moral behavior than the fearful restraint which some encourage in the name of religion.

The emotional climax of David's life may have been the day he brought the Ark of God into Jerusalem. Carrying this symbol of Hebrew religion to his new capital was a politically important maneuver, because Jerusalem had not previously been part of the covenanted "holy land." Since Hebrews believed that the Ark did not travel safely where the Lord did not wish it to go, David's success on his second attempt was occasion for great celebration. "David and all Israel danced for joy before the LORD without restraint to the sound of singing, of harps and lutes, of tambourines and castanets and cymbals" (2 Samuel 6:5, NEB).[1] David experienced that magnificent sense of identity in which his ambitions and God's desires were in accord and were coming into fruition. Dressed in a linen ephod, symbol of God's priesthood, he whirled in a dance of ecstasy. Later his first wife Michal, Saul's daughter, rebuked him for thus exhibiting his genitals to the crowd:

> "What a glorious day for the king of Israel, when he exposed his person in the sight of his servants' slave-girls like any empty-headed fool!" David answered Michal, "But it was done in the presence of the LORD . . . . Before the LORD I will dance for joy, yes."
> (vs. 20, 21)

With his unrestrained capacity for emotional release, David was never shy about revealing his feelings to the Lord. The lyrical quality and emotional intensity of the Psalms are, in part, a legacy from this religious confidence.

David was also very active sexually, and his many relationships with women raise problems for us. It is hard to keep track of all his wives: first Michal in Saul's court; then Abigail and another in the wilderness; then four more wives at Hebron; then more wives plus a cluster of concubines in Jerusalem; and finally, when he was old and feeble, the beautiful Abishag just to keep him warm at night. When Michal first fell in love with David, Saul sought to entice David to his death by setting a bride-price of a hundred Philistine foreskins. David returned with two hundred. Women were trophies in this warrior culture, and David frequently rewarded himself with a new one. The problem, I believe, was not David's lack of sexual discipline, but that heterosexual relationships were frustrating because David did not relate to women as full human beings. Although David was heterosexual, his friendship with Jonathan proved emotionally satisfying because it involved deep engagement with a person he respected. David's relationship with the Lord was also mutual and fulfilling. The Hebrew culture, however, discouraged David from full, complex, enduring relationships with women, and as a result his household of too many wives and competing children was burdensome to him.

David was a moral agent: a sinner, yet always morally aware. He would have been a better man, and a happier one, if Hebrew culture had supported more responsible sexual ethics. Prescriptions in the Ten Commandments—"You shall not commit adultery" and "You shall not covet your neighbor's wife" (Exodus 20:14, 17, RSV)—were inadequate. Relations between men and women, like those between parents and children, needed broader and more positive guidelines, such as honor your wife or your husband as a full participant in life. So long as women were considered property, sexuality was incomplete, and human personality—both male and female—was diminished.

\* \* \*

"In the spring of the year, the time when kings go forth to

battle" (2 Samuel 11:1, RSV), David's troops were in the field while he—now too valuable to risk at the front—paced the roof of his Jerusalem palace, bored. Seeing in the distance a beautiful woman bathing, he had the woman, Bathsheba, brought to him. In time, Bathsheba discovered she was pregnant, and since her husband Uriah was still away with the regiment he commanded, she appealed to David for some protective strategy. David summoned Uriah, made small talk, gave him a gift, and urged him to go home, hoping that Uriah would attribute Bathsheba's pregnancy to himself. This clumsy deception aroused Uriah's suspicions; he refused to return home and slept instead with his troops. When the army prepared to return to battle, David instructed Joab, his commander, to place Uriah in the most dangerous position. Joab botched the battle and sustained heavy casualties, an ineptness that angered David until he heard "your servant Uriah the Hittite is dead also" (vs. 24). Then he forgave Joab, and after her time of mourning passed, brought Bathsheba to the palace as his wife. Some time later the prophet Nathan visited David with a story about a man with large herds who was so stingy he stole a poor neighbor's only lamb to feed his guests. The story hit its mark:

> David was very angry, and burst out, "As the LORD lives, the man who did this deserves to die! He shall pay for the lamb four times over, because he has done this and shown no pity." Then Nathan said to David, "You are the man." (2 Samuel 12:5–6, NEB)

Humbled and repentant, David acknowledged his sin: not just adultery, not just murder, but yielding to the temptations of power and substituting intrigue for ethics. When Bathsheba's baby was born sickly, David became deeply depressed, fasting, praying, and lying on the ground until the boy eventually died. According to tradition, during this period David wrote Psalm 51:

> Have mercy upon me, O God, according to thy loving-
>     kindness:
> According unto the multitude of thy tender mercies blot
> out my transgressions.
> Wash me thoroughly from mine iniquity,
> And cleanse me from my sin.
> For I acknowledge my transgressions:

And my sin *is* ever before me.
Against thee, thee only, have I sinned,
And done *this* evil in thy sight.
(vs. 1–4, KJV)

Kingship was fraught with temptations. David had been anointed by leaders of Israel in a covenant ceremony; he expanded the kingdom to an empire, however, not by covenant but by conquest. In fact, he obtained so much booty, tribute, and captive labor that he hardly needed to tax the tribes of Israel. Yet an empire subdued by force undermined the social morality that had been nurtured so long and so expectantly within the tribal structure. Those conquered people who did not choose to be Hebrews had no stake in covenant law or sabbath ethics. Aliens were ruled, not liberated; the moral dynamic of Hebrew development yielded to imperialism. Distinctive ethical traditions, such as the forgiveness of debts, became even more difficult to enforce in this small but culturally diverse empire.[2]

The remarkably candid biblical narratives of Israel's foremost king convey a sense of history's pardon for most of David's offenses. His notorious census, however, was remembered bitterly as a sin against Israel itself. Even hardheaded Joab, David's field commander, objected to it, for he understood that Israel's strength depended upon her voluntary spirit. Nevertheless, David insisted upon counting the people. The first purpose of the census was to determine "the number of able-bodied men, capable of bearing arms" (2 Samuel 24:9, NEB), though it might also be used for taxation and other forms of central administration. There is no evidence that David put the census to this latter use, as Solomon later did, but the blame for this violation of the covenant was laid at his door. Census broke faith because it bypassed the traditional tribal authority embodied in family agreement; it provided the information which a central bureaucracy would need to institute a military draft, implement national taxation, or control the ownership of property. Only people who feel confident of their influence in government will support centralized information, and the Hebrews feared that the census was a first step toward their reenslavement.

David loved his sons and indulged them. What was said of

Adonijah appears to have been true for them all: "Never in his life
had his father corrected him or asked why he behaved as he did"
(1 Kings 1:6, NEB). Life within this complex family approached
anarchy. When David's son Amnon raped his half-sister Tamar,
David did nothing. When Absalom, Tamar's brother, murdered
Amnon in revenge, David allowed him to hide in exile for a while;
but "David's heart went out to him with longing" (2 Samuel 13:39,
NEB) and so he invited his son to return. Absalom, a charmer who
despised his father, plotted for years with the tribal leaders until
he persuaded them to forsake David and anoint him instead. The
deposed king left Jerusalem mourning this loss of the people's
favor and God's: "David wept as he went up the slope of the Mount
of Olives; he was bare-headed and went bare-foot" (2 Samuel
15:30, NEB). When he recovered himself, the wily old warrior sent
to Absalom's court a double agent, whose misleading advice to the
new king allowed David to reach the wilderness safely. Again
David was a Hebrew, although this time he was protected by his
palace guard of foreign mercenaries, not by the poor of the land.
When the decisive battle approached, David gave his commanders a revealing order: "For my sake, treat young Absalom gently!"
(2 Samuel 18:5, NJB). David's mercenaries routed the army of Israel, which fled through the woods; and Absalom, riding away on
the royal mule, impaled himself in the branches of an oak tree.
When Joab was summoned to the spot, he killed Absalom and
called a halt to the battle. In one of the Bible's most moving
scenes, a runner brought the news to David,

> "Good news for my lord the king!" the Cushite shouted. "Today
> Yahweh has vindicated your cause, by ridding you of all who had
> risen up against you." "Is all well with young Absalom?" the king
> asked the Cushite. "May the enemies of my lord the king," the
> Cushite answered, "and all who rise up to harm you, share the
> fate of that young man!"
> The king shuddered. He went up to the room over the gate and
> burst into tears; and, as he wept, he kept saying, "Oh, my son
> Absalom! My son! My son Absalom! If only I had died instead
> of you! Oh, Absalom my son, my son!" (2 Samuel 18:31–19:1, NJB)

Later Joab rebuked David for undermining army morale, charg-
ing that David would not have wept that way if his own men had

been slaughtered and Absalom spared. To be moral, to be feeling, and yet to struggle for power is a hard and painful task.

* * *

Subsequent generations, burdened with their own disappointments, looked back to David's reign as a time when kingship worked. They developed an image of the ideal king who was benevolent—not a source of oppression, but one who intervened on behalf of the weak. Remembering one king who, whatever his sins, was indeed a moral agent, they imagined that other kings might by the grace of God achieve righteousness. The last of the psalms that is attributed to David's inspiration depicts such a worthy ruler:

> God, endow the king with your own fair judgement,
>   the son of the king with your own saving justice,
> that he may rule your people with justice,
>   and your poor with fair judgement.
>
> Mountains and hills,
>   bring peace to the people!
> With justice he will judge the poor of the people,
> he will save the children of the needy
>   and crush their oppressors. . . .
>
> For he rescues anyone needy who calls to him,
>   and the poor who has no one to help.
> He has pity on the weak and the needy,
>   and saves the needy from death.
>                     (Psalm 72:1–4, 12–13, NJB)

Not many rulers, however, have been able to follow this call.

Biblical ethics grew from the Lord's compact with the powerless, who could see clearly the need for justice. As we ourselves gain power we find many reasons to depart from standards that now appear rigorous, costly, and inefficient. We come to trust, instead, the resources we now possess and the techniques we have devised, and we may even believe that our power over others is really for their benefit. Power tempts us to such self-justification.

The beauty of David is that even when he sinned, he did not rationalize. Caught between ethics and practicality, he cried to the Lord in his distress.

# 16. *Solomon's Technique*

Israel's first two kings had been designated by the prophet Samuel and anointed by tribal elders in covenant ceremonies. Samuel was now gone, and David, old and feeble, avoided the question of succession. Perhaps he was reluctant to offend any of his sons, or perhaps he could no longer negotiate with the tribal leaders. Adonijah, his oldest surviving son, assembled conservative tribal supporters who were prepared to proclaim him king. While this assembly was meeting, however, Bathsheba and the prophet Nathan persuaded David to anoint Solomon, Bathsheba's second son, immediately. This news reached Adonijah in the midst of his assembly; he panicked, fled to seek sanctuary, and offered no resistance. After David died, Solomon employed the palace guard of foreign mercenaries to rout his opponents and consolidate his power. The luckless Adonijah was executed. Old Joab, commander of the troops of Israel, was murdered as he clung to God's altar claiming sanctuary. The frank, dramatic narrative of David's reign, which scholars have called the "Court-history of David," concludes the description of this purge with the laconic comment "Thus Solomon's royal power was securely established" (1 Kings 2:46, NEB). The subsequent biblical record of Solomon's reign is more circumspect and less revealing than the Bible's candid accounts of David's virtues and temptations.

Even though he had eliminated his rivals, Solomon still needed legitimacy. He did not propose a covenant with the tribal leaders, nor did he ask a prophet for a word from the Lord; rather,

Solomon unfurled the technique he would use brilliantly
throughout his forty-year reign: he dazzled the people. First he
arranged a marriage alliance with Egypt, bringing to Jerusalem
a daughter of the pharaoh. Egypt was comparatively weak, and
the daughter might have been an offspring of a huge harem, but
the union appealed to the Hebrews' pride, for they remembered
where their ancestors had once been slaves. Next, adopting a religious strategy common to Egyptian rulers but novel in Israel,
Solomon arranged a personal vision.[1] At the Lord's shrine in Gib-
eon he offered a grand sacrifice and then retired to sleep; the next
day he reported to his court a dream conversation with the Lord:

> "Now, Yahweh my God, you have made your servant king in
> succession to David my father. But I am a very young man,
> unskilled in leadership. . . . So give your servant a heart to
> understand how to govern your people, how to discern between
> good and evil, for how could one otherwise govern such a great
> people as yours?" It pleased Yahweh that Solomon should have
> asked for this. "Since you have asked for this," God said, "and not
> asked for long life for yourself or riches . . . I give you a heart wise
> and shrewd . . . What you have not asked I shall give you too: such
> riches and glory as no other king can match."
>
> (1 Kings 3:7–13, NJB)

Solomon divided Israel into twelve administrative dis-
tricts, sacrificing the ancient tribal jurisdictions in favor of a
more efficient system. He appointed governors to insure that
each district would furnish provisions for the royal household one
month every year. Since Solomon's court grew to number in the
thousands, it became a heavy burden upon the dry landscape and
its modest farmers to provide the flour, meal, grain, cattle, sheep,
stags, gazelles, roebucks, and fowl mentioned in the biblical lists,
as well as barley and straw for thousands of horses in the
elaborate regional stables that Solomon built. The people's first
duty became the support of a lavish, distant court. In the boasts
of the court recorder, Solomon's administrative system was so
efficient that "the regional governors . . . never fell short in their
deliveries" (1 Kings 4:27, NEB) and "the people of Judah and Israel
. . . ate and they drank, and enjoyed life . . . every man under his
own vine and fig-tree" (4:21, 25). That was the official view from

the palace. In the countryside, however, things no doubt seemed less idyllic. With the heavy burden of official contributions, farmland probably received few sabbatical rests during this era, and likely the poor found little to glean. Solomon's deliberate disruption of tribal government and culture was not at all conducive to forgiveness of debts or release from slavery. As oppression trickled down through society, those at the bottom paid for the luxury at court.

* * *

The ambitious Solomon wanted to build a new royal city, one that would include a permanent temple for the Lord on a hilltop adjacent to David's Jerusalem. Hiram of Tyre, the king who had furnished cedar for David's house, offered Solomon the means. The two rulers' initial correspondence, preserved in the Bible, launched new exploitation of both workers and nature:

> When Hiram King of Tyre heard that Solomon had been anointed king in his father's place, he sent envoys to him, because he had always been a friend of David. Solomon sent this answer to Hiram: "...The LORD my God has given me peace; there is no one to oppose me, I fear no attack. So I propose to build a house in honour of the name of the LORD my God.... If therefore you will now give orders that cedars be felled and brought from Lebanon, my men will work with yours, and I will pay you for your men whatever sum you fix; for, as you know, we have none so skilled at felling timber as your Sidonians."
>
> When Hiram received Solomon's message, . . . he sent this reply to Solomon: "I have received your message. In this matter of timber, both cedar and pine, I will do all you wish. My men shall bring down the logs from Lebanon to the sea and I will make them up into rafts to be floated to the place you appoint; I will have them broken up there and you can remove them. You, on your part, will meet my wishes if you provide the food for my household." So Hiram kept Solomon supplied with all the cedar and pine that he wanted, and Solomon supplied Hiram with twenty thousand kor of wheat as food for his household and twenty kor of oil of pounded olives; Solomon gave this yearly to Hiram.... King Solomon raised a forced levy from the whole of Israel amounting to thirty thousand men. He sent them to Lebanon in monthly relays of ten thousand, so that the men spent one month in Lebanon and two at home.... Solomon also

had seventy thousand hauliers and eighty thousand quarrymen, apart from the three thousand three hundred foremen in charge of the work. (1 Kings 5:1–17, NEB)

To obtain the timber, Solomon imposed upon Israel the notorious *courvée* system of forced, unpaid labor.[2] His compensation for Sidonian help did not go to feed the workers: these payments in wheat and olive oil, taxed from Israel's farmers, instead went to support Hiram's royal household in Tyre.

So far as we know, this began the region's first vast logging operation, which provided materials for twenty years of construction in Jerusalem. The famed cedars of Lebanon grew seventy to eighty feet tall with long, spreading branches and trunks ten feet or more in diameter. On the coastlands where Hiram once logged for Solomon, only a few of these trees now survive. The prophet Ezekiel, who glimpsed the cedar's environmental significance, described it as a metaphor for empire:

> . . . a cedar in Lebanon,
>   whose fair branches overshadowed the forest,
> towering high with its crown finding a way through the
>     foliage.
> Springs nourished it, underground waters gave it height,
> their streams washed the soil all round it
> and sent forth their rills to every tree in the country.
> . . . . . . . . . . . . . . . . . . . . . . . . . . . . . . . . . . . . . . . .
> Its boughs were many, its branches spread far;
>   for water was abundant in the channels.
> In its boughs all the birds of the air had their nests,
> under its branches all wild creatures bore their young.
> . . . . . . . . . . . . . . . . . . . . . . . . . . . . . . . . . . . . . . . .
>   I, the LORD, gave it beauty
>     with its mass of spreading boughs,
>   the envy of all the trees in Eden,
>     the garden of God.
>                                    (Ezekiel 31:3–6, 9, NEB)

These grand trees crowned the Lebanese landscape and sustained a rich ecosystem by absorbing, expiring, and circulating water through the forest environment. To expand Jerusalem, Solomon began logging on a scale that led to their depletion.

Continued cutting gradually dried up the springs, eroded the
land, diminished the birds and wildlife, and reduced the Lebanese coastlands to their present arid condition. Solomon's records proclaim his knowledge of trees "from the cedar of Lebanon
down to the marjoram that grows out of the wall" (1 Kings 4:33,
NEB), but his was the technical expertise of an exploiter, not the
wisdom of a protector. We cannot blame Solomon for lacking
modern ecological awareness. We can, however, hold him responsible for systematically overturning a Hebrew social ecology that
fostered moral concern for natural life and discouraged prideful
imperial projects. Solomon's violations of the Hebrew covenant
opened the way for him to join with Hiram to ravage the land
Ezekiel called "the garden of God."

Although the temple was not the largest of Solomon's
buildings, it was the centerpiece of his scheme. David, who had
thought about constructing a temple to honor the Lord, had given
in to the tradition that God must remain free from physical constraint; Solomon, however, was prepared to replace tradition
with cosmopolitan splendor. He hired Phoenician craftsmen to
supervise construction of a temple, designed from both Canaanite and foreign models, that would house the ancient Ark of the
Lord. Conscripts and slaves mined, quarried, and felled indis-
criminately, and the moral considerations of the Hebrew covenant were all but forgotten. Centuries after the event, editors of
the books of Kings composed a long prayer of dedication to har-
monize the temple with the Hebrew tradition. A verse imbedded
in this sermon may indeed be Solomon's own:

> O LORD who hast set the sun in heaven,
>   but hast chosen to dwell in thick darkness,
> here have I built thee a lofty house,
>   a habitation for thee to occupy for ever.
>             (1 Kings 8:12–13, NEB)

"Yahweh is now cornered in the temple," Walter Brueggemann
responds caustically. "His business is support of the regime, to
grant legitimacy to it. . . . He is guest and not host. Religion
becomes a decoration rather than a foundation."[3]

Despite the temple's inauspicious beginnings, centuries of faithful worship, inspired prophets, and thoughtful priests incorporated the temple into Hebrew experience of the Lord. In Jerusalem the culture of faith outlasted Solomon's reign of oppression, and it survived other oppressive times as well, redeeming a number of ambiguous monuments through the spirit of God's people. We who believe, however, may examine the monuments of our faith, both physical and institutional, with the eye that Jesus used to scrutinize the Jerusalem temple in his day. Jesus saw that the temple needed to be cleansed, and he knew that even if the temple were destroyed, faith would continue.[4]

\* \* \*

Some good things, too, happened during the reign of Solomon. The king's innovative development of international trade, coupled with his lavish patronage of court and temple, created a community of intellectuals who made valuable contributions to Israel's cultural and spiritual growth. For the first time some of Israel's important religious traditions were committed to writing, including the magnificent Yahwist narrative. Psalms and liturgy received encouragement and support. Solomon's court also began the "wisdom" tradition that has remained associated with his name. At its best this was a creative interaction of the Hebrew ethical tradition with cosmopolitan influences, for the development of Jerusalem stimulated the agrarian Hebrew society, causing people to reflect on the particular opportunities and problems of urban culture. There were undoubtedly excesses and perversions in each of these developments, but subsequent generations eliminated much of the chaff from the wheat to form the biblical literature that we now read.

An imaginative administrator, Solomon mobilized Israel's limited resources to participate creatively—and profitably, for himself—in international trade and cosmopolitan life. He married many foreign wives, joined in the worship of their gods, and appropriated the technical advances of their countries. Trading chariots and horses between Egypt and Arabian kingdoms, he acquired a large chariot corps, which he used for display rather than combat. He hired Sidonian seamen for trading expeditions on both the Mediterranean and Red Seas, and mastered the technologies of his time to achieve fortune and reputation. George Mendenhall notes, however, that Solomon's reign provided Hebrews with their first experience of the fact that "Technology has no built-in self-control"; it must be curbed by ethical principles.[5]

If "wisdom" is a moral quality, not simply a technical ability, then the reports of Solomon's wisdom are mere self-promotion. The queen of Sheba grasped the real character of Solomon's reputed wisdom when she made a trading visit to Jerusalem:

> When the queen of Sheba saw how very wise Solomon was, the palace which he had built, the food at his table, the accommodation for his officials, the organisation of his staff and the way they were dressed, his cupbearers, and the burnt offerings which he presented in the Temple of Yahweh, it left her breathless, and she said to the king, "The report I heard in my own country about your wisdom in handling your affairs was true then! Until I came and saw for myself, I did not believe the reports, but clearly I was told less than half . . . How fortunate your wives are!"
>
> (1 Kings 10:4–8, NJB)

Although Solomon lacked true wisdom, he was exciting, flashy, and sophisticated. To those who were easily impressed—subjects and visitors alike—these traits were sufficient.

*  *  *

Behind its splendid facade, Solomon's empire gradually decayed. Early in the reign, portions of Edom southeast of Judah, which David had pacified, were liberated by refugees from a sanctuary in Egypt. Then a band of Aramaic adventurers captured Damascus, the principal city of Solomon's northernmost province, which in subsequent generations became the region's strongest power.[6] There was a threat of internal insurrection as well. During his building program Solomon noticed the administrative energy of a youth named Jeroboam, and "seeing how the young man worked, he put him in charge of all the labour-gangs in the tribal district of Joseph" (1 Kings 11:28, NEB). Once on home territory, however, Jeroboam was aroused by the plight of his people. He joined with the prophet Ahijah, who was appalled at

Solomon's practice of worshiping all the gods represented in his harem, and they called the ten northern tribes to revolt. But Solomon quickly pursued Jeroboam, and the rebels fled to Egypt. The cagey Solomon managed to avoid big military conflicts, relying instead upon his diplomatic skills. Difficulties arose, though, largely because the king's compulsive acquisitiveness exceeded what he could tax from his people or win in trade:

> King Solomon was a lover of women, and besides Pharaoh's daughter he married many foreign women, Moabite, Ammonite, Edomite, Sidonian, and Hittite. . . . He had seven hundred wives, who were princesses, and three hundred concubines.
>
> (1 Kings 11:1–3, NEB)

These numbers may be exaggerated, but Solomon's court was certainly extensive, and the problem of supporting it became acute. At one time Solomon needed gold so badly that he sold Hiram of Tyre twenty towns near their common border.[7]

After a forty-year reign Solomon died, and with the accession of his son Rehoboam dissatisfaction among the northern tribes threatened the unity of the empire. Rehoboam traveled north to Shechem, where Joshua had originally confederated the twelve tribes, to confront tribal leaders. They made their offer: "Your father laid a cruel yoke on us; if you will lighten your father's cruel slavery, that heavy yoke which he imposed on us, we are willing to serve you" (1 Kings 12:4, NJB). Rehoboam's senior advisors who retained sympathy for the people recommended compromise, but his younger counselors, who knew only life at court, urged him to be ruthless. Unfortunately Rehoboam tried to intimidate the tribal leaders: "My father made your yoke heavy, I shall make it heavier still! My father controlled you with the whip, but I shall apply a spiked lash!" (vs. 14, NJB). Hearing this, those from the north withdrew, passing the cry:

> What share have we in David?
> — No heritage in the son of Jesse!
> Away to your tents, Israel!
> Now look after your own House, David!
>
> (vs. 16, NJB)

After stoning to death Rehoboam's commander of forced labor, the ten northern tribes joined and chose as their king the erst-while rebel, Jeroboam. Thus, only seventy years after David created the empire, it crumbled because of the greed of kings.

This loss of empire, however, was less of a tragedy than the erosion of Hebrew ethics during the imperial period. David had emerged as a Hebrew with moral sensitivity, but he had found conquest more rewarding than his duty to protect the moral community within Israel, and he neglected his opportunity to extend liberation beyond the twelve tribes. He ruled with a light hand, yet by the end of his reign he had so lost contact with tribal leaders and with covenant traditions that he had to rely upon the protection of foreign mercenaries. Absalom's death in battle with his father conveyed to David the tragic consequences of this loss of integrity. Solomon learned to compete for power within David's anarchic household, and he also learned how to manipulate his father, the symbols of the Lord, and the Hebrew moral tradition. He secured his kingdom through terror and maintained it through exploitation. "Remarkably," Walter Brueggemann ob-serves, "in one generation he managed to confiscate Israel's freedom and reduce social order to the very situation of Egyptian slavery."[8] Solomon force-marched Israel into the cosmopolitan world, employing both technology and self-advertisement. Al-though he undermined the ancient Hebrew morality, Solomon created cultural institutions that led to the written preservation of his people's heritage.

Empires are commonplace, but the Hebrew covenant was unique. By the end of Solomon's reign this moral ecology—a delicate yet balanced alternative to the ways of empires—had unraveled. It had never become a whole cloth, a viable weave of cultural and natural relationships. It was a vision of God's will for a holy people and holy land, fortified by several generations of inconclusive experience. Now the struggle to build a covenant society had to start over in two small, vulnerable sister kingdoms. Dark centuries followed, lighted by fierce flashes of moral convic-tion from a few like Elijah, until the prophetic tradition flowered again with Amos, Hosea, Isaiah, and the Deuteronomist.

At first, when God called Hebrews to withdraw from Egyptian and Canaanite oppression, the covenant people imagined they could separate themselves from the enemy. Their experience with empire taught them that the enemy was also within.

# 17. *The Serpent*

During these times, when a court and priesthood of literate and thoughtful people were assembled in Jerusalem, the ancient Hebrew stories were written down by the Yahwist in a form similar to the narrative which is now a principal strand in the books of Genesis, Exodus, and Joshua. While it is difficult to interpret how political events shaped these tales through the centuries of their oral transmission, we may assume that the stories held meaning for people who shared that history. Indeed these stories—most particularly the narratives of creation and fall—have been meaningful to many ages and cultures, from the time of Solomon to the present.

In the Yahwist narrative the hopeful creation stories were balanced by tales of disintegration that helped people cope with personal and historical tragedy. The fall of humanity from the beauty and satisfactions of Eden appeared not just in the one story of the serpent in the garden, but in a progressive narrative from the forbidden fruit to the great flood. These tales also convey an ecological awareness that corresponds to the breadth of Hebrew moral concern. Though the narrative portrays the role of humanity as decisive, all elements of creation contributed to the fall, and each element suffered in consequence.

Eden's plant community participated significantly in the interaction that led to human disobedience. Since natural beauty stimulates human desire, the fruit of the forbidden tree was enticing, "good for food, and . . . a delight to the eyes" (Genesis 3:6, RSV). The attractiveness of nature—both its beauty and its usefulness—makes humans wish for contact with it and thus requires us to select what form our contact will take: in this instance, whether to tend it or to consume its fruit. Because God created such a beautiful garden, to ignore the tree of knowledge—to simply leave it alone — was never a possibility for human beings. The serpent, by contrast, was a moral agent who intended to do harm (and so was punished at the conclusion of the story). Those who hunt or work with livestock, as did the Hebrews, know that animals can mislead people and sometimes appear to do so deliberately. Hebrews included animals within the universe of moral responsibility: in this instance the serpent, "more subtle than any other wild creature that the LORD God had made" (3:1, RSV), embodied the deviousness of which animals are capable.

Note that the narrator portrayed Eden as a good and beautiful place, but not a *perfect* place. Perfection, a Greek notion, implies static rigidities quite inappropriate to a biblical appreciation of growth, change, complexity, and creativity. In Eden's healthy ecosystem, interdependence counterbalanced the competitive tensions. Biblical images of "goodness" and "beauty" embrace these vital characteristics of earthly life; they can even incorporate a modern understanding of biological evolution and of ecological relationships. Eden was a good and beautiful place, but it nevertheless had problems which challenged the integrity of its inhabitants.

The Eden story concerns the human temptation to disrupt the moral ecology that the Lord had established on earth. We can imagine that the serpent, embodying the potential for rebelliousness among animals, was jealous of God and resentful of human dominion. Perhaps its subtle strategy meant to suggest that God was jealous of human potential and to provoke human distrust of God in the hope that animals could then escape supervision and moral obligation. Initially, the woman responded to the serpent with creative intelligence:

> Now the serpent . . . said to the woman, "Did God say, 'You shall not eat of any tree of the garden'?" And the woman said to the serpent, "We may eat of the fruit of the trees of the garden; but God said, 'You shall not eat of the fruit of the tree which is in the midst of the garden, neither shall you touch it, lest you die.'"
> (Genesis 3:1–3, RSV)

Not only did the woman recall accurately the Lord's command not to eat from one particular tree—a command given before God separated the original person into male and female—but she also made a prudent inference of her own: "neither shall you touch it." This budding rabbi, however, soon became intrigued by the serpent's wiles. Her misjudgment was the same error that later tempted some Hebrews to worship Baal. The woman accepted the serpent's implicit claim that true knowledge of God's will for humanity did not come from direct conversation with the Lord, but was more reliably learned in dialogue with creation. God was not to be trusted. The serpent tempted the woman to abandon the Lord's ecology and to impute the image of God to nature: Listen to us, it seemed to hiss, and you will learn more about God than the Lord would willingly disclose. In the words of the Yahwist,

> The serpent said, "Of course you will not die. God knows that as soon as you eat it, your eyes will be opened and you will be like gods knowing both good and evil." When the woman saw that the fruit of the tree was good to eat, and that it was pleasing to the eye and tempting to contemplate, she took some and ate it. She also gave her husband some and he ate it. (vs. 4–6, NEB)

Although the woman evinced moral agency in this story, as did the serpent, the man merely ate without comment. The story was told by men; the reticent description of the man's role may illustrate the common temptation to mask moral agency, to avoid responsibility, and to blame one's actions upon other persons or upon circumstances beyond one's control. Man sinned not only in the act but in the telling: he repressed his desire so that he might conceal moral responsibility from himself. Later in the story he was pitiable, blaming the woman and even implicating God: "It was the woman you put with me" (vs. 12, NJB).

The specific human sin was disobeying the Lord by eating fruit from "the tree of the knowledge of good and evil" (2:17, KJV). We should not understand this to mean that moral insight, or the capacity for moral judgment, comes from human sin. Whatever the myth might have meant in some pre-Hebrew form to people terrified by authority, Hebrews understood that the capacity for moral judgment was the foundation of life in Eden. They knew that the Lord broke the chains of arbitrary obedience and revealed instead an understandable moral framework which gave them freedom to act responsibly, not fearfully. Moral understanding and accountability are presumed by this story in its biblical setting. The couple's sin, then, was violating this morality and disobeying the Lord with the intention to take possession of "good and evil" and redefine those terms to suit themselves. The man and the woman coveted spurious "wisdom" like that of Solomon: autonomous human action that simply seizes what it desires and constructs its own rationalizations. The serpent in the garden effectively suggested that if humans master nature, they will be equal to God and will be able to shape the character of good and evil for their own convenience.

The serpent lied; violating the moral ecology does not make people godlike, but leaves them lost and confused. Instead of wanting to discover more, the man and woman wished to see less. Their enthusiasm turned into apprehension, and because their sexual feelings now made them anxious, they hid their genitals from each other. Indeed human existence itself—with its yearnings to express, create, and possess—now felt embarrassing. When they heard the Lord walking in the garden, the couple tried to hide themselves completely. Discovered, they neither acknowledged moral responsibility nor protected each other; reverting to childish behavior, they each made excuses. No longer responsible, no longer adult, they had not become godlike and powerful but rather victims of each other and candidates for exploitation. This story is part of a myth of human origins, but it is also a cautionary tale. Politically, it warns that those who isolate themselves from their moral community become weak and vulnerable; Hebrews who break covenant risk being enslaved again. Psychologically, this story tells us that freedom depends upon the maintenance of moral integrity. If we fall into moral confusion, like this man and woman, we become vulnerable to manipulative leaders who will exploit our sexual shame and reinforce our apprehension about our own desires, urging us to surrender a freedom that has become burdensome to us.

In appraising the fundamental human temptation, I replace the traditional distinction, obedience versus disobedience, with a contrast between moral responsibility and arrogance. The story does not simply warn us to be obedient. Our world is full of powers that demand our obedience and cults that invite us to follow blindly; the Lord, instead, calls us to moral responsibility. Isolated from other values, obedience can encourage a slavish disposition that is inconsistent with the liberating implications of God's covenant. Obedience without initiative requires God to furnish instructions for every circumstance; when God does not do so, we substitute inflexible traditions and oppressive hierarchies. The biblical Lord prefers to give us clear, general instructions, as well as inspiring examples, and then challenges us to act responsibly in relation to those around us. A *morally responsible* person recognizes God's presence and God's claim, as well as the presence and claims of the others who complete the landscape of earthly life. The arrogant, on the other hand, doubt that God is relevant or that the rest of life has needs and interests independent of human welfare. They do not acknowledge that they are upheld by a culture, an ecosystem, and a moral universe which lay claims upon them.

God's punishment, the expulsion from Eden, made tangible what had already happened implicitly. When the moral ecology is ignored, peaceful relationships between humans and animals fall into antagonism:

> I will put enmity between you [the serpent] and the woman,
> between your brood and hers.
> They shall strike at your head,
> and you shall strike at their heel.
>
> (Genesis 3:15, NEB)

The relationship between man and woman, too, suffered from the corruption of their partnership. From God's judgment, "Your yearning will be for your husband, and he will dominate you" (vs. 16, NJB), Phyllis Trible draws these implications:

> To defend himself, the man turned against the woman and betrayed her to God. Yet, according to God, she still yearns for the original unity of male and female: "for your man is your

desire." Alas, however, union is no more; one flesh is split. The man will not reciprocate the woman's desire; instead, he will rule over her. Thus she lives in unresolved tension. Where once there was mutuality, now there is a hierarchy of division. The man dominates the woman to pervert sexuality. Hence, the woman is corrupted in becoming a slave, and the man is corrupted in becoming a master. His supremacy is neither a divine right nor a male prerogative. Her subordination is neither a divine decree nor the female destiny. Both their positions result from shared disobedience. God describes this consequence but does not prescribe it as punishment.[1]

Because the man and woman violated the moral ecology, the positive connection between the human family, and the soil from which God shaped them, weakened. Eden had required human work "to cultivate and take care of it" (2:15, NJB), work that was engaging and productive. Now, since the human family had alienated themselves from the land by exercising their power arbitrarily, cultivating the earth would be a difficult and frustrating labor:

> Painfully will you get your food from it
> as long as you live.
> . . . . . . . . . . . . . . .
> By the sweat of your face
> will you earn your food,
> until you return to the ground,
> as you were taken from it.
> (Genesis 3:17–19, NJB)

Later in this same Yahwist narrative, after God flooded the earth in anger, the Lord repented, lifted the curse from the ground, and inaugurated the covenant within which humans could again anticipate the possibility of satisfying, productive agriculture. The purpose of the covenant, which embraced holy people and holy land, was to recreate the moral ecology so that God, humanity, and nature might again have just and fruitful relationships.

God's judgments characterize the consequences of violating the moral ecology, consequences which in historical accumulation saturate the life of the world. Arrogance builds institutions from the mistakes of the past, and they, in turn, stimulate new abuses. Culture transmits fears and hatreds from one generation to the next. Similarly, torn landscapes erode their own vitality, reducing the quality of life for succeeding generations. The Christian doctrine of "original sin" names the paradox that while each generation is brought to life by the culture into which it is born, it is also seduced by the distortions within that culture. However, we must not regard any of the Genesis judgments as an inevitable pall over human existence. God's offer of covenant invites us to join an alternate culture—to repair the damage and to rebuild each of the corrupted relationships.

Although Christian theology has portrayed the relationship of sin and salvation in sequential images—paradise, followed by the fall, then a time of suffering until redemption restores hope of wholeness, and finally, a new earth and heaven —the biblical emphasis is more dynamic, and human experience confirms that any of these elements may be present. We know both desire and fear, both communion and discord, in our daily lives. Perhaps we can recall better times; certainly, we hope for times to come when we will know communion, love, and beauty more fully, and when society will truly support these virtues. Yet God's covenant promises that in the worst of times we can still know and love other persons, both men and women; we can have empathetic and productive relationships with animals, plants, and the earth itself; we can still emerge from hiding and show ourselves to the Lord without fear. In the present age, no curse places these things beyond our reach.

# 18. *Horses and Chariots*

Like the Bible in general, the Yahwist narrative conveys ambivalent feelings about human culture and particularly about the technologies that spring from human ingenuity. After the story of the first family's expulsion from Eden, there follows a tale of cultural rivalry between two brothers—one a shepherd, one a farmer—that led to murder. The earth, polluted by this violence, was so weakened as to make resident agriculture impossible; the murderer, Cain, was forced to wander. His descendants developed three migratory vocations which would later thrive on the margins of settled, agricultural society: nomadic herding, music, and the forging of bronze and iron tools.[1] After the great flood, when God covenanted with all living creatures and lifted the curse from the ground, cultural problems nevertheless persisted. Noah, the first to return to agriculture, was so delighted by his initial harvest of grapes from the now responsive soil that he got drunk and embarrassed his sons with his nakedness. Then in the last of these mythic tales before the narratives of Abraham and the patriarchs, the Yahwist tells of the human family assembling to construct a city with a high tower. The scale of this technological initiative made the Lord both anxious and determined:

> [N]ow they have started to do this . . . nothing they have a mind to do will be beyond their reach. Come, let us go down there and confuse their speech. (Genesis 11:6–7, NEB)

The Lord, as understood by the Hebrews, preferred human diversity to monolithic power, and thought that slow development through moral reflection was better than huge, spontaneous constructions leading to unknown consequences.

These Hebrew attitudes toward technology arose from a history of vulnerability. The Hebrews were marginal people facing neighbors with superior agricultural and military equipment. When the Philistines were ascendant, for example, they did not allow Hebrews to practice blacksmithing: "The Israelites had to go down to the Philistines for their ploughshares, mattocks, axes, and sickles to be sharpened" (1 Samuel 13:20, NEB). This economic oppression was one reason the Hebrews turned to Saul, anointing him to be their first warrior-king. It was later, during Solomon's reign, that Hebrews themselves began to employ more up-to-date technology such as iron-tipped plows which scratched more deeply into the soil. However, benefits from this improvement were probably diluted by changes in the social structure, since Solomon was undermining covenant traditions. When the wealthy and powerful obtained improved tools, they might use this advantage to increase their landholdings at the expense of the less fortunate. When the ecology of sabbath relationships was overturned, technological improvements in food production might lead, paradoxically, to spreading poverty and even slavery among rural peasants.[2] In addition, unless the land itself retained rights within the moral fabric of society, the benefits of improved tools might be short-lived. The introduction of even these primitive iron tools could tempt farmers to extend tillage to steeper slopes and harder soils. Without care to preserve ground cover, to nourish the earth, and to give land periods free from cultivation, this expansion could stimulate erosion and evaporation—depleting topsoil and drying the land—and so reduce soil fertility after a few generations. Potential, long-term social benefits from the spread of iron tools may have been undermined by Solomon's administrative weakening of Hebrew land ethics.

King Solomon may also have introduced mining of precious minerals to Hebrew economy. In a poetic meditation from a later generation, Job expresses fascination with this technology, yet raises ethical concerns. The dangers of mining required slave labor, the techniques violated natural environmental relationships, and the whole enterprise reeked of presumption:

> There are mines for silver
> and places where men refine gold;
> where iron is won from the earth
> and copper smelted from the ore;
> the end of the seam lies in darkness,
> and it is followed to its farthest limit.
> Strangers cut the galleries;
> they are forgotten as they drive forward far from men.
> While corn is springing from the earth above,
> what lies beneath is raked over like a fire,
> and out of its rocks comes lapis lazuli,
> dusted with flecks of gold.
> No bird of prey knows the way there,
> and the falcon's keen eye cannot descry it;
> proud beasts do not set foot on it,
> and no serpent comes that way.
> Man sets his hand to the granite rock
> and lays bare the roots of the mountains;
> he cuts galleries in the rocks,
> and gems of every kind meet his eye;
> he dams up the sources of the streams
> and brings the hidden riches of the earth to light.
> But where can wisdom be found?
> And where is the source of understanding?
> . . . . . . . . . . . . . . . . . . . . . . . . . . . . . . . . . .
> The fear of the Lord is wisdom,
> and to turn from evil is understanding.
>
> (Job 28:1–12, 28, NEB)

To Job, technology was no substitute for ethics. Not even the most stunning feats of the age deserved acceptance if they appeared to lack a moral context.

The technology which the Bible most thoroughly scrutinizes is the horse and chariot—the battle tank of the ancient world. From the time when Moses' band eluded the chariots of Egypt, to the early struggles for Canaan when God sent rain to mire the chariots of Sisera, to the battles of David's foot soldiers against the chariots of the Syrians, Hebrew warriors nearly always fought under technological disadvantage. They learned to trust bravery, cunning, guerrilla tactics, and most importantly the favor of the Lord. While David was king, he kept only a few chariots, preferring combat tactics with which he had more experience. Although Solomon quartered throughout Israel large regiments of horses and chariots, which must have appeared intimidating to his subjects and to foreign visitors, apparently he never used them in battle. Hebrews disparaged chariots, but they applauded the bravery of the horses that carried their riders into battle—the typical Hebrew attitude of admiring moral agents while denigrating heavy equipment. The poet of the book of Job heard the Lord, too, boast about horses' courage:

> Are you the one who makes the horse so brave
>     and covers his neck with flowing mane?
> Do you make him leap like a grasshopper?
>     His haughty neighing inspires terror.
> Exultantly he paws the soil of the valley,
>     and charges the battle-line in all his strength.
> He laughs at fear; he is afraid of nothing,
>     he recoils before no sword.
> On his back the quiver rattles,
>     the flashing spear and javelin.
> Trembling with impatience, he eats up the miles;
>     when the trumpet sounds, there is no holding him.
> At each trumpet blast he neighs exultantly.
>     He scents the battle from afar,
>     the thundering of the commanders and the war cry.
>                                         (Job 39:19–25, NJB)

Above all, the Hebrews were convinced that the Lord was more potent than chariots and that God's favor must be retained by faithfulness and moral purpose. Some ethics of Hebrew warfare may today seem offensive, especially the practice of destroying both persons and property to avoid the temptations of taking slaves and booty. However, the Hebrew desire to remain faithful to the Lord was commendable. Even during the divided kingdom there were rulers who retained this sense of moral priority. When the prophet Elisha, who gave military advice on the Lord's behalf, lay on his deathbed, "Jehoash king of Israel went down to him and wept over him and said, 'My father! My father, the chariots and the horsemen of Israel!' " (2 Kings 13:14, NEB). God's word, not royal equipment, was the nation's strength.

Hebrew prophets eventually developed an ethical critique of military power. Shortly before the northern kingdom was overrun by the Assyrian empire in 721 B.C., Hosea criticized Israel's rulers for turning this small country into a garrison state that neglected justice to pursue defense:

> You have ploughed wickedness,
> you have reaped iniquity,
> you have eaten the fruit of falsehood.
> Because you have trusted in your chariots,
> in your great numbers of warriors,
> turmoil is going to break out among your people,
> and all your fortresses will be laid waste.
> (Hosea 10:13–14, NJB)

In Judah, the southern kingdom, the prophet Micah also understood how the technologies of war competed with the general welfare. He yearned for the time when

> they will hammer their swords into ploughshares,
> their spears into sickles.
> (Micah 4:3, JB)

From their experience of the perpetual struggles for power, Hebrews learned an invaluable lesson: their future as a people depended upon their unique morality. An Old Testament song contains the most characteristic and also the most profound Hebrew comment on technology:

> Some *trust* in chariots, and some in horses:
> But we will remember the name of the LORD our God.
> (Psalm 20:7, KJV)

* * *

Modern anxiety about technology helps us to notice a pattern of meaning in these biblical fragments, although technology was only occasionally a concern in the foreground of Hebrew moral reflection. We have an acute need for criteria to guide technological development, because the accelerating pace of innovation during the nineteenth and twentieth centuries has created unprecedented technological opportunities within human culture, even while their consequences threaten the survival of both the natural environment and humanity itself. New technologies have had such overwhelming impact upon life in the industrialized world that we are both enticed and coerced into trusting technological innovation to solve our problems, despite our fear of unbridled inventiveness. We ride a roller coaster of excitement and anxiety. "Science and technology" is the idol which fascinates us, arousing hope and inspiring devotion. To the modern sensibility this idol outshines God, and so it also eclipses values such as social justice and political rights.

The Bible does not sufficiently illumine our technological issues; since our problems are more acute than those of the Hebrews, we need to pioneer a moral understanding. Hebrew anxiety about technology should inspire us neither to Luddite attacks upon the machinery of our age nor to a primitivist withdrawal from our culture. There are, indeed, some technologies which modern society should abandon altogether, such as atomic weapons, nuclear power, and strip-mining for coal. But most advancements, including many which now harm society and nature, are not inevitably destructive if they can be supervised and limited. Our problem is not technological creativity as such, but inadequate moral principles and political strategies to guide technological development, deployment, and use. To attack technology avoids the issue. Even after we forge relevant principles and policies from the fires of inspiration and experience, we will need *more* creative technology, not less, to support human welfare and protect natural life in an increasingly crowded and complex world.

Hebrew insight can help us decide where to place our trust. When our innovations spring from moral awareness, then we can serve society and protect the fabric of earthly life. We can harness technological power with sensitivity to the impact of our means, and drive it toward just goals. Unbridled power, however, can trample the life of the world. We must resist the glorification of power for its own sake, whether technological, political, or—most dangerous—the union of the two. "The history of Western man,"

George Mendenhall observes, "is a history of the alternation between the ethical principle and the technological-political one. This is the battle between Yahweh and Baal."[3]

From Hebrew experience with technology we can also learn another truth: when as followers of the Lord we feel marginal and overwhelmed, we must simply return to our proven moral insights and devise ways to bypass the strengths of the enemy.

# 19. *Pollution*

In the first English version of the Bible, 1382, John Wycliffe translated a passage from the Holiness Code concerning ritual purity of priests: "Holi thei shulen be to ther God, and thei shulen not polute his name" (Leviticus 21:6).[1] The early English *polute* translates a Hebrew word for ceremonial impurity. The Hebrew image expanded, however, to connote moral corruption and also to describe, in broadest reference, the fouling of the landscape. In Jerusalem the temple cult nurtured concern for liturgical purity and the avoidance of ritual pollution. At the height of Hebrew prophecy, Isaiah and Jeremiah, who realized that a once-coherent moral order was being corrupted, used the concept of pollution to express both their judgment against the moral fouling of the covenant, and the impact of human degradation upon the holy earth. Our modern application of the word *pollution* to environmental contamination resonates with this biblical usage.

The Bible's concern for pollution of the land first appears as anxiety about the impact of murder—the unjust spilling of blood. The Yahwist tells that Cain's murder of his brother Abel weakened the ability of the soil to produce crops and forage.[2] Likewise, in the book of Numbers, laws relating to murder conclude with a warning against degrading the landscape:

> You shall not thus pollute the land in which you live; for blood pollutes the land. . . . You shall not defile the land in which you live, in the midst of which I dwell; for I the LORD dwell in the midst of the people of Israel. (Numbers 35:33–34, RSV)

This association of murder with pollution may have liturgical or even magical origins. The prophets, however, broadened the reference to a general association of human misbehavior with environmental degradation. In words which speak to our day as well as his, Hosea preached that all forms of human violence damage nature:

> [Children] of Israel, listen to the word of Yahweh,
> for Yahweh indicts the inhabitants of the country:
> there is no fidelity, no tenderness,
> no knowledge of God in the country,
> only perjury and lies, slaughter, theft,
> adultery and violence, murder after murder.
> This is why the country is in mourning, and all who live in it
>     pine away,
> even the wild animals and the birds of heaven;
> the fish of the sea themselves are perishing.
>
> (Hosea 4:1–3, JB, alt.)

While Hosea addressed those words to the northern kingdom, Isaiah, his contemporary in Judah, came to the same poignant insight:

> The earth mourns and withers,
>     the world languishes and withers;
>     the heavens languish together with the earth.
> The earth lies polluted
>     under its inhabitants;
> for they have transgressed the laws,
>     violated the statutes,
>     broken the everlasting covenant.
> . . . . . . . . . . . . . . . . . . . . . . . . . . . .
> The wine mourns,
>     the vine languishes,
>     all the merry-hearted sigh.
>
> (Isaiah 24:4–5, 7, RSV)

The most creative Hebrew reflections on human pollution of the earth occurred during a period of acute political anxiety. In 721 B.C. the Assyrian army captured Samaria, capital of the northern kingdom, and forced principal citizens into exile in the hope that, without leadership, the remainder of the Hebrew population would become submissive. Judah, the southern kingdom, maneuvered among Assyrian, Babylonian, and Egyptian pressures in order to survive as a society—sometimes independent,

sometimes a vassal state—for 134 more years until Nebuchadnezzar of Babylon, angered by King Zedekiah's inept double-
dealing among the rival powers, laid siege to Jerusalem and
marched a large population into exile in Babylon. During the
troubled decades before the fall of Jerusalem in 587 B.C., while the
shifting political alliances tempted both kings and commoners
into religious apostasy, sensitive moralists anguished over the
possibility that the Lord's covenant people might be dispersed
and the holy land returned to alien gods and empires.

New and terrible eventualities had to be considered. The
Holiness Code, which may have been edited during this period,
suggested that the land might become so sickened by Hebrew
iniquity that it would expel the polluting agent: "You shall keep
my statutes and my ordinances and do none of these abominations ... lest the land vomit you out, when you defile it" (Leviticus
18:26–28, RSV). More hopefully, Deuteronomy proclaimed that if
the people would "fear the LORD your God and keep all [God's]
statutes and commandments," they and their children could yet
enjoy "a land flowing with milk and honey" (Deuteronomy 6:2–3,
NEB, alt.). The Code's publication inspired King Josiah to attempt
religious reform. During this same reign, however, the prophet
Zephaniah feared the worst. He felt that the Lord was about to
abrogate the covenant with Noah, cancel the promise of the
rainbow, and begin again:

> I will sweep the earth clean of all that is on it,
>    says the LORD.
> I will sweep away both man and beast,
> I will sweep the birds from the air and the fish from the sea,
>    and I will bring the wicked to their knees
> and wipe out mankind from the earth.
>    This is the very word of the LORD.
>
> (Zephaniah 1:2–3, NEB)

After Ezekiel was led away to Babylon, he maintained contact
with the poor who remained in Judah. However, he feared that
the holy land might revert to barren wilderness because the
leaderless rabble persisted in idolatry and wickedness:

You eat meat with the blood in it, you lift up your eyes to idols,
you shed blood; and yet you expect to possess the land! You trust
to the sword, you commit abominations, you defile one another's
wives; and you expect to possess the land! Tell them that these
are the words of the Lord GOD: As I live, among the ruins they
shall fall by the sword; in the open country I will give them for
food to beasts; in dens and caves they shall die by pestilence. I
will make the land a desolate waste; her boasted might shall be
brought to nothing, and the mountains of Israel shall be an
untrodden desert. (Ezekiel 33:25–28, NEB)

Among the great prophets of this period, however, only Jeremiah
plumbed the depths of pollution and found there the Lord's own
pain.

\* \* \*

During the forty years prior to the fall of Jerusalem,
Jeremiah pronounced God's judgment upon this tiny nation's
fickle twisting among the political powers and regional gods, and
condemned the people's unwillingness to trust radically and
faithfully in the Lord alone. The prophet's words convey what
the great Jewish scholar Abraham Joshua Heschel has named a
"divine pathos"—the pain and sorrow in God's mourning over the
apostasy of this people.[3] Jeremiah's first great prophecy opens
with God's lament over Israel's moral pollution of the holy land
and culminates with the Lord's touching query: "Have I been a
wilderness to Israel?" (Jeremiah 2:31, RSV):

I brought you into a fruitful land
  to enjoy its fruit and the goodness of it;
  but when you entered upon it you defiled it
  and made the home I gave you loathsome.
The priests no longer asked, "Where is the LORD?"
Those who handled the law had no thought of me,
  the shepherds of the people rebelled against me;
  the prophets prophesied in the name of Baal
  and followed gods powerless to help.
. . . . . . . . . . . . . . . . . . . . . . . . . . . . . .
Is Israel a slave? Was he born in slavery?
If not, why has he been despoiled?
. . . . . . . . . . . . . . . . . . . . . . . . . . . . . .

> Have I shown myself inhospitable to Israel
> like some wilderness or waterless land?
> Why do my people say, "We have broken away;
> we will never come back to thee"?
>                  (Jeremiah 2:7, 8, 14, 31, NEB)

Jeremiah brought Hebrew prophecy a giant step toward modern sensibility, for although he was possessed by God's spirit, he was also seriously reflective. Two hundred years before Plato introduced detached reflection to Greek philosophy, Jeremiah brought an emotionally engaged self-consciousness into Hebrew religious experience. Prodded by his personal anguish, he not only conveyed the Lord's words to the people, but also imagined the divine Personality behind the message.

Jeremiah's pain was complex, because he loved the people he was called to condemn. He was bound to try to convince them of the inevitability of their fate, a future he wished they could avoid:

> How can I bear my sorrow?
> I am sick at heart.
> . . . . . . . . . . . . . . .
> I am wounded at the sight of my people's wound;
> I go like a mourner, overcome with horror.
> Is there no balm in Gilead,
>    no physician there?
> Why has no new skin grown over their wound?
>                  (Jeremiah 8:18, 21–22, NEB)

Hearing Jeremiah's words, the people despised him; the rulers either scorned him or attempted to silence him in prison. Although he could not restrain the fire of prophecy that burned within him, Jeremiah knew that the words were God's, not his own. He felt that the Lord he loved had violated his person:

> O Lord, Thou hast seduced me,
> And I am seduced;
> Thou hast raped me
> And I am overcome.
> (Jeremiah 20:7, Heschel's translation)[4]

Jeremiah's burden was to announce the impending destruction of Judah. He told rulers and people that they must trust the Lord through a time of judgment, must submit to Nebuchadnezzar without resistance, and must avoid the temptations of power politics. He saw that the fall of the northern kingdom had inspired its southern counterpart not to genuine repentance, but instead to a desperate flirtation with the idols of the powerful and a contemptible reversion to the superstitions of Canaan. Judah now figuratively "polluted the land, committing adultery with stone and tree" (3:9, RSV). Even the resulting droughts did not recall the nation to its senses:

> [T]his people has a rebellious and defiant heart.
> . . . . . . . . . . . . . . . . . . . . . . . . . . . . . . . . . . . . .
> They did not say to themselves,
> "Let us fear the LORD our God,
> who gives us the rains of autumn
>   and spring showers in their turn,
> who brings us unfailingly
> fixed seasons of harvest."
> But your wrongdoing has upset nature's order,
> and your sins have kept from you her kindly gifts.
>                     (Jeremiah 5:23–25, NEB)

While we may see in these words an arbitrary or even magical relationship between human apostasy and natural calamity, we should keep in mind the Hebrews' complex moral ecology. Hebrews lacked scientific understanding; they knew nothing, for example, of how agricultural techniques relate to soil moisture and rainfall. Nevertheless they drew from the Lord's covenant a sophisticated *moral* understanding that respected natural life and guided agriculture into patterns likely to sustain a frugal and responsible society. Jeremiah was certainly aware of this "sabbath ecology"; indeed, the Jerusalem editors of the Holiness Code may have codified these ancient laws during Jeremiah's forty-year prophetic career there. Jeremiah understood that wholesale violation of God's covenant had ethical and material impact upon the health of the holy landscape.

As drought deepened, the distressed prophet argued with God: "O LORD, I will dispute with thee, for thou art just" (Jeremiah 12:1, NEB). He asked why the landscape itself must suffer while the most unscrupulous people seemed to evade the consequences of their behavior:

> How long must the country lie parched
>     and its green grass wither?
> No birds and beasts are left, because its people are so wicked,
> because they say, "God will not see what we are doing."
>                                         (Jeremiah 12:4, NEB)

God responded by warning Jeremiah that he must endure the drought in training for greater calamities to follow. The prophet heard God speak blunt, pathetic words:

> I have forsaken the house of Israel,
>     I have cast off my own people.
> I have given my beloved into the power of her foes.
> . . . . . . . . . . . . . . . . . . . . . . . . . . .
>     Is this land of mine a hyena's lair,
>     with birds of prey hovering all around it?
> Come, you wild beasts; come, all of you, flock to the feast.
> Many shepherds have ravaged my vineyard
>     and trampled down my field,
> they have made my pleasant field a desolate wilderness,
> made it a waste land, waste and waterless, to my sorrow.
> The whole land is waste, and no one cares.
>                                         (Jeremiah 12:7–11 NEB)

Thus chastened, unable to flee his painful vocation, Jeremiah composed a beautiful liturgy conveying the desperation of people and animals alike:

> Judah droops, her cities languish,
>     her [people] sink to the ground;
>     Jerusalem's cry goes up.
> Their flock-masters send their boys for water;
> they come to the pools but find no water there.
>     Back they go, with empty vessels;
>     the produce of the land has failed,
>     because there is no rain.
>     The farmers' hopes are wrecked,
>     they uncover their heads for grief.
>     The hind calves in the open country
>         and forsakes her young
>     because there is no grass;

> for lack of herbage, wild asses stand on the high bare places
>   and snuff the wind for moisture,
> as wolves do, and their eyes begin to fail.
> Though our sins testify against us,
>   yet act, O LORD, for thy own name's sake.
>               (Jeremiah 14:2–7, NEB, alt.)

When Jeremiah turned from drought to contemplate the military disaster awaiting Judah, he felt as if the whole of nature might slip back toward chaos:

> I looked to the earth—it was a formless waste;
> to the heavens, and their light had gone.
> I looked to the mountains—they were quaking
> and all the hills rocking to and fro.
> I looked—there was no one at all,
> the very birds of heaven had all fled.
> I looked—the fruitful land was a desert,
> all its towns in ruins
> before Yahweh,
> before [God's] burning anger.
>               (Jeremiah 4:23–26, NJB, alt.)

Blow after blow fell upon Judah during its final twenty-two years. The first was King Josiah's death. His long reign, which included genuine religious reform modeled on Deuteronomy, ended in 609 B.C. when he was killed in battle against Pharaoh Necho of Egypt. Judah submitted to Egyptian sovereignty and then—when Nebuchadnezzar defeated Necho—to the power of Babylon. When King Jehoiakim attempted a revolt, Nebuchadnezzar allowed Judah to be ravaged by the raiding parties from surrounding vassal kingdoms. Jeremiah prefaced his condemnation of Jehoiakim with grief for the bruised landscape: "O land, land, land" (Jeremiah 22:29, RSV). In 598 B.C. Nebuchadnezzar himself invaded Judah, besieged Jerusalem, exiled king and court to Babylon, and installed Zedekiah to rule. Jeremiah continued to preach political submission to Babylon, a strategy which would have saved thousands of lives and tens of thousands from exile. However, his words were not popular among the conspiratorial nobility in Jerusalem. They persuaded Zedekiah to join a rebellion spreading through the empire and to strike an alliance with Egypt. Nebuchadnezzar again laid siege to Jerusalem, though an advancing Egyptian army forced him to withdraw temporarily. Nebuchadnezzar routed the Egyptians and returned. After eighteen months' siege, with only this brief interruption, he overwhelmed the starving defenders. The city was burned in 589 B.C., some of the nobility were executed, and a large population from Judah, this time, was marched into exile.

Throughout this siege Jeremiah was imprisoned to silence his cries for surrender. Nevertheless, his final prophetic act before the fall of the city was a witness to hope. He learned that he was the surviving heir to farmland in the tribal territory of Benjamin, far out beyond the siegeworks. From his cell in the palace guardhouse he exercised his Hebrew right of redemption, purchased the field from the family's creditors, and arranged safekeeping for copies of the deed. "For these are the words of the LORD of Hosts the God of Israel," he said. "The time will come when houses, fields, and vineyards will again be bought and sold in this land" (32:15, NEB). The covenant was not abrogated, the rainbow not removed. In God's mercy the landscape was to be restored again:

> The time is coming, says the LORD, when I will sow Israel and Judah with the seed of man and the seed of cattle. . . .
> The time is coming, says the LORD, when I will make a new covenant with Israel and Judah. . . . I will set my law within them and write it on their hearts. . . . No longer need they teach one another to know the LORD; all of them, high and low alike, shall know me, says the LORD. . . .
> I will enter into an eternal covenant with them, to follow them unfailingly with my bounty. . . . I will rejoice over them, rejoice to do them good, and faithfully with all my heart and soul I will plant them in this land.
> (Jeremiah 31:27, 31, 33–34; 32:40–41, NEB)[5]

Just before the fall of Jerusalem, Jeremiah heard the Lord promise that the biblical ecology would one day be realized.

* * *

Modern knowledge of the pollution from industrial and cultural activities is far more sophisticated than anything Jeremiah could have imagined. This scientific understanding, however, lags behind the challenges we face. It is usually driven by crises; it is rarely anticipatory. Although Hebrew prophets lacked scientific knowledge, they had a moral awareness of pollution which was more sensitive than the ethics we employ today toward nature.

Many of our political and scientific leaders interpret pollution as something incidental to necessary human activities, an unavoidable side effect which needs some correction but which does not cast doubt upon fundamental human behavior in a technological age. They prefer to treat specific pollution situations in isolation and to design technical fixes for them, such as a filter at the source or an ameliorating treatment at the point of impact. We are encouraged to regard pollution within an *anthropocentric* perspective: to remain unconcerned until a problem threatens human welfare; to attribute pollution to technical imperfections in human mastery of the environment; and to trust new techniques for remedy.

The Hebrew prophetic understanding of pollution was more ecological. While prophets lacked our knowledge of specific pollutants, they were sensitive to the interactions that knit the human community to the natural landscape and divine purpose. They suspected that pollutants which enter this sensitive web at one point spread quickly through the whole. Although concerned about the impact of pollution upon human welfare, they were equally concerned about God's honor and the health of the natural landscape. They knew that correction would require changes in human behavior, but more than that, they believed that correction required *repentance:* acknowledging transgressions and reestablishing just, respectful relationships with God, with society, and with nature. Renewed sensitivity to the complex moral ecology surrounding human action was necessary before specific changes in human behavior could achieve healthy results. The prophetic approach to pollution was thus radical—going to the root—rather than technical, adjusting the details.

In the biblical ecology, conscientious respect substituted both for knowledge of natural processes, which was not yet available, and for those technical skills that had not been developed. For example, the sabbatical requirement to leave fields fallow every seventh year was a partial substitute for knowledge of

the complex ecology of soil recovery. Building environmental relationships on the basis of such respect required projecting
human characteristics—including sensory awareness, needs for
independence, and moral responsiveness—upon other species of
life and upon the landscape in general. This imaginative posture
was probably quite effective in implementation. Hebrew agricultural ethics were far superior, ecologically, to the principles of the
peoples who surrounded them.

Were we to practice such moral respect for nature, it would
guide but not inhibit the application of modern biological knowledge. Ethical regard for the land, which the Hebrews expressed
by sabbatical rest, is only deepened when we—assisted by modern science—understand the processes of soil recovery. Our
knowledge may help us devise patterns of crop rotation and rest
even more beneficial than the ancient sabbatical, while our respect for nature helps us resist new techniques that abuse the
soil. If we recognize our responsibility, in the image of God, to
take care of the land, ethics and knowledge can stimulate each
other.

Scientific knowledge and technique do not substitute for
moral regard. When the prophets insisted upon justice in human
relationships with God and nature, they were responsive to the
lure of mastery over nature which even now entices Western
society. Like Eve in the garden, we are excited by the prospect of
knowledge and are tempted to act precipitously on the basis of
new discoveries, disregarding the possible consequences of mistakes or misinformation. Although modern analysis of environmental pollution expands rapidly, our knowledge trails our
actions. The known threats to our biosphere are frightening
enough to contemplate, and beyond these there will always be
unknown dangers. Only ethics can reach beyond knowledge to
guide our course, ethics which inspire respect for other life and
which humble us before the judgment and mercy of God. Only
moral respect and humility can temper knowledge and stay rash
acts that might destroy the garden.

Within biblical ecology, human violence and social injustice were understood to cause drought, to weaken the soil, and to

spread malaise through the natural world. The links between cause and effect seem arbitrary: perhaps the land noticed injustice and became discouraged; perhaps the Lord sent drought to punish sin. Hebrew prophets were sure, however, that some interaction existed. Today, environmentalists trace many surprising connections between social injustice and environmental degradation. The impact of human culture upon the biosphere is now so profound that we may be sure there are many more connections which we have not analyzed, and some that we may never know. A moral ecology remains our best protection: justice and compassion within the human community, along with respect and concern for other species and the systems of natural life.

Biblical concern about pollution began with cultic anxiety that priests who ministered to the Lord might carelessly deviate from the elaborate rules that governed their personal and liturgical behavior, and thereby pollute God's name with dishonor. As Hebrew sensitivity to pollution underwent extensive ethical development, care for the holy land came to occupy a place equivalent to concern for the holy liturgy. When the holy land suffered or when it was abused, God was dishonored. Pollution struck the land, and the Lord, together.

Other prophets had realized that human injustice offended God and damaged the earth, and Jeremiah completed the triangle of insight when he grasped that the Lord suffered with the bruised landscape. Although Jeremiah's initial reaction to the great drought was to complain to God on behalf of the thirsty earth, the prophet came to realize that it was Israel who had abused and forsaken the holy landscape. While people complained of their own hunger, Jeremiah knew that only God shared the humiliation of the doe who could not feed her young; and only God felt the pain of the earth itself. Jeremiah heard the Lord's anguished cry: "The whole land is waste, and no one cares" (12:11, NEB); he knew that the forsaken Lord empathized with the parched earth. So, as his last prophetic act before the fall of Jerusalem, Jeremiah responded to God's spirit and redeemed a field in hope.

# Part V.

# *Ecological Visions*

Where *there is* no vision, the people perish.
(Proverbs 29:18, KJV)[1]

Hope for the future inspires life and guides our actions. Indeed, both ancient prophets and modern futurists have envisioned the future primarily to arouse appropriate attitudes and stimulate useful actions in the present. People need realistic forecasts of problems in order to prepare for difficulties. We need hope to inspire creativity, and ideals to help us build the society we desire. Since the whole biosphere is now vulnerable to human society, we need visions that embrace a future for nature as well as for ourselves. Biblical ecology projects such moral visions.

I interpret the fall not primarily as a past event which inevitably corrupts the present, but as human beings' ever-present temptation to grasp for power while disregarding our responsibilities to society, to the natural environment, and to the Lord. It is true that we have fallen: ancestral choices have left their stamp on our culture and our environment. It is equally true that we choose whether to continue falling. Today's choices, implemented by more potent instruments than our ancestors could imagine, compound the legacy we leave our children.

At the same time, however, we can take hope from the growth of knowledge, improved technical skills, and fresh moral sensitivities. The human race is maturing, and we have constantly unfolding opportunities for good. Modern biology makes an informed, moral relationship with nature far more possible for us than for ancient Hebrews. The environmental movement combines new scientific insight with emotional commitment to foster a deep respect for nature. "So," as the Apostle Paul pointed out to the sophisticated in his day, "no matter who you are, . . . you have no excuse" (Romans 2:1, NJB).

Biblical hope for covenant fulfillment includes the full earthly ecosystem. The vision of a few disembodied human souls escaping from a perishing landscape is less prominent than the inclusive vision of a new earth which not only gives hope for the future but challenges us to redemptive acts right now. "There will be no saying, 'Look, here it is!' or 'there it is!' " Jesus insisted, "for in fact the kingdom of God is among you" (Luke 17:21, NEB).

This part begins with a chapter clarifying biblical ecology through comparisons with alternative perspectives on environmental awareness, and then examines religious implications of the environmental crises that human society is likely to trigger as we overload our biosphere. We are condemning both our own children and other species to deep distress; nevertheless, the Lord's promise of redemption extends to the whole created ecosystem. The biblical vision is not so much a "perfect end" as a new beginning, a jubilee, after which righteous relationships between humanity and nature will produce abundance never before imagined. As ancient prophets' visions of peace between human culture and wild nature expand through modern ecological insight, all species can find reconciliation in Jesus, the Lamb of God, who is sufficient sacrifice for each of them.

# 20. *Comparisons*

Religious concern for environmental protection is spreading. Within American society, several interesting movements seek a religious experience with nature and a moral understanding of our environment: the animistic spirituality of Native American tribes; three forms of Christian pantheism—a revival of medieval nature mysticism, Teilhard's evolutionism, and process theology; and three perspectives that have emerged directly from the modern environmental movement—the Gaia hypothesis, deep ecology, and Buddhist communion with nature. I review each of these briefly to illustrate the modern religious context for recovering a biblical understanding of nature. I cannot convey these stimulating alternatives adequately, for real knowledge of another viewpoint must come from emotional engagement as well as intellectual analysis—from within a tradition, not from the outside looking in. I alert the reader to alternative perspectives so we may deepen our understanding of the biblical perspective.

* * *

*Animism* is a term applied to religious relationships with particular objects, such as animals, special trees, or sacred mountains believed to manifest a vitality transcending their physical characteristics. *Pantheism* characterizes religions which identify a god or several gods with the forces of nature, rather than ascribing to the deity a personality distinct from such forces. In ancient Canaan, during the time when Hebrew faith was forming, popular relationships with nature were often animistic, while the worship of Baal, along with that of other deities representing natural forces, was pantheistic.

Many traces of animism are evident within the Hebrew tradition. Genesis stories of the Patriarchs, for instance, dwell on the sacredness of particular places and special objects such as trees and stone pillars. Nevertheless, an anti-animist polemic runs through the Old Testament. Prophets heaped scorn upon religious devotion to natural objects, while Priestly and Deuteronomic editors, loyal to the Jerusalem temple, wove a critique of localized worship into the historical books of the Bible. These editors condemned kings who tolerated worship at the many sacred places within Israel; sometimes they implied that proper worship of the Lord could take place only in front of the Jerusalem temple—a reverse idolization of a particular sacred spot. Obviously, faithful Hebrews worshiped and experienced the Lord in many places.

To develop a biblical ecology, I have focused on the Hebrew ethical tradition rather than on these cultic traditions. Covenant faith drew the people as well as their environment into the realm of holiness, sanctifying them by God's selection and blessing. Hebrews, like their pagan neighbors, saw more vitality and personality in animals, plants, trees, and even natural features such as waters and mountains, than we who are schooled by modern science may deem reasonable. Ancient imagination may have exaggerated the scope of such vitality; modern sensibility, however, deliberately ignores vital characteristics of other species to rationalize human manipulation and abuse of them. Within biblical ecology, the holiness of nature arose not from its vitality but from its election by God, and the human capacity to act morally, rather than manipulatively, was also considered a gift from the Lord. In fact, the Hebrew conception of God's holy people and God's holy land held that every species and natural feature had moral characteristics, rights, and responsibilities. I believe that this perspective taught *care and respect for others*— whether persons, animals, trees, or ground—through attentive interactions during the days, years, and generations of human experience.

Native American tribes today preserve animistic attitudes toward the American landscape and its creatures. Tribal spirituality may appeal to other Americans because it includes sensual awareness of the earth and ethical sensitivity to other species—qualities which we miss in the modern Christian tradition. We may marvel, for example, at the Eskimo hunter's respect for, and politeness toward, the animals he must kill for food. As environmental crises make us more sensitive to nature, we begin to feel a loneliness which Native Americans have known for generations. Melvin Gilmore, of the Omaha tribe, recalls:

> When I was a youth, the country was very beautiful. Along the rivers were belts of timberland, where grew cottonwood, maple, elm, ash, hickory, and walnut trees, and many other shrubs. And under these grew many good herbs and beautiful flowering plants. In both the woodland and the prairies I could see the trails of many kinds of animals and could hear the cheerful songs of many kinds of birds. When I walked abroad I could see many forms of life, beautiful living creatures which *Wakanda* had placed here; and these were, after their manner, walking, flying, leaping, running, playing all about. But now the face of all the land is changed and sad. The living creatures are gone. I see the land desolate and I suffer an unspeakable sadness. Sometimes I wake in the night and I feel as though I should suffocate from the pressure of this awful feeling of loneliness.[1]

Chief Luther Standing Bear associates white America's alienation from Native Americans with our alienation from the landscape itself:

> The white man does not understand the Indian for the reason that he does not understand America. He is too far removed from its formative processes. The roots of his tree of life have not yet grasped the rock and soil. . . . The man from Europe is still a foreigner and an alien. . . . But in the Indian the spirit of the land is still vested; it will be until other men are able to divine and meet its rhythm.[2]

Although biblical ecology is not animistic, American Christians should listen to the prophetic words that Native Americans speak to us. They relate to our common landscape with an integrity which most modern Christians have never considered. In the Hebrew tradition, ethical sensitivity to creatures and landscape was inspired by a Lord who, though distinct from nature and from humanity, loved and chose them both. Our current ecological crisis calls American Christians to complete our faith and show to nature the image of a redeeming Lord. We cannot do this by merging Christian faith in the Lord with Native American animism: such an attempt would undermine the integrity of each of these very different religious traditions. However, Native American theologians such as Vine Deloria, Jr., and Christian theologians such as John Hart, have shown that dialogue between these two traditions can stimulate both of them to ecological reflection.[3]

* * *

The biblical God transcends natural forces: the Lord cannot be confined in a temple or limited to a territory, and Yahweh manifests a personality distinct from the characteristics of nature. Nevertheless, several contemporary theologies attempt to rehabilitate Christian relationships with nature by closely associating the Lord with natural processes. Matthew Fox, an American Dominican priest, is developing an "ecological spirituality" which draws from four medieval Rhineland mystics: Hildegard of Bingen, Mechtild of Magdeburg, Meister Eckhart, and Julian of Norwich, whose lives spanned three centuries from A.D. 1100 to 1400. Three were women, and the other led a women's community; together they present a distinctive feminine spirituality. Fox calls their perspective "panentheism": it does not equate God with natural forces, but it affirms the full interpenetration of God with natural life. Julian postulated that "God is everything which is good, as I see it, and the goodness which everything has is God," while Meister Eckhart wrote that "God created all things in such a way that they are not outside himself. . . . Everything that God creates or does, he does or creates in himself, sees or knows in himself, loves in himself." Furthermore, Julian pictured the cosmos as the womb of God, "our true Mother in whom we are endlessly carried and out of whom we will never come." Though celibates, all these mystics affirmed sensuality, and they also emphasized human relationships with the earth. Eckhart believed that "the soul loves the body," and Julian, extending that relationship, declared, "I understand that our sensuality is grounded in Nature, in Compassion and in grace. I saw that God is in our sensuality. For God is never out of the soul." Together these mystics embraced the earth with a spiritual passion. "Holy persons draw to themselves all that is earthly," Hildegard wrote, while Julian expressed the sacramental character of gardening:

> There is a treasure in the earth that is a food tasty and
>     pleasing to the Lord.
> Be a gardener. Dig and ditch, toil and sweat.
> Turn the earth upside down and seek the deepness and water
>     the plants in time.
> Continue this labor and make sweet floods to run and noble
>     and abundant fruits to spring.
> Take this food and drink and carry it to God as your true
>     worship.[4]

Early in the twentieth century, Pierre Teilhard de Chardin, a French Jesuit priest and paleontologist, recast the foundations of Christianity in the light of Darwinian biology. He was fascinated by the thrust of evolution toward greater complexity and by the evolutionary emergence of consciousness:

> We should use the following as an absolute principle . . . : "It is
> better, no matter what the cost, to be more conscious than less
> conscious." This principle, I believe, is the absolute condition of
> the world's existence.

Teilhard imagined, indeed, that evolution might yet create from human stock a more transcendent being with superior capacities. He emphasized God's presence within this process of becoming: Christ is the origin, character, and goal of evolution. "In him everything in heaven and on earth was created," the Apostle Paul had written, ". . . and all things are held together in him" until the end, when "God will be all in all" (Colossians 1:16–17; 1 Corinthians 15:28, NEB). Teilhard merged the cosmos into Christ, whose incarnation was "an act co-extensive with the duration of the world." Writing prior to the modern environmental movement, Teilhard focused on the emergence of evolution through human, and especially Christian, consciousness. He slighted ecological interdependence, however, and he did not emphasize the value of lower species.[5]

Process theology shares some important characteristics with Teilhard's thought, while addressing his particular deficiencies. Based on the philosophies of Alfred North Whitehead and Charles Hartshorne, process theology emphasizes *becoming* over being, and stresses the primacy of environmental relationships over individual existence. John B. Cobb, Jr. explains that

> the actual entities of which the world is ultimately made up are better thought of as organisms than as material or mental substances.
> The main significance of the idea of organism here is that each entity exists only in its relation to its environment.

Pantheism is complete here, for God is understood to be *within* this organismic system, not beyond it. "God, too, is constituted by relations to all things."[6] Unlike Teilhard or the Rhineland mystics, though, process theologians do not see God as consistently good, but recognize both ambiguity and uncertainty in evolution. Adaptation and creativity are important for humanity and for other organisms if goodness is also to evolve.

Writing with Australian biologist Charles Birch, Cobb accentuates the cost of human social evolution. While I have associated the biblical image of "fall" with a collapse of agricultural ethics, Birch and Cobb suggest instead that the fall of humanity may have occurred when hunters and gatherers turned to farming:

> It was the agricultural revolution that introduced opposition between human nature and human activity. People were forced into drudgery in order to live. In consequence they became acquisitive and violent. Contented hunters became unhappy farmers.

Birch and Cobb define the moral value in environmental relationships in terms of *aliveness,* which includes sensory awareness, responsiveness, and creativity. Moral worth is relative to aliveness: to "how rich is the world to which one is attuned and how fresh is the response of feeling, thought and action to that world."

All species, and even natural relationships and processes of change, exhibit some characteristics of aliveness and therefore have some value. Everything which exists is, in reality, a composition of events, and each of these possesses some awareness:

> In this model subjectivity or experience is attributed to all such events. Since experience is always valuable, events have intrinsic value. All things therefore have some intrinsic value either in themselves or in their constituent parts.[7]

In contrast to these theologians, I have not turned to pantheism to modify a biblical understanding of the Lord or to convey a moral ecology. Rather, I have emphasized the primacy of moral relationships over both relationships of being (stressed by classic philosophy) and relationships of becoming (stressed by evolutionary philosophies). The biblical Lord inspires moral awareness, which leads to respect for each species; this God also requires that ethics permeate all relationships. This is the distinctive gift to creatures from the biblical Lord, who stands beyond humanity, nature, and our joint evolution, while choosing to be passionately engaged with us all. I do not think that moral relationships can be built upon a single value such as Teilhard's "consciousness" or Birch and Cobb's "aliveness." Ironically, moral relationships are more complex, ecological, and evolutionary than the theories of evolutionary theologians suggest. Ethics are also less rational than systematic theologians might wish. Moral relationships between humanity and nature include sensory awareness, emotional engagement, cultural memory, respect, and a humbling appreciation of God's presence and concern. Moral relationships grow through both insights and mistakes— haltingly, politically, historically, and without guarantees— among those who have faith enough to reach beyond themselves.

The beauty of the Lord is what undergirds the being of God: that is, our experience of God's benevolence precedes and shapes our recognition of God's existence. The living God is never merely a hypothesis, nor is the God we experience limited by our apprehension. The Lord, passionately engaged with the world, is more self-giving than pantheist theologies can express because

God has more identity than such theories can convey. God delights in a world of creatures who find life within themselves as well as interdependence with others; the quality of their identity is enhanced because it is not God's identity. Though I admire the intimacy of Julian's image, I do not believe God holds the world forever in the womb, but gives birth and then delights in the maturation of creatures and the development of just and caring relationships among them. Through creativity, the biblical Lord gives freedom.

\* \* \*

Several interesting religious perspectives have been born from new environmental awareness. While advising America's space program about instrumentation that might detect chemical requirements for life on other planets, British scientist James Lovelock came to believe that the life-support system on earth was more sophisticated than science had appreciated. He hypothesized that for millions of years, and despite enormous stresses from the earth's evolving biotic community, a planetary system of feedback and biological self-regulation has maintained the precise saline balance in oceans and the distinctive atmospheric composition necessary to support life. He argued that

> the Earth's living matter, air, oceans, and land surface form a complex system which can be seen as a single organism and which has the capacity to keep our planet a fit place for life.[8]

Lovelock called this system *Gaia* after the Greek earth-goddess. His stimulating presentation of this hypothesis has provoked lively discussion among scientists, even though his conception of a complex earth-organism challenges important aspects of evolutionary theory. Some environmentalists admire the Gaia hypothesis as a corrective to the image of an insensate earth, an image which has characterized scientific imagination since the days of Francis Bacon and René Descartes. Others respond spiritually toward Gaia, causing Lovelock to call his hypothesis "the first religion to have a testable scientific theory embedded within it."[9] The ethical implications of Gaia, however, are unclear. Lovelock, whose research receives substantial support from industry, believes that the self-regulating biosphere may respond to pollutants far more effectively than conventional science can predict. "The evidence for accepting that industrial activities either at their present level or in the immediate future may endanger the life of Gaia as a whole," he writes, "is very weak indeed." Lovelock also looks forward to more sophisticated human management of the biosphere so that Gaia may become even more "awake and aware of herself."[10]

The "deep ecology" movement, in contrast, asks human culture to withdraw its influences from the natural environment. Norwegian philosopher Arne Naess has used the phrase "deep ecology" to propose a radical redefinition of the human place in the earthly community. Because all organisms and earthly systems are of equal worth, he believes, humanity should exercise no more claims than any other species. We should instead reorient ourselves to finding human fulfillment in the good of the whole ecosystem:

> The material standard of living should be drastically reduced and the quality of life, in the sense of basic satisfaction in the depths of one's heart or soul, should be maintained or increased. . . .
>
> There is a basic intuition in deep ecology that we have no right to destroy other living beings without sufficient reason. Another norm is that, with maturity, human beings will experience joy when other life forms experience joy and sorrow when other life forms experience sorrow. . . .
>
> For deep ecology, there is a core democracy in the biosphere. . . . We have the goal not only of stabilizing human population but also of reducing it to a sustainable minimum without revolution or dictatorship. I should think we must have no more than 100 million people if we are to have the variety of cultures we had one hundred years ago.[11]

The deep ecology movement serves as an umbrella for many radical, and sometimes insightful, critiques of human relationships with nature. Although the values of deep ecology are biologically inclusive, they tend to be culturally sectarian, spurning all human endeavors that alter the earthly landscape. Deep ecology, in fact, expresses a dualism that reverses the exploitative scientific ethos: it sees nature as good, and human culture as almost always evil.

Some who wish to improve their sensitivity to nature are turning to Buddhist spirituality. Gary Snyder, a California poet, represents this tendency. Cultivating a simple, rural lifestyle, he aims "to be a good member of the great community of living creatures. True affluence is not needing *anything*."[12] Snyder proposes that the phrases "wild land, sacred land, good land" are interrelated and equivalent. Australian Aborigines helped him to realize that places recognized as "sacred" are often ideal habitats for particular species: "sacredness comes together with a sense of optimal habitat of certain kinfolk that we have out there—the wallabies, red kangaroo, bush turkeys, lizards." The remaining wilderness areas in California, Snyder suggests, should be considered sacred places:

> The backpacker-pilgrim's step-by-step, breath-by-breath walk up a trail, carrying all on the back, is so ancient a set of gestures as to trigger perennial images and a profound sense of body-mind joy.... The point is in making intimate contact with wild world, wild self. *Sacred* refers to that which helps take us out of our little selves into the larger self of the whole universe.[13]

When I was preparing the first book of this series concerning John Muir, I benefited from Michael Cohen's sensitive study of Muir, written from an American Buddhist perspective.[14] Although his appreciation of Muir's experience with wilderness was profound, Cohen could not empathize with Muir's decades of devotion to public education and political activities on behalf of wilderness preservation. The Buddhist way points toward reflection rather than action.

Biblical ecology is activist. It is a moral strategy for a liberating intervention in a world where relationships have been corrupted by greed, pride, and power. While it summons us to empathy and respect for others, it inspires engagement rather than withdrawal. Nature had already been drawn into history, exploited, and degraded, before the Lord first chose a holy people and a holy land. When we look for values to guide modern environmental relationships, it is no longer helpful for us to view nature as a self-sufficient, self-regulating system which can be isolated from humanity and which needs no God. Nature looks to the Lord for liberation, and God calls humanity to complete the earth's ecology. Human culture can be creative even when it modifies nature, though the Bible is sensitive to the destructive capabilities of human technology and is wary of human presumption. Human awareness of the world's beauty is an important aspect of that beauty; without our consciousness, reflection, and appreciation, the ecosystem would be incomplete. The biblical tradition is complex enough to prophesy judgment upon human abuse of nature, while also hoping for covenant completion, a time when people and all creatures can live together in peace.

# 21. *The Day of the Lord*

I have not been called like Jeremiah to announce God's judgment upon modern society for environmental abuse, and I have no unique insight into what may lie ahead. There is ample evidence available to the public, however, that pathological cycles triggered by human abuse of the biosphere may profoundly disrupt life on earth. Some of these destructive interactions may be beyond recall—though prompt, responsible action might mitigate their severity. Humanity is at risk, as are most other species and the natural systems which support us. Our children and grandchildren may live in a crowded, painful world of dwindling vitality—a world of wounds.

Information about threats to the world's ecosystem is incomplete, and the implications of what we know are controversial. Nevertheless, it is reasonable to assume that several of the following cycles of destruction are already beyond the point where we might limit their impact to incidental damage:

• *Acid rain and toxic air pollution.* Mature forests are weakening and dying in central and eastern Europe; the decline, first noticed in 1972, has spread to eleven tree species. Similar problems are now being detected in Quebec, New England, and the higher elevations of southern Appalachian forests. The principal cause appears to be increasingly acid rain and airborne toxic metals. Acid rain results from the discharge of sulfur dioxide into the atmosphere by electric power plants, industries, automobiles, and indeed every building which heats with coal or oil.

Many of these same sources also discharge toxic metals. Lakes in these regions are acidifying, becoming less and less able to sustain life; toxic metals are accumulating in aquatic food chains, particularly in the Great Lakes, and may soon render some species of fish unfit to eat. Corrective measures, requiring major changes in production of electricity and use of energy, will take decades to implement. Since I make maple syrup from the sap of one of these weakened species, I am drawn into the pain of the forests.[1]

• *Ozone depletion.* Chlorofluorocarbon gases, emitted by aerosol spray cans, by the discharge of freon from air-conditioning units, and by supersonic jets, migrate to the stratosphere through a complex chemical interaction which no one fully understands. There they diminish the valuable ozone layer that reflects harmful solar radiation outward, away from the surface of the earth. It may take decades for emissions at ground level to affect stratospheric ozone; scientists are divided over the extent and rate of depletion. But in 1979 the National Academy of Sciences warned that as more ultraviolet radiation reaches the earth, the incidence of human skin cancer will increase; crop yields may be reduced; the larvae of shrimp, crabs, and other important seafood species may be killed; and microorganisms at the base of the marine food chain may be destroyed. In October 1983, an enormous hole opened in the ozone layer above Antarctica—and it took two years for scientists to accept the evidence that their instruments recorded. This hole reappears each October, probably the first major depletion from pollutants released many years before. Ocean life, therefore, is already at risk. In 1988 the major industrial nations signed a treaty that will slowly reduce the production and use of chlorofluoro-carbons. Even so, deterioration of the ozone layer is likely to continue for decades.[2]

• *The greenhouse effect.* Carbon is released to the atmosphere by forest fires and by the burning of fossil fuels: coal, oil, and natural gas. Later it is reabsorbed by oceans and by green plants, particularly trees. Throughout the world, annual carbon emissions from the burning of fossil fuels have tripled since 1950 and now account for most carbon releases. During the same period, deforestation—particularly rapid in the tropics—has reduced the earth's capacity to reabsorb carbon. Consequently, carbon dioxide levels in the earth's atmosphere are rising, and since $CO_2$ helps to hold the earth's heat and prevent its radiation into space, the earth's mean temperature is rising also. Though measurements are still uncertain, $CO_2$ concentrations in the earth's atmosphere appear to have risen about thirty percent since 1860. Even small changes in the earth's temperature can produce large effects: mean temperatures during the last ice age were only five degrees cooler than today. If $CO_2$ concentrations should double—a condition likely by the middle of the next century—the earth's mean temperature could rise between 1.5 and 4.5 degrees centigrade, reaching the highest levels since humanity appeared on earth. Such warmth would melt large portions of polar ice caps, raising sea levels and flooding coastal areas; it could, as well, dry out the major grain-producing regions of the world. Were remedial steps begun immediately, it would still take a generation or more to replace fossil fuels and to reforest extensively.[3]

•  *Rain forest destruction.* Forests are lungs for the landscape. They do not discharge net oxygen, as people often suppose, but they do absorb net carbon dioxide, and their respiration of water is crucial to world climate. A tropical rain forest is directly responsible for fifty percent of the rainfall it receives, because it absorbs, stores, and expires water so efficiently. When such forests are cut, regional rainfall decreases drastically. Except for energy from the sun, nearly all the nourishment for plants and animals within a rain forest must circulate through their complex aboveground ecosystem; these forests draw little from the poor soils on which they stand. Tropical rain forests—occurring in the Amazon basin, Guatemala, and Panama; in Zaire, Sierra Leone, and the Ivory Coast; in Thailand, Malaysia, and the Philippines—cover less than two percent of the globe. Yet between forty and fifty percent of the earth's species live in these environments. Forty thousand square miles of rain forests are being cut each year, primarily to provide lumber for North America, Europe, and Japan, and to raise cheap beef that is sold to fast food outlets. A tropical forest, once cleared, will not regenerate itself as a temperate forest will. At the present rate, within sixty years all rain forests will have been cut, yet the pace of cutting is not diminishing but accelerating. In these forests, laments Peter Raven of the Missouri Botanical Garden, "over a million species or a quarter of the total biological diversity on earth are at risk of extinction during the next 15 to 20 years or so." There are as yet no plans to halt or even to slow this vast biological genocide.[4]

• *Desertification.* Although agriculture has always been hard on soil, modern agriculture is particularly destructive. Soils from a wide area, stretching across Greece through Asia Minor and Palestine to the Euphrates River, were exhausted and eroded centuries ago. Today the rapid depletion of the world's soils is masked by heavy applications of fertilizer manufactured from petroleum. The United Nations estimates that one-third of the earth's remaining agricultural soil may be lost during the final quarter of the twentieth century. Trees, which play a critical role in the circulation of water between earth and atmosphere, are being depleted for firewood in overcrowded agricultural regions. Heavy grazing by domestic cattle is destroying grasslands that once supported abundant wild game for meat. This desertification is proceeding most rapidly on the African continent.[5]

• *Mineral depletion.* High-grade reserves of petroleum, metals, and minerals vital to industrial production will be wholly consumed in the next fifty years. From the perspective of economic theory, this is a self-correcting problem. As a fuel or material becomes scarce it commands a higher price. High price then encourages conservation, the substitution of another commodity, and the exploitation of lower-grade reserves. However, the burden of scarcity falls most heavily upon those who can no longer afford fuel or tools made from newly expensive materials. So long as societies resist conserving their resources and delay developing substitutes for commodities likely to become scarce, mineral depletion will widen the chasm between the affluent and the growing numbers of the poor.[6]

• *Population explosion.* The more insecure one's life is, the stronger the motivation to have children who may repay parental love with care for their parents in old age. Over two billion people now live in the more stable half of the world—the principal industrial regions plus China—where the rate of annual population growth has been reduced to 0.8 percent. Even at this rate, however, population within this stable half will double in eighty-seven years. A frightening reality is that 2.6 billion people now live in the unstable half of the world, including Latin America, Africa, the Middle East, India, and Southeast Asia; and in this half, population growth averages 2.5 percent, which will double the population in only twenty-eight years. The Worldwatch Institute notes that in these areas,

> where birth rates remain high, rapid population growth is beginning to overwhelm local life-support systems in many countries, leading to ecological deterioration and declining living standards. . . .
> Once populations expand to the point where their demands exceed the sustainable yield of local forests, grasslands, croplands, or aquifers, they begin directly or indirectly to consume the resource base itself. Forests and grasslands disappear, soils erode, land productivity declines, and water tables fall. This in turn reduces per capita food production and incomes, triggering a decline in living standards.[7]

When childhood mortality increases, adults without confidence in social welfare produce more children in the hope that a few of their own may survive to provide for their parents. The vicious circle intensifies:

> Once this deterioration begins, rapid population growth and ecological deterioration feed on each other, pushing countries into a demographic trap. In effect, ecological deterioration, economic decline, and political instability reinforce each other, confronting governments with the prospect of social disintegration.[8]

• *Threat of nuclear war.* Nuclear war is a political decision, not an ecological necessity. Unfortunately, environmental deterioration and its resulting social tensions may increase the risks of war. This is only one reason why political action to reduce the likelihood of nuclear confrontation is urgent. Unlike environmental stress, which advances incrementally, nuclear war would devastate quickly. Radiation might render the northern hemisphere—or perhaps the whole earth—uninhabitable by humans and other species high on the food chain. Additionally, clouds from intense fires might shield the landscape from sunlight until the earth returned to an ice age. Even short of war, however, serious threats to human health and environmental stability remain from the operation of nuclear power plants and the disposal of nuclear wastes.[9]

\* \* \*

Thinking about these possibilities has agitated, angered, and depressed me. I would rather not anticipate such destruction. I feel guilty: just living the life of an affluent American, I exacerbate each of these world problems. I also feel helpless: I want God to intervene to rescue me, my wife, my sons and their families, the country and culture that I love, and the landscapes I treasure, from the consequences of human arrogance and folly. I want to use my faith to escape, but I know this is not what the Bible teaches. Instead, God's saving covenant aims at bringing people to maturity and responsibility so that we can practice justice, express compassion, experience the repercussions of our actions, and become free people within a moral universe. When some Hebrews imagined that God might terminate history in time to rescue them from the results of their apostasy and folly, the prophet Amos blocked such moral evasion and assured them that God would not provide an escape. Indeed, Amos declared, the Lord was at the heart of the punishment that awaited them:

> Fools who long for the day of the LORD,
> what will the day of the LORD mean to you?
> It will be darkness, not light.
> It will be as when a man runs from a lion,
>    and a bear meets him,
> or turns into a house and leans his hand on the wall,
>    and a snake bites him.
> The day of the LORD is indeed darkness, not light,
>    a day of gloom with no dawn.
>
>                    (Amos 5:18–20, NEB)

Like other prophets in Israel prior to the fall of Samaria, and in Judah prior to the fall of Jerusalem, Amos insisted that the engulfing disasters were the work of the Lord, not simply natural perversity or spontaneous turns in the course of history. He proclaimed in God's voice,

> It was I who kept teeth idle
>    in all your cities,
> who brought famine on all your settlements;
>    yet you did not come back to me.
>    This is the very word of the LORD.
>
> It was I who withheld the showers from you
> while there were still three months to harvest.
>    I would send rain on one city
>    and no rain on another;
>    rain would fall on one field,
> and another would be parched for lack of it.
> From this city and that, [people] would stagger to another
> for water to drink, but would not find enough;
>    yet you did not come back to me.
>    This is the very word of the LORD.
>
> I blasted you with black blight and red;
>    I laid waste your gardens and vineyards;
> the locust devoured your fig-trees and your olives;
>    yet you did not come back to me.
>    This is the very word of the LORD.
>                                        (Amos 4:6–9, NEB, alt.)

Amos wanted Israel to consider the moral implications of their disaster, for if they would ponder that dimension, they would again meet the Lord. Those who followed Baal tried manipulative techniques to force sprouts from barren soil and to entice rain from a cloudless sky. Within the covenant, however, Hebrews were required to look first to their moral relationships with God, with each other, and with the landscape—trusting that when these were put right, the heavens and the earth would respond fruitfully.

To find the Lord within our own environmental crisis, we too will need to ponder moral dimensions. During two centuries we have constructed an idol which most people—even Christians —have come to trust more than the Lord. That idol is technology: the machinery and techniques of modern production.[10] We have come to believe that technical expertise can substitute for moral sensitivity. Our idol stimulates the fantasy that we can satisfy all human desires with products of our own manufacture, while it sedates our awareness that the means we employ to do this have consequences of their own. Power, the idol assures us, does not corrupt; it only frees those who wield it. The "invisible hand" of the idol's economy will turn the greed of a few into blessings for all. "Side effects" can be ignored. Manufacturers of each new product rush it into use and advertise what it will accomplish; later, when they are forced to address its dangers, they claim they had no way of knowing. Enthralled by our technology, we think we are masters of the universe. If we are caught up short by impending disaster, however, we complain like children that we are victims of consequences no one could have anticipated.

Jesus, like the prophets, insisted that we grow up. He expected from his followers foresight and moral accountability:

> Whoever does not bear their own cross and come after me, cannot be my disciple. For which of you, desiring to build a tower, does not first sit down and count the cost, whether there is enough to complete it? Otherwise, when the foundation is laid and the tower cannot be finished, all who see it begin to mock.
> (Luke 14:27–29, ILL)[11]

Our binge of technological idolatry and productive anarchy is nearly exhausted. To keep the world alive, we must recognize the consequences of our means. Human society needs to awaken to maturity and moral sensitivity that exceed prior human achievements. Furthermore, we must innovatively protect, comfort, and sustain the afflicted within the human family and in our biological community, harnessing technology to the service of morality. Such a fundamental turn from idolatry is unlikely unless we awaken to the day of the Lord—unless we feel the sharp pain and also accept its moral meaning.

As Jeremiah complained, the pain often is not distributed

fairly. The wicked, who have power to resist necessary reforms, may be the last to feel it. Poor people and helpless creatures suffer first. Another Jerusalem prophet, Joel, empathized with this early suffering of the victimized landscape:

> Alas! the day is near,
> the day of the LORD: it comes,
> a mighty destruction from the Almighty.
> Look! it stares us in the face;
> the house of our God has lost its food,
>   lost all its joy and gladness.
>   The soil is parched,
>   the dykes are dry;
>   the granaries are deserted,
>   the barns ruinous;
>   for the rains have failed.
>   The cattle are exhausted,
>     the herds of oxen distressed
> because they have no pasture;
> the flocks of sheep waste away.
> To thee I cry, O LORD;
>   for fire has devoured the open pastures
> and the flames have burnt up all the trees of the country-side.
> The very cattle in the field look up to thee;
>   for the water-channels are dried up,
>   and fire has devoured the open pastures.

(Joel 1:15–20, NEB)

Amid the unfairness of all-embracing disaster, practical and moral comfort can come from knowledge that the Lord suffers with the afflicted. This knowledge can be conveyed by people who, in the image of God, empathize with their fellow creatures and with the earth itself.

\* \* \*

Although I do not feel commissioned to prophesy destruction, I urge close attention to those who are called to warn modern civilization: those who combine technical insight with moral sensitivity. Some Christians may find it disorienting to listen to modern prophets, many of whom stand outside the conventional limits of our faith. John Muir, the subject of the first book in this series, is a good early example of the type.

We may also feel disoriented when we realize that it is too late to respond with the traditional evangelical strategy, calling everyone to faith in the Lord so we may then talk together about ethics—including environmental ethics. The crisis is coming so quickly that most people will depend upon secular images to interpret it. Nevertheless, believers will need to join with all perceptive citizens to acknowledge the crisis and to fashion strategies for change. It will not be useful for Christians to adopt a superior stance; we ourselves are late in accepting God's commission to attend nature with love. It is not too late, however, to stand in solidarity with an afflicted world and to serve it alongside all others who care.

I do have one prophetic word to add. Among Christians who repent and accept kinship with nature, one calling may be laid upon those who, because of their biblical faith, have special courage. This is the task of Jeremiah. When society at large awakens to the dimensions of the environmental crisis, many of our leaders will want to cling to the idol of technology. They will want to save some people—while claiming to serve all—by intensifying control over the weak and dominion over the landscape. Those who wish to manage the crisis in this way will ask us to surrender our freedoms. Ever more elaborate schemes to subdue nature will be proposed. Ever more rigorous requirements will be placed on the poor, especially those of the Third World, who will be blamed for their own starvation. Subsidized by the rest of us, a few of the elite will design means to rocket from this strangled planet to colonize another, hailing this as a victory for humanity. If the world ends, I believe it will end in just such a fury of repression. Before such an end, however, the Lord will call Jeremiahs to risk imprisonment and death by demanding that the powerful stop manipulations which only deepen the plight of the world. These Jeremiahs will also have to tell anxious, desperate people that they must accept suffering, loosen their reins from the world, and nurse it to recovery with love. This will be a thankless calling, but an essential one if any are to survive.

# 22. *Redemption*

When Jesus entered Jerusalem, filled with the spirit of the new kingdom, the crowd accompanying him burst into enthusiastic praise: *"Hosanna! Blessed is he who is coming in the name of the Lord! Blessed is the coming kingdom of David our father! Hosanna in the highest heavens!"* (Mark 11:9–10, NJB). Intertwined with the stories of Jesus' triumphal entry and his cleansing of the temple, however, there is another incident which seems uncharacteristic: Jesus cursed a fig tree. This act was puzzling, but it was duly recorded; and though few have been able to make sense of it, perhaps we can now understand why Jesus commanded nature to bear fruit in anticipation of his new kingdom.

Jesus asked the disinherited to take hope, and this day they did. The next morning he set forth to demand holy reform from money managers in the temple court:

> as they were leaving Bethany, he felt hungry. Seeing a fig tree in leaf some distance away, he went to see if he could find any fruit on it, but when he came up to it he found nothing but leaves; for it was not the season for figs. And he addressed the fig tree, "May no one ever eat fruit from you again." And his disciples heard him say this. (Mark 11:12–14, NJB)

The disciples who witnessed this bizarre incident inferred that hunger had caused Jesus to be disappointed, but I suspect that he wanted more from the tree than breakfast. Jesus came to Jerusalem to revive the ancient covenant. He asked people to risk behaving justly in order to bring in the righteous age. With this same intention Jesus approached the fig tree, a member of the holy landscape, calling it to risk premature fruitfulness. Although it was not the calendar season for fruit, this was *the time* for all who desired covenant renewal to exert themselves. Within covenant understanding, all nature should respond to righteousness with fruitfulness. Earlier, fish had clogged Peter's nets when Jesus entered the boat, but now the fig tree failed to respond. Nature's failure was soon matched by others: the failure of temple officials whom Jesus had to drive from its court; the failure of religious leadership and civil government; the failure of the disinherited, who, angered by Jesus' refusal to use force, turned against him; and finally the failure of his own frightened disciples. Jesus' frustrating encounter with the fig tree was part of his *passion*, one of many painful disappointments on his way to the cross.

According to Mark, shortly after cleansing the temple Jesus told the parable of the vineyard, suggesting that those who possessed the holy land unjustly would go so far as to kill the son of its rightful owner. Jesus implied that God would form a new people to redeem the vineyard and restore it to righteous productivity: "Now what will the owner of the vineyard do? He will come and make an end of the tenants and give the vineyard to others" (12:9, NJB). This call to people of the new kingdom to restore just and fruitful relationships with the holy landscape went unheard, largely because the church came to life among the seaports and trading towns of the Mediterranean basin, beyond the traditional holy land. Perhaps for this same reason, Jesus' encounter with the fig tree was not understood.[1]

* * *

Hebrew visions of redemption usually encompassed the holy land as well as the holy people. When Nebuchadnezzar took Hebrews to Babylon and left behind a desolate landscape, Ezekiel prophesied that God would restore both people and lands in order to vindicate the Lord's integrity:

> It is not for your sake, you Israelites, that I am acting, but for the sake of my holy name, which you have profaned. . . . I will take you out of the nations and gather you from every land and bring you to your own soil. I will sprinkle clean water over you, and you shall be cleansed from all that defiles you; I will cleanse you from the taint of all your idols. I will give you a new heart and put a

> new spirit within you; I will take the heart of stone from your
> body and give you a heart of flesh. I will put my spirit into you
> and make you conform to my statutes, keep my laws and live by
> them. You shall live in the land which I gave to your ancestors;
> you shall become my people, and I will become your God. I will
> save you from all that defiles you; I will call to the corn and make
> it plentiful; I will bring no more famine upon you. I will make the
> trees bear abundant fruit and the ground yield heavy crops. . . .
> It is not for your sake that I am acting; be sure of that, says the
> Lord GOD. Feel, then, the shame and disgrace of your ways. . .
>
> (Ezekiel 36:22–32, NEB)

Ezekiel's deep anger at the apostasy of his own generation conditioned the way he expressed hope for the future. He despaired
of human nature. Like his contemporary, Jeremiah, he used coercive language—"I will . . . make you conform"—to convey how
a "new heart" and a "new spirit" might function, even though
"heart" and "spirit" are properly vital, responsive images.[2] It is
plain, however, that Ezekiel looked forward to an age when the
full dynamics of covenant community would be realized. A people
cleansed from idolatry will live obedient to God's will, he believed,
and nature will respond fruitfully. Both apostasy and oppression
will cease. Hearts will no longer be hardened but will become
natural "flesh" again, sensitive to the needs of others. Spirits will
not be selfish but will respond to God's will. Nature, humanity,
and the Lord will live in covenant relationship.

Ezekiel stressed that restoration of the covenant community depended upon God's integrity. He did not draw hope from
the evolution of nature or from the promise of humanity; indeed,
he despaired of both. Nevertheless, as Paul said of Abraham, "in
hope he believed against hope" (Romans 4:18, RSV). Hebrews had
learned to consider natural, social, and cosmic interactions in
moral terms—a liberating understanding which inspired hope
and guided ethical behavior. The prophets believed that the
integrity of God's work with the created world required a historical resolution. God would punish the disobedient and might even
ask the chosen to suffer on behalf of others. Beyond the tragedy
experienced today and the calamity glimpsed for tomorrow, however, prophets expected a moral resolution to fulfill the cove-

nant's liberating promise. The very character of the Lord required such resolution: "I will vindicate the holiness of my great name" (Ezekiel 36:23, RSV).

Ezekiel portrayed the age of redemption as a great jubilee. Pondering the problem of just redistribution of the holy land among the inhabitants, he proposed a significant advance in social justice. In God's name he instructed the redeemed that when they divided the farmland they must give place not only to the Hebrew poor but also to alien families in the community:

> "You must distribute [this country] as a heritage for yourselves and the aliens settled among you who have fathered children among you, since you must treat them as citizens of Israel. . . . You will give the alien his heritage in the tribe where he has settled—declares the Lord Yahweh. " (Ezekiel 47:22–23, NJB)

The new covenant would embrace all the people who dwelt on the land, regardless of their race or heritage.

A century before Ezekiel, Isaiah had prophesied that the Lord would bring the holy land and holy people to fruition together:

> On that day the plant that the LORD has grown
> shall become glorious in its beauty,
> and the fruit of the land shall be
> the pride and splendour
> of the survivors of Israel.
> (Isaiah 4:2, NEB)

In the century after Ezekiel, following their return from exile in Babylon, disciples of Isaiah imagined that the culture of the new covenant would radiate from Jerusalem, beyond the original holy people and the landscape of Canaan, to embrace the whole created order:

> For behold, I create
> new heavens and a new earth.
> Former things shall no more be remembered
> nor shall they be called to mind.
> Rejoice and be filled with delight,
> you boundless realms which I create;
> for I create Jerusalem to be a delight

and her people a joy;
I will take delight in Jerusalem and rejoice in my people;
    weeping and cries for help
shall never again be heard in her.
There no child shall ever again die an infant,
    no old [persons] fail to live out [their] life.

· · · · · · · · · · · · · · · · · · · · · · · · · · · · · · · ·

[People] shall build houses and live to inhabit them,
plant vineyards and eat their fruit;
    they shall not build for others to inhabit
    nor plant for others to eat.
My people shall live the long life of a tree,
and my chosen shall enjoy the fruit of their labour.
They shall not toil in vain or raise children for misfortune.

· · · · · · · · · · · · · · · · · · · · · · · · · · · · · · · · · · · · · · · · · ·

[B]efore they call to me, I will answer,
and while they are still speaking I will listen.
The wolf and the lamb shall feed together
and the lion shall eat straw like cattle.
They shall not hurt or destroy in all my holy mountain,
    says the LORD.

(Isaiah 65:17–25, NEB, alt.)

Isaiah's disciples did not believe that the familiar cosmos would be destroyed to be replaced by another, although many Christians have so understood these passages. The sun and moon are not to be removed, but the usefulness of their light to guide our steps will pale in comparison with the vividness of God's presence. The new creation will not terminate human relationships with the land, but will establish them:

The sun shall no longer be your light by day,
nor the moon shine on you when evening falls;
    the LORD shall be your everlasting light,
    your God shall be your glory.
Never again shall your sun set
    nor your moon withdraw her light;
but the LORD shall be your everlasting light
    and the days of your mourning shall be ended.

Your people shall all be righteous
and shall for ever possess the land,

a shoot of my own planting,
a work of my own hands to bring me glory.
(Isaiah 60:19–21, NEB)

\* \* \*

Even though the early Christian movement spread beyond the ancient holy land and lost touch with the ethics of that relationship, the Apostle Paul continued to teach that redemption applies to the whole earth. Jesus Christ has inaugurated a new creation within which human relationships with nature are redeemable. Paul argued that for Christians all foods are clean, including foods once prohibited by Hebrew dietary laws as well as those marketplace foods which, in the Roman world, were routinely blessed in pagan ceremonies. Christ revealed the integrity of all God's creations and provided the basis for wholesome relationships among all things:

> Well then, about eating food sacrificed to idols: . . . even if there were things called gods, either in the sky or on earth—where there certainly seem to be "gods" and "lords" in plenty—still for us there is one God, the Father [and Mother], from whom all things come and for whom we exist; and there is one Lord, Jesus Christ, through whom all things come and through whom we exist. (1 Corinthians 8:4–6, JB, alt.)

Once we know Christ, Paul affirmed, we can never again imagine that God is remote from this world, never again conclude that anything earthly is beyond God's redeeming power. In his letter to the Philippians, Paul explained that Christ's *passion* as the suffering servant of all was not a departure from the character of God but the clearest revelation that he was God.[3] Christ's humility is sufficient to inspire every creature—if Christians will also give similar witness:

> Let your bearing towards one another arise out of your life in Christ Jesus. For the divine nature was his from the first; yet he did not think to snatch at equality with God, but made himself nothing, assuming the nature of a slave. Bearing the human likeness, revealed in human shape, he humbled himself, and in obedience accepted even death—death on a cross. Therefore God

raised him to the heights and bestowed on him the name above all names, that at the name of Jesus every knee should bow—in heaven, on earth, and in the depths—and every tongue confess, "Jesus Christ is Lord," to the glory of God the Father [and Mother]. (Philippians 2:5–11, NEB, alt.)

The letters to the Colossians and Ephesians—which may be from Paul's disciples rather than from his own hand—make explicit this cosmic understanding of Christ's redemption: "Through him God chose to reconcile the whole universe to [God's] self, making peace through the shedding of his blood upon the cross—to reconcile all things, whether on earth or in heaven, through him alone" (Colossians 1:20, NEB, alt.), "that the universe, all in heaven and on earth, might be brought into a unity in Christ" (Ephesians 1:10, NEB). Christ did not come to rescue a handful of believers from this world. He came to renew creation, to restore humanity and nature to full communion with God, and to bring all creatures into just and compassionate relationships with each other through the inspiration of his own humble sacrifice.

In his most complete and thoughtful statement of faith, Paul explained to Roman Christians that Christ was the new Adam, sent to renew the human species, and that all who confessed Christ would share his relationship with God. Such sharing, however, meant entering into Christ's humility and suffering for the sake of our fellow creatures—not just other people, but all living things. Liberation must reach to all:

> In my estimation, all that we suffer in the present time is nothing in comparison with the glory which is destined to be disclosed for us, for the whole creation is waiting with eagerness for the children of God to be revealed. It was not for its own purposes that creation had frustration imposed on it, but for the purpose of [God] who imposed it—with the intention that the whole creation itself might be freed from its slavery to corruption and brought into the same glorious freedom as the children of God. (Romans 8:18–21, NJB, alt.)

The new humanity is called to be both redeemed and redeeming. Paul invited Christians to renew the image of God in themselves by joining to serve all of creation. As Christ's example suggests, the image of God does not authorize mastery over others through power, but requires liberating others through care and sacrificial service. The goal is for all species, through Christ, to recognize each other as God's children.

\* \* \*

In some places the Bible's vision is more anxious: an elect few are to be rescued from a burning world and transported beyond dying nature and wicked culture to a realm where, passive and receptive, they will receive comfort forever. Many Christians prefer this vision to a comprehensive biblical hope. Those immersed in despair, those who toil the earth under the curse of injustice, and those who feel alienated from a society which has shown them little compassion, may hope that God in love rescues them and in justice consigns the rest to eternal fire.

I believe, however, that as we are strengthened by our participation in the redeemed community we may be able to grasp a hope that is broader and deeper. Biblical hope begins, surely, with a promise of mercy to those who in faith suffer alienation from a wicked society. This hope is symbolized by the divine whirlwind that lifted Elijah to heaven, and it is confirmed by Jesus' promise to prepare a place for his disciples.[4] It extends, however, to the redemption of human culture—a new Jerusalem from which truth and health will flow out to the world. And it embraces the whole panoply of life which the Lord created and which Christ suffered to redeem—expanding from Eden, to the holy land, and finally to embrace "heaven and earth."

In Christ, redemption is environmental. The health of one relates to the health of all. We are not rescued *from* others but redeemed *for* others. Christians need not imagine, as some radical environmentalists do, that nature would be improved by the withdrawal of the human species; though we should understand that nature is in peril until humanity repents of pollution. Nor need we conclude that our true home is in some other place without all our beautiful friends who also share this planet. The "world" we are asked to shun is the culture of injustice, not environmental relationships. Humanity and other species are created to nurture each other. Scientific ecologists understand how species live *from* other species; biblical moralists may perceive how we live *for* others.

At the height of medieval Christendom, when it seemed possible that one faith might embrace all, theologians claimed, "Outside the church there is no salvation." Now, in a difficult era when Christians must be the example of humility, we must affirm: *apart from the earth there is no salvation.* Our future, and the future of all who share this landscape with us, are joined.

# 23. *Abundance*

These were exciting days around the Sea of Galilee. Jesus had sent pairs of his disciples—people from this area—through the surrounding villages to proclaim the new kingdom and to heal. Crowds now followed him everywhere. It was a time of abundance:

The apostles rejoined Jesus and told him all they had done and taught, and he said to them, "Come away to some lonely place all by yourselves and rest for a while"; for there were so many coming and going that there was no time for them even to eat. So they went off in the boat to a lonely place where they could be by themselves. But people saw them going, and many recognised them; and from every town they all hurried to the place on foot and reached it before them. So as he stepped ashore he saw a large crowd; and he took pity on them because they were like sheep without a shepherd, and he set himself to teach them at some length. By now it was getting very late, and his disciples came up to him and said, "This is a lonely place and it is getting very late, so send them away, and they can go to the farms and villages round about, to buy themselves something to eat." He replied, "Give them something to eat yourselves." They answered, "Are we to go and spend two hundred denarii on bread for them to eat?" He asked, "How many loaves have you? Go and see." And when they had found out they said, "Five, and two fish." Then he ordered them to get all the people to sit down in groups on the green grass, and they sat down on the ground in squares of hundreds and fifties. Then he took the five loaves and the two fish, raised his eyes to heaven and said the blessing; then he broke the loaves and began handing them to his disciples to distribute among the people. He also shared out the two fish among them all. They all ate as much as they wanted. They collected twelve basketfuls of scraps of bread and pieces of fish. Those who had eaten the loaves numbered five thousand.

(Mark 6:30–44, NJB)

Generosity, hospitality, and abundance are signs of the renewed covenant. They may seem to emerge spontaneously, unaccountably, from the spirit of the new kingdom. Often, however, one can connect these effects to the moral character of the holy society and its redeemed environment. The several Gospel versions of the great feeding offer no explanations. The provisions may have multiplied miraculously as they passed through the hands of Jesus and his disciples. Perhaps good organization, and Jesus' own confidence that there would be enough, made it possible for each family to bring forth and share, without anxiety, provisions they had held back for their own use. Whatever the explanation, no story from Jesus' ministry is better attested. It reminds me of a prophecy from Zechariah, five hundred years before, concerning new covenant hospitality among rural families: "On that day, says the LORD of Hosts, you shall all of you invite one another to come and sit each under his vine and his fig-tree" (Zechariah 3:10, NEB). When we know the presence of the Lord, and feel secure, we are more willing to share.

* * *

The Bible views the ecology of redemption from several different aspects. The most common perspective is that of the farmer. From the northern kingdom, Amos's prophecies close with a delightful vision of farmers reunited to their soil, hardly able to keep pace with its fertility:

> A time is coming, says the LORD,
>   when the ploughman shall follow hard on the reaper,
> and he who treads the grapes after him who sows the seed.
>   The mountains shall run with fresh wine,
>   and every hill shall wave with corn.
>   I will restore the fortunes of my people Israel;
> they shall rebuild deserted cities and live in them,
> they shall plant vineyards and drink their wine,
>   make gardens and eat the fruit.
>   Once more I will plant them on their own soil,
>   and they shall never again be uprooted
>     from the soil I have given them.
>   It is the word of the LORD your God.
>
> (Amos 9:13–15, NEB)

In the southern kingdom Isaiah had a similar vision of the time
when empires would be overthrown and farmers could return to
their fields in peace:

> When that day comes the cattle shall graze in broad pastures; the
> oxen and asses that work your land shall be fed with well-
> seasoned fodder, winnowed with shovel and fork. On each high
> mountain and each lofty hill shall be streams of running water,
> on the day of massacre when the highest in the land fall. The
> moon shall shine with a brightness like the sun's, and the sun
> with seven times his wonted brightness, seven days' light in one,
> on the day when the LORD binds up the broken limbs of [God's]
> people and heals their wounds. (Isaiah 30:23–26, NEB, alt.)

Sometimes the redeemed community is viewed from the
perspective of nature. Isaiah imagined that the trees will sing of
their own liberation when the Babylonian king dies and his
minions withdraw:

> The whole world is at rest and calm,
> shouts of joy resounding,
> the cypresses, the cedars of Lebanon,
> rejoice aloud at your fate,
> "Now that you have been laid low,
> no one comes up to fell us."
>                        (Isaiah 14:7–8, NJB)

Ezekiel envisioned trees sprouting fresh branches and ripening
new fruit to welcome the return of Hebrews from their Babylonian captivity: "But you, O mountains of Israel, shall shoot forth
your branches, and yield your fruit to my people Israel; for they
will soon come home" (Ezekiel 36:8, RSV). Jesus may have had this
verse in mind when he approached the fig tree near Jerusalem.

The Bible also shows us the redeemed community from
God's perspective. Hosea's prophecy closes with a vision of the
Lord as the tree of life:

> They will come back to live in my shade;
> they will grow wheat again,
> they will make the vine flourish . . .
> What has Ephraim to do with idols any more
> when I hear him and watch over him?.

> I am like an evergreen cypress,
> you owe your fruitfulness to me.
> 
> (Hosea 14:8–9, NJB)

In Isaiah there is a poem—difficult to translate and interpret—which presents a charming image of the caring Creator. The Lord, high-spirited as in the days of creation, nearly drowns the renewed landscape with devoted attention. When weeds threaten, the Lord is first tempted to counterattack but then relents and offers peace to them as well. Such an ecosystem, integrating all species in fruitfulness, will spread to embrace the whole world:

> That day,
> sing of the delightful vineyard!
> I, Yahweh, am its keeper;
> every moment I water it
> for fear its leaves should fall;
> night and day I watch over it.
> 
> I am angry no longer.
> If thorns and briars come
> I will declare war on them,
> I will burn them every one.
> Or if they would shelter under my protection,
> let them make their peace with me,
> let them make their peace with me.
> 
> In the days to come, Jacob will put out shoots,
> Israel will bud and blossom
> and fill the whole world with fruit.
> 
> (Isaiah 27:2–6, JB)

When interpreted as an allegory, this poem complements Jesus' parable of the vineyard, suggesting that the new, fruitful Israel will embrace people once regarded as "thorns and briars."

Isaiah explains that in the redeemed community the moral ecology will interpenetrate nature to revive the vitality of the landscape. Covenant justice will reach beyond the agricultural domain to embrace the wild and to establish peace between the two. In a prophecy addressed to the women of Judah, who did much of the farm work, Isaiah describes a progression of judgment, repentance, and suffering. . .

until the spirit is poured out on us from above,
and the desert becomes productive ground,
so productive you might take it for a forest.

In the wilderness justice will come to live
and integrity in the fertile land;
integrity will bring peace,
justice give lasting security.

My people will live in a peaceful home,
in safe houses,
in quiet dwellings ...
Happy will you be, sowing by every stream,
letting ox and donkey roam free.

                    (Isaiah 32:15, NJB; 16–20, JB)

Ezekiel, prophet of the Jerusalem temple, received the most complex vision of moral ecology: many Christians are familiar with John of Patmos's summary of this vision in Revelation 22:1–2. The river of new life will flow from the temple, gaining strength as it advances through the landscape. It will reach the most lifeless of all earthly places, the Dead Sea, which will be redeemed by the sweet waters and restored to vitality. However, some salt marshes will remain—did Ezekiel know that brackish pools are vital to the regeneration of life? Fish will abound in this new river, and nets will be spread in the Dead Sea for ocean species. The trees that cluster beside these holy waters will bear fruit continually and put forth healing leaves. Ezekiel reports that in his vision, God's messenger

brought me back to the entrance of the Temple, where a stream flowed eastwards from under the Temple threshold, for the Temple faced east.... The man went off to the east holding his measuring line and measured off a thousand cubits; he then made me wade across the stream; the water reached my ankles. He measured off another thousand and made me wade across the stream again; the water reached my knees. He measured off another thousand and made me wade across the stream again; the water reached my waist. He measured off another thousand; it was now a river which I could not cross; the stream had swollen and was now deep water, a river impossible to cross. He then said, "Do you see, son of man?" He then took me and brought me back to the bank on the river. Now, when I reached it, I saw an enormous number of trees on each bank of the river. He said, "This water flows east down to the Arabah and to the sea; and flowing into the sea it makes its waters wholesome. Wherever the river flows, all living creatures teeming in it will live. Fish will be very plentiful, for wherever the water goes it brings health, and life teems wherever the river flows. There will be fishermen on its banks. Fishing nets will be spread from En-Gedi to En-Eglaim. The species of fish will be the same as the fish of the Great Sea. The marshes and lagoons, however, will not become wholesome, but will remain salt. Along the river, on either bank, will grow every kind of fruit tree with leaves that never wither and fruit that never fails; they will bear new fruit every month, because this water comes from the sanctuary. And their fruit will be good to eat and the leaves medicinal."

(Ezekiel 47:1–12, NJB)

* * *

What are we to make of these florid visions? Christian theology, which matured in the world of Greek philosophy, has usually spiritualized them. Lush environmental details have been considered as allegories conveying the relationship of Christ to believers. Many Christians exclude from their hope the abundance of nature and even the bodily character of human existence, treating both as impediments to the spiritual journey. Often, in Christian imagery, the new creation is portrayed as radically separate from the earth: the present cosmos will be destroyed, and from it only incorporeal souls of believers will enter the realm of the blessed. In such a depiction, environmental details become mere poetic expression of the exalted feelings of the redeemed, and their truth becomes psychological rather than geographical. I believe that through such spiritualization, Christianity has lost the scope of biblical concern. Christian hope has grown timid, wholly unlike vital biblical promise. Spiritualization has also undermined the relevance of Christian hope for modern society caught in environmental crisis.

In the Bible, most visions of redemption are worldly. They propose no escape from history, but instead offer hope for moral fulfillment within a historical framework. Prophets who feel the tension between God's will and fallen society project visions of redemption not only to convey a future hope, but also to guide present behavior. In moments of faithfulness within the Hebrew community and among followers of Jesus, this fulfillment comes to life.

Biblical visions give me hope that the redeemed community will be realized on this earth among the species and cultures familiar to us. Those trees, so productive and healthful, will grow from varieties we have known. We will experience their healing as we give them appropriate respect, care, and love. The new Jerusalem will not be a gold-plated amusement park for the redeemed, but a center of urban life where human culture is purified and completed. As the nations are healed by the spread of the holy ecology, other urban centers and other cultures will also reach wholesome fulfillment. In some of these the works of Shakespeare, Bach, and Mozart will flourish; in others, the arts of different cultures will thrive. New human expressions will be staged as well. Surrounding the cities will be extensive forests to help people breathe, productive agricultural regions where farmers live close to the soil, and wild areas where society refrains from disrupting natural integrity. There will be fewer people but more life: we will have deeper communion among species, broad faithfulness to the Lord, and great beauty. New things will happen which we cannot now anticipate. These are the hopes that biblical visions encourage in me.

These visions of abundance suggest infusing earthly life with new energy. In this new creation God's presence will be more immediate and more nourishing as "the spirit is poured out on us from above" (Isaiah 32:15, NJB). A few biblical images, however, suggest energy which becomes dazzling and even overwhelming: "the sun with seven times his wonted brightness" (Isaiah 30:26, NEB). Some Christian theology has exploited the coercive character of these images at the expense of their moral dynamics. It is common within my Calvinist tradition to honor God by ascribing redemption entirely to overwhelming divine energy without regard to the responsiveness of the redeemed. Images of redemption can easily become mechanical rather than ecological. Indeed, when we despair of the moral struggle, like

Jeremiah and Ezekiel, we may hope for a "new heart" and "new spirit" that produce virtue automatically under God's constant and direct supervision. When we are tired, we want redemption to be passive.

After sabbath rest, however, we may appreciate more engaging and creative images. Jeremiah and Ezekiel, like other prophets and Jesus himself, were not merely passive humans beneath divine power. Redemption does not replace moral effort, but rebuilds the moral ecology. It recreates affectionate relationships with God, among humanity, and with nature. Those in turn support ethical choices and therefore deepen the opportunities for righteousness. When we respond creatively to the moral challenges that now trouble us, we will not only be happier and more fulfilled, but our moral vision will expand to encompass new challenges as well. The Bible does not portray redemption as a static community but as a changing, spreading, life-giving society.

The rich language of redemption conveys a moral ecology. The city, the temple, the river, the fish, the hills of waving grain, and the excited farmers are not vague images of heavenly emotions but depictions of a worldly society which prophets believed the Lord would bring. Not photographic, to be sure, the visions portray a future for this earth. They exaggerate in order to call attention to the moral dynamics of relationship. I doubt that Ezekiel expected a river to spring from beneath the temple bearing incredible fertilizing powers. But he did expect that as God's truth flowed from the temple and was drunk by all, vitality would return both to the human community and to the natural environment: "life teems wherever the river flows" (Ezekiel 47:9, NJB). Ezekiel believed that no place on this earth was so barren as to be beyond revitalization from this expansive ecology. In the modern world, therefore, even desertification is reversible. Ecologists can indeed prepare theoretical models for such a reversal. Change, however, will depend upon our moral commitment to refrain from destroying the world and to assist the recovery of life. This, in turn, will require a vivid and persuasive religious realization. Ezekiel helps us toward such a vision.

Except perhaps in moments of despair, Hebrews understood that moral relationships are not coercive but liberating. Therefore their visions depict abundance rather than constraint. The trees lining the river of life will not be forced into constant productivity by genetic manipulation. Instead, they will respond to the love of God and the respect of humanity, for they live in a moral ecology which supports ever more exuberant growth. They, like us, are redeemed.

# 24. *Peaceable Kingdom*

The image of a peaceable kingdom is from Isaiah, chapter 11. I see it as Benjamin West, the early American Quaker, painted it. In the right foreground, wild beasts and domestic animals gather around a child. A young lion leans against the child, who is protecting it with one arm, while a cow drapes her head lovingly across the lion's back. A leopard, lying next to a plump goat, looks out at us with a puzzled expression, but a dozing wolf is content to shelter a baby lamb. The child is pointing with an olive branch to a nearby scene beside a river, where William Penn and other Quakers, having landed from their ship, confer with a native chief who sits beneath an oak tree, flanked by his council. They are preparing the scrolls for a peace treaty. These hopeful settlers have arrived from the Old World in the spirit of Christ's new covenant. They do not desire conquest, but rather seek accommodation with this landscape and its inhabitants. They will respect their treaty with the human representatives of this wild land. Although subsequent history did not fulfill the artist's hopes, West proclaimed on canvas after canvas that such peaceful covenanting would bring the kingdom of God.[1]

\* \* \*

Reconciling human culture to the wild was a challenge to the Hebrews' imagination. They understood the holy land primarily in pastoral and agricultural terms. Though their ancestors had passed through the wilderness, though Hebrew bands continued to use wilderness for refuge, and though prophets retreated there as well, nothing in biblical literature portrays Hebrews as being at home in the wild. Their culture was not hunting and gathering, and although they told stories of nomadic Abraham moving from place to place with his flocks, the Hebrews were a settled people. If they found food in the wilderness, they saw it as a special mercy from God, not as the result of their skillful adaptation to a challenging environment. Although sabbatical law gave gleaning privileges to wild animals and conferred other protections upon wildlife, as we have seen, these important moral insights remained rudimentary in their application to wildlife. Throughout the biblical period, full flowering of the Hebrews' distinctive morality was constrained by fear of the wilderness.

When Hebrew prophets imagined a world transformed by covenant renewal, they portrayed with diffidence the place of wild beasts, much as they hesitated over the place of foreign nations. Ezekiel did not wish the redeemed people to be troubled by either of these threats: "No more will they be a prey to the nations, no more will the wild animals of the country devour them. They will live secure, with no one to frighten them" (Ezekiel 34:28, NJB).[2] Biblical writers tended to imagine that if wild beasts and hostile nations did not disappear altogether from the restored creation, then both must change their character. Nations would stream to Jerusalem to worship the true Lord, while predatory animals would alter their diet and merge with the pastoral scene. These fantasies sidestepped moral questions concerning both wildlife and cultural diversity.

In Isaiah's imagination, when God healed the world and turned even the desert into a verdant marsh, the redeemed would march back to Zion on a splendid raised roadway—separated from the wicked, the ignorant, and predatory animals:

> Then shall blind . . . eyes be opened,
>   and the ears of the deaf unstopped.
> Then shall the lame . . . leap like a deer,
>   and the tongue of the dumb shout aloud;

for water springs up in the wilderness,
and torrents flow in dry land.
The mirage becomes a pool,
  the thirsty land bubbling springs;
    instead of reeds and rushes, grass shall grow
    in the rough land where wolves now lurk.
And there shall be a causeway there
which shall be called the Way of Holiness,
  and the unclean shall not pass along it;
it shall become a pilgrim's way,
  no fool shall trespass on it.
No lion shall come there,
no savage beast climb on to it;
  not one shall be found there.
But those [God] has ransomed shall return
  and the LORD's redeemed come home;
they shall enter Zion with shouts of triumph,
crowned with everlasting gladness.
                          (Isaiah 35:5–10, NEB, alt.)

In his finest messianic vision, however, Isaiah found a way to include predators—even venomous serpents—within the holy community of the redeemed. He changed their eating habits and domesticated their personalities so they would no longer be aggressive or dangerously defensive:

The lion shall eat straw like cattle;
the infant shall play over the hole of the cobra,
and the young child dance over the viper's nest.
They shall not hurt or destroy in all my holy mountain;
  for as the waters fill the sea,
so shall the land be filled with the knowledge of the LORD.
                          (Isaiah 11:7–9, NEB)

In the twentieth century, wildlife biologists have come to appreciate how predators strengthen the wild ecosystem and serve the species upon which they prey. We are learning, as well, that domestication and genetic manipulation may damage species. Through selective breeding we have developed livestock more dependent upon our care and more vulnerable to our abuse, and we have diminished their sensibilities. A century ago John Muir compared the alert individuality and dexterity of wild sheep running free on mountain peaks with the stupid conformity of the domesticated breeds that ravaged the Sierra mountainsides. Clearly the wild sheep had a better life, even though they were more exposed to wolves. In addition, they fit within an environment which domestic sheep, driven in great hungry herds, destroyed.

In modern times it is not the threat to people posed by predatory animals or poisonous serpents which sets humanity and nature at odds, but rather the oppressive character of human culture. Humanity is far more dangerous to other species than they are to us. The earth's peace and health are threatened primarily by industrial technologies, cultural patterns of consumption, and proliferation of the human species; each of these continues today without regard for natural life.

Hosea's grasp of the tension between human society and nature is more relevant to modern sensibilities than is Isaiah's. As noted in an earlier chapter, Hosea's vision of covenant renewal included the disarming of human society so that other species could live without fear. When restoring the covenant, Hosea prophesied, the Lord will pay special attention to the weakest party, nature:

> I will make a covenant on behalf of Israel with the wild beasts, the birds of the air, and the things that creep on the earth, and I will break bow and sword and weapon of war and sweep them off the earth, so that all living creatures may lie down without fear.
>
> (Hosea 2:18, NEB)

As we come to realize that earthly peace will not be achieved by domesticating the wild, but rather by disarming our human oppression of nature, new moral vistas open to us. We can affirm the goodness of God's creation with greater confidence. The system of life support on this planet, including predators and the species which defend themselves with poisons, is not inherently blemished but remains a magnificent network through which life nourishes life. Occasional pain, and the certainty of death, contribute to the earth's vitality. The "savagery" of nature has been exaggerated: sometimes this characterization results from projecting onto nature aggressive feelings of our own we prefer not to acknowledge; sometimes it serves to rationalize human social competitiveness. Savagery is the sickness of human culture, not of the natural environment. Nature, inherently beautiful, does not need to be modified or replaced. Instead, ecological intricacy must be protected from human society's tendencies to appropriate all natural life as human "resources," to simplify ecosystems in favor of desired crops, and to eliminate competing predators. John Muir called modern men and women to restrain this compulsion to manage and, instead, to reenter the earth's ecosystem as constructive participants in the life of the world. "A little pure wildness," he declared, "is the one great present want, both of men and sheep."[3]

This vision, however, suggests enormous sacrifices. To achieve peace with nature, human society will have to lighten its burden upon the biosphere. To curtail pollution we will need to redesign much of our industry, power generation, agriculture, transportation, and even our housing. To limit dissipation of the earth's resources we will need to improve the efficiency of manufacture and the durability of products, recycle what we use no longer, and restrain our desires for many things. We must also halt the growth in human population and begin a steady course of population reduction, although we do not know how many people can be supported without damage to the health of the biosphere. The pollution we generate, the materials we consume, and the wild areas we destroy are more important variables than human numbers. Population size is significant to the extent that it aggravates these other impacts. If we are thrifty rather than profligate in our patterns of life, the earth will accommodate more people.

As we make peace with nature, we will surrender the humanocentric arrogance which assumes that all the world must be adjusted to serve human welfare. We will replace a material image of human welfare with a moral one. The health of other species and the vitality of natural ecosystems are fully as significant as human health and cultural vitality. Nature also has rights to life which are compromised by human overpopulation and too much cultural stress upon the earth. Reborn humanity will find fulfillment not in consuming the earth but in delighting in it: respecting, protecting, and enjoying the earth, as well as harvesting appropriate sustenance with care.

Purposeful reform, built upon moral vision, can protect freedom and assure order within society. Only when we undertake such reforms willingly, however, can we strengthen the human social covenant and also build a peaceable kingdom with nature. Without popular support for needed changes, existing social trends are likely to precipitate environmental disasters which panic the public, induce social chaos, and invite tyranny. If social reforms are to be just and environmental reforms are to be peaceful, reformers must convey the attractiveness of sensible alternatives to modern destructive trends.

At the heart of the biblical vision is a promise that if we love nature and treat the life of the earth with respect, we will fulfill our human vocation and find personal satisfaction. Furthermore, we will be happy with the earth's response. The harvest which the earth yields is far more than meat and fruit, oil and wine. Interactions with nature differ from the interpersonal, social, and cultural relationships which predominate in modern life, so that natural relationships may expand our sensibilities and enrich our lives. Work with the species and materials of the biosphere can be uniquely satisfying. The natural environment is also a field for justice, and it can stimulate our moral sensitivity. Nature is beautiful: if we do not engage with this beauty we are deprived. Culture and manufacture provide us many things that are both essential and desirable, but they are not worth placing nature at risk. To make peace with God we are called to make peace with nature as well, so that God's glory may return to our landscape:

> Let me hear the words of the LORD:
> are they not words of peace?
> . . . . . . . . . . . . . . . . . . . . . . .
> Deliverance is near to those who worship [God],
> so that glory may dwell in our land.
> Love and fidelity have come together;

justice and peace join hands.
Fidelity springs up from earth
and justice looks down from heaven.
The LORD will add prosperity,
and our land shall yield its harvest.
                              (Psalm 85:8–12, NEB, alt.)

* * *

When we appreciate God's new kingdom in its full, ecological vitality, we may wish to modify several images of Christian hope that we have previously taken for granted. The life of a renewed earth cannot be portrayed adequately with terms suggesting static rest. Life filled with God's spirit is active, not passive: it grows, blossoms, and changes. Jürgen Moltmann affirms that "In the kingdom of glory there will be time and history, future and possibility." He explains:

> We have termed creation in the beginning an open system, and have interpreted the creative activity of God in history as the opening up in time of closed systems. . . . If the process of creation is to be completed through God's indwelling, then . . . the indwelling of the unbounded fullness of God's eternal life means the openness *par excellence* of all life systems, and hence also their eternal livingness, not their finite petrification. The openness of all life systems . . . also leads to their perfected communication among themselves. . . . So the "kingdom of God" is also the kingdom of universal "sympathy of all things."[4]

The biblical vision of jubilee can help us comprehend the environmental vitality that flows from the new kingdom. Hebrews understood jubilee as a time when social relationships are put right and all people can return to beloved landscapes that have meaning for them. There they can distribute opportunities with equity, as did the holy people when God first called them into covenant. If Jesus announced a jubilee, then in the fullness of the kingdom we will again walk this land with our Lord, taking hope and risking faithfulness. In jubilee, the meek will be blessed; poor people and parched lands will find redemption together:

> The wretched and the poor look for water and find none,
> their tongues are parched with thirst;

> but I the LORD will give them an answer,
> I, the God of Israel, will not forsake them.
> I will open rivers among the sand-dunes
>     and wells in the valleys;
> I will turn the wilderness into pools
> and dry land into springs of water;
> I will plant cedars in the wastes,
> and acacia and myrtle and wild olive;
> the pine shall grow on the barren heath
> side by side with fir and box,
> that [people] may see and know,
> may once for all give heed and understand
> that the LORD . . . has done this,
>     that the Holy One of Israel has performed it.
>             (Isaiah 41:17–20, NEB, alt.)

Jubilee will not bring history to a stop, but it will draw the living—all people and all species—into just relationships. When we envision the new covenant as a great jubilee, we expect life and growth to continue after this gracious restoration. People and nature joined in wholesome relationships can then flower in unprecedented ways—like the life along Ezekiel's holy river. There will be expansion and discovery. There will even be mistakes and abuses, for the jubilee vision implies that the risks of growth can be tolerated within a context of moral alertness. God will be so present, and love for the covenant so deeply imbedded in human culture and natural environment, that we can expect to notice our mistakes, learn from them, and overcome them. The sabbath days and sabbatical years will bring to mind true justice, so that it can no longer be overlooked.

In a redeemed environment, death will continue to play a vital role, for death is essential to renewal. The enmity between death and life will be reconciled, and the sting of death will be removed.[5] Untimely death, death before we have known life and enjoyed its beauty thoroughly, will no longer afflict us. God will walk among us, and we will meet death at ripe age when our cup of experience is full and our understanding is satisfied. We will die in peace. As we have drawn nourishment from the lives and deaths of others and given thanks for them, we will also freely present our lives to others, so our bodies may fertilize the ground while our passing makes room in a finite landscape for our grandchildren and for the offspring of other species as well. Death will have meaning when all creatures live in communion with both God and nature.

# 25. *The Lamb*

The principal annual remembrance in the Hebrew tradition is the Passover meal: unleavened bread of oppression, bitter herbs, a sacrificial lamb or kid like those whose blood identified the courageous households prepared to escape Egyptian slavery. The Priestly narrator peered back through the annual reenactment to grasp the tense excitement on the eve of the Hebrews' deliverance:

> On the tenth day of this month each man must take an animal from the flock for his family. . . . It must be an animal without blemish, a male one year old; you may choose it either from the sheep or from the goats. You must keep it till the fourteenth day of the month when the whole assembly of the community of Israel will slaughter it at twilight. Some of the blood must then be taken and put on both door-posts and the lintel of the houses where it is eaten. . . . This is how you must eat it: with a belt round your waist, your sandals on your feet and your staff in your hand. You must eat it hurriedly: it is a Passover in Yahweh's honour. That night, I shall go through Egypt and strike down all the first-born in Egypt, man and beast alike, and shall execute justice on all the gods of Egypt, I, Yahweh! The blood will be a sign for you on the houses where you are. When I see the blood I shall pass over you, and you will escape the destructive plague when I strike Egypt.
> (Exodus 12:3–13, NJB)

Passover celebration recalls the character of slavery and the risks of deliverance, helping Hebrews appreciate what it means to be a free people. Only a culture which remembers its oppression is likely to protect its freedom. Michael Walzer, a Jewish political philosopher, observes,

> Holiness makes for liberty and justice, but it is effective only insofar as it describes a way of life, a religious and political

culture. The Israelites will not be a holy nation until they are, all
of them, participants in a world of ritual remembering; until they
celebrate the Passover, rest on the Sabbath, study the law; until
they actively "break every yoke" and learn to live with . . . the
"ineradicable subversion" of the Exodus story. This is God's
kingdom and, in some ultimate sense, every place else is Egypt.[1]

We have seen that the covenant community into which
these Hebrews were called was ecological, embracing holy land as
well as holy people. This community, redeemed from oppression
by the Lord, was not to resemble the Hebrews' experience of wilderness, that anxious encounter between a people and landscape
who did not understand each other. Nor was it to resemble Egypt,
where technology controlled productivity and the earth was
enslaved along with those who labored upon it.[2] The redeemed
community offered moral interaction between people and land, in
faithfulness to the Lord, so that each might nurture the freedom
of the other.

In the Jerusalem temple a tradition of sacrifice began to
contradict this moral ecology. The fruits of agriculture and hus-
bandry fell into a system of tithes and offerings, becoming commodities instead of companions. Despite abuse of land, livestock,
and laborers, a farmer could appease the Lord by offering a
portion of the harvest; thus morality became a commercial transaction, and agriculture evaded moral relationships. The prophet
Micah realized that a religious system which put sacrificial
offerings in the place of justice would itself become a means of
oppression:

Wherewith shall I come before the LORD,
*And* bow myself before the high God?
Shall I come before [God] with burnt offerings,
With calves of a year old?
Will the LORD be pleased with thousands of rams,
*Or* with ten thousands of rivers of oil?
Shall I give my firstborn *for* my transgression,
The fruit of my body *for* the sin of my soul?
[God] hath showed thee . . . what *is* good;
And what doth the LORD require of thee,
But to do justly, and to love mercy,
And to walk humbly with thy God?
                                        (Micah 6:6–8, KJV, alt.)

When Jesus entered Jerusalem, filled with the spirit of the new kingdom, his anger at this sacrificial system burst forth: "He upset the tables of the money changers and the seats of the dove sellers. . . . 'Does not scripture say: *My house will be called a house of prayer for all peoples?* But you have turned it into *a bandits' den*'" (Mark 11:15–17, NJB).[3] Instead of anxious transactions to appease endless guilt, Jesus offered the opportunity to stand forth and live the new kingdom.

Jesus knowingly risked death by bringing this dramatic call for covenant renewal to Jerusalem. However, his purpose was to revive the covenant community, not to court martyrdom. He did not offer himself as a substitute for justice; rather, his submission to religious and civil powers unmasked their hypocrisy. Jesus endured death rather than employing tactics which might ensnare the new kingdom within the world of power politics, and thus compromise it at its inception. So potent was his integrity that death could not hold him. Believers found him alive in their midst as they continued to experience the new kingdom among each other.

When early Christians reflected on the meaning of Jesus' death, they were more likely to draw from the liberating tradition of Passover than from the temple tradition.[4] The Apostle Paul portrayed Christ as taking the place of the Passover offering: "Christ our passover is sacrificed for us: Therefore let us keep the feast . . . with the unleavened *bread* of sincerity and truth" (1 Corinthians 5:7–8, KJV). A generation later, the opening chapter of John's Gospel proclaimed that Jesus would become the Passover lamb. In this most stylized and theological account of Jesus' life, John the Baptist exclaimed at his first sight of Jesus, "Behold, the Lamb of God, who takes away the sin of the world!" (John 1:29, RSV).

\* \* \*

From the perspective of biblical ecology, we can find new meaning in the metaphor of Christ as the Passover lamb. The original Passover was occasioned by the plagues that disrupted life in Egypt—plagues that the Hebrews would remember as the hand of the Lord. Eager to protect their children and to escape oppression, Hebrew families slaughtered a young sheep or goat, marked their doorways with its blood, ate in faith, and prepared to flee. At another level this story, like the story of Abraham's sacrifice of Isaac, may have served as commentary on the practice of child sacrifice common in the ancient world.[5] As a first step in their liberation, the Lord assured the Hebrews that a lamb from their household flock—eaten in confident expectation by those prepared to take risks for their faith—was sufficient sacrifice.

The night before his crucifixion, Jesus celebrated Passover with his disciples. When he shared with them the unleavened bread of haste, he gave it special relevance by naming it a metaphor for his own body—about to be broken as he gave his life for the world. Then, in a hopeful gesture, he shared the cup of wine to signify the new covenant that would continue whenever his followers joined together in faith. Jesus' blood, shed once, remained a sufficient mark of liberation for his people. They could go forth from the Egypt of oppression in the strength of the Lord. "This cup is the new covenant sealed by my blood," Paul quoted Jesus. "Whenever you drink it, do this as a memorial of me" (1 Corinthians 11:25, NEB).

Hebrew prophets had developed a moral critique of the sacrificial system practiced in the temple. Now God substituted Christ for the Passover lambs whose blood marked the doorways of those willing to step forth for freedom. Furthermore, as the Lord once assured Hebrews that child sacrifice was not necessary, in Christ we are assured that the sacrifice of natural life is not required of us. Jesus died in moral substitution for sinners, taking the burden of their offenses upon himself. He also died in literal substitution for the lamb itself, terminating the notion that the religious slaughter of weaker species is an offering pleasing to the Lord.

Christ's death did not inspire his followers to a new asceticism toward natural life. Indeed, the reverse was true. As we have seen, the Apostle Paul's understanding that redemption applied to all species led to his conviction that each one was therefore clean and might be eaten appropriately. This belief affirmed the ecology of biological interdependence and removed religious inhibitions. Paul also called the men and women of the new covenant to be instruments for nature's liberation and thus renew the ecosystem. Paul believed, as did John of Patmos, that all species would have reason to praise Christ, the Lamb of God, as their redeemer.[6]

The Christian affirmation, "Jesus is Lord!" (1 Corinthians 12:3, NEB), is a joyful claim but not a triumphal one. This profession implies that integrity will redeem the course of history —as naked power cannot—and will achieve a just society, although integrity may sometimes seem a weakness and may even lead to suffering or death. Faith in Jesus commits us to liberation through personal and corporate example rather than through coercion. Those who practice justice and compassion, in the teeth of an unjust world, will attract others who desire life, and their integrity can inspire relevant strategies for change. Commitment to Jesus is deeper, however, than an expectation of success. To follow Jesus is to taste the beauty of holiness. As followers we sample the fruits of loving attitudes and restored relationships; we learn that even if integrity should fail, no alternative is so satisfying. Integrity validates itself in defeat as well as in victory.

When we profess that Christ is the redeemer of nature, we affirm that the ecology of integrity will prevail over the depredations of the powerful who strip-mine the biosphere. Life-giving relationships between humanity and nature, encouraged by the Lord's love, will triumph over exploitation. This affirmation may not make the gospel more popular or easier to believe. We should not mistake it for a theological compromise that makes religion more amenable to a culture that has difficulty seeing beyond the material. Biblical ecology does not permit believing less; it requires believing more! It expands the traditional Christian faith—that God will redeem faithful people—to embrace natural species and the systems of earthly life. Those who doubt that God can redeem believers will not find it any easier to imagine how God might redeem "all the living things in creation—everything that lives in the air, and on the ground, and under the ground, and in the sea" (Revelation 5:13, JB). A cosmology that anticipates a renewed earth, a life in covenant faithfulness with the Lord, will not be any more acceptable to scientists than are heaven-centered cosmologies—so long as science cannot recognize the Lord and places no value on either covenant or faithfulness.

Nevertheless, through the Hebrew and Christian Scriptures the Lord gives us a vision of jubilee: people and nature joined in freedom, justice, and integrity; working, loving, growing, and praising the Lord. I find this the most beautiful vision of all. I choose to follow it.

* * *

Awakened to this biblical vision, which embraces nature within the covenant of God's faithfulness, what do we do? I suggest that we experience nature, defend it, learn to live in harmony with it, and worship the Lord in conscious communion with other species and the fabric of earthly life.

Experience is the key to moral relationships. We may find that opening ourselves to new experiences with life will liberate and engage us. Some of us may need to renew our trust in the Lord in order to overcome our fears of life. We need long-term, intimate relationships with the natural world: both the practice of nurture, such as cultivating a garden, and the sensory stimulation of repeated engagement with a wild area, apart from human cultivation. Such experience can lead to knowledge, insight, and emotional bonding with nature, helping us recover the image of God.

Organized efforts to protect nature are particularly valuable if they arise from personal experience. With our traditional volunteerism, Americans excel at such efforts, so those who wish to participate in protection will find many opportunities. Our collective efforts, however, remain small in comparison with the need. Many natural tragedies persist—both local losses and remote catastrophes, such as the cutting of rain forests—because too few of the people who experience the loss acutely have the capacity to resist. Especially effective are those organizations uniting people who are directly affected by environmental abuse and others who can assist them.

Learning to live in harmony with nature is our most complex challenge. It involves personal ethics and demands responsible social interactions with nature where we live, work, and play. Since culture embraces our lives and influences our choices, learning to live with nature requires changes in economic structures and public policies. To achieve personal integrity, committed individuals must also help their culture to grow and change. Men and women, families and groups, can alter their own habits and patterns to reflect their respect for nature, while also participating in social and political action to correct larger patterns of abuse. None of us is too weak to make a difference, yet none is so self-sufficient as not to be implicated in our society's massive environmental degradation. Even while we reach out to become part of the solution, we remain part of the problem. We need forgiveness.

Christians who become aware of natural relationships will want to reform our worship as well. The Lord has joined us with nature through the covenant of redemption. When we realize this, our human isolation in worship—cut off from other species —becomes an offense. Churches may expand their sense of *parish* to embrace a natural environment as well as a human fellowship. Experiments in inclusive worship can help develop new liturgies that incorporate the surrounding species and systems of life—not as objects of worship, but as recognized co-participants. Together we can praise the Creator:

> Sing a new song to Yahweh . . .
>
> The whole wide world has seen
> the saving power of our God.
> Acclaim Yahweh, all the earth,
> burst into shouts of joy!
>
> Play to Yahweh on the harp,
> to the sound of instruments;
> to the sound of trumpet and horn,
> acclaim the presence of the [LORD].
>
> Let the sea thunder, and all that it holds,
> the world and all who live in it.
> Let the rivers clap their hands,
> and the mountains shout for joy together,
>
> at Yahweh's approach, for [God] is coming
> to judge the earth;
> [God] will judge the world with saving justice
> and the nations with fairness.
>
> (Psalm 98, NJB, alt.)

* * *

Jesus began his public life by asking John the Baptist to immerse him in the Jordan River, in fellowship with others who were responding to John's call for a new beginning. When Jesus retreated into the wilderness to ponder his strategy, the wild beasts drew near him. He entered Peter's boat and the fish schooled about it. On his way to purify the temple, he asked the fig tree to manifest faith in the covenant renewal. John of Patmos, in a vision of completion, saw all creatures honoring Christ, the Lamb of the new Passover, as their Savior.

Let us regard Jesus as the Lamb, God incarnate, embracing human flesh and all the earth's liveliness as well as the soil from which we are formed. When we think about Jesus, let us remember the weak of all species and the vulnerable systems of life support, for we may meet Christ among them. And when we deal directly with the natural world, let our love, respect, and careful behavior express the image of God and the Lamb. William Blake describes this communion simply and beautifully:

> Little Lamb who made thee
> Dost thou know who made thee
> Gave thee life & bid thee feed,
> By the stream & o'er the mead;
> Gave thee clothing of delight,
> Softest clothing wooly bright;
> Gave thee such a tender voice,
> Making all the vales rejoice:
> Little Lamb who made thee
> Dost thou know who made thee
>
> Little Lamb I'll tell thee,
> Little Lamb I'll tell thee;
> He is called by thy name,
> For he calls himself a Lamb:
> He is meek & he is mild,
> He became a little child:
> I a child & thou a lamb,
> We are called by his name.
> Little Lamb God bless thee,
> Little Lamb God bless thee.[7]

# Suggestions for Reading

The Bible is the most important book we can read. It is an especially rewarding book when the words engage our feelings as well as our understanding. If you are familiar with a text, choose an unfamiliar translation to help you hear with fresh ears. The *King James Version* remains the most beautiful expression of the English language, although the archaic style may frustrate new readers. Among modern versions, the *New English Bible* is often the most graceful. The *New Jerusalem Bible,* because it does not echo the King James, is stimulating to those accustomed to Protestant versions; furthermore, it avoids sexist wording. Although I have read the *Revised Standard Version* all my life, it now seems stilted and pedestrian to me, and the *Inclusive Language Lectionary,* which substitutes non-sexist language in many RSV passages, is clumsy. Any reader who wishes to prepare Scripture for public worship should be able to select a better version and alter its usage if necessary. See pages 6–7 for additional comments on these versions; and see chapter 1, endnote 9, for publication information. Northrop Frye offers a fine literary study of biblical language in *The Great Code: the Bible and Literature* (New York: Harcourt Brace Jovanovich, 1982).

George Mendenhall presented the Hebrews as a liberating community in "The Hebrew Conquest of Palestine," first published in *The Biblical Archaeologist* 25 (Sept. 1962), 66–87, and then reprinted in *The Biblical Archaeologist Reader 3* (Garden City, NY: Doubleday, 1970). Read this clear statement before considering Mendenhall's elaboration of his thesis in *The Tenth Generation: The Origins of the Biblical Tradition* (Baltimore: Johns Hopkins University Press, 1973). Michael Walzer, a Jewish political philosopher, makes quite a different argument to a similar conclusion in *Exodus and Revolution* (New York: Basic

Books, 1985). Walter Brueggemann pioneered a fresh perspective on the relation of Hebrew faith to the landscape in *The Land* (Philadelphia: Fortress Press, 1977). In *The Politics of Jesus* (Grand Rapids, MI: William B. Eerdmans, 1972), John Howard Yoder discusses Jesus' use of the jubilee theme; this discussion continues in Sharon H. Ringe, *Jesus, Liberation, and the Biblical Jubilee* (Philadelphia: Fortress Press, 1985) and Karen Lebacqz, *Justice in an Unjust World* (Minneapolis: Augsburg Publishing House, 1987). It is fascinating to read Adam Michnik's *Letters from Prison and Other Essays* (Berkeley: University of California Press, 1985), to see how a similar strategy of moral and political integrity was attempted in modern Poland. Phyllis Trible shows us the nuances of gender in biblical usage in *God and the Rhetoric of Sexuality* (Philadelphia: Fortress Press, 1978): her concluding essay on Ruth is particularly beautiful.

If you want a brief primer on ecology, Paul E. Lutz has an excellent essay, "Interrelatedness: Ecological Pattern of the Creation," in *Cry of the Environment*, edited by Philip Joranson and Ken Butigan (Santa Fe: Bear & Co., 1984). I mention stimulating readings on eight specific ecological problems in the endnotes for chapter 21. The endnotes for chapter 20 list interesting writings from the nine religious perspectives discussed in that chapter. Lynn White's important indictment of Christian attitudes toward nature, "The Historical Roots of Our Ecologic Crisis," was first published in *Science*, 10 Mar. 1967, and has been reprinted in *Ecology and Religion in History,* ed. David and Eileen Spring (New York: Harper & Row, 1974).

# Series Relationships

Each of the four books in this series may be read independently, yet together they form an integrated *Environmental Theology*. Book 1, *Baptized into Wilderness: A Christian Perspective on John Muir*, invites Christians to deepen our relationships with nature and illustrates principal themes of the series through the life and reflection of John Muir, America's first advocate of wilderness protection. Book 2, *Beauty of the Lord: Awakening the Senses,* is intended to help Christians dissolve impediments to expressive interactions with life on this earth. Through a dialogue with Jonathan Edwards, founding philosopher of the American evangelical tradition, it concludes that experience of beauty may knit us to God and to the natural world as well. Book 4 applies the biblical ecology developed here, as well as theological understanding from Books 1 and 2, to personal ethics and contemporary environmental issues. It proposes constitutional rights for species, ecosystems, and unusual natural features; suggests a moral reconstruction of agriculture; and recommends that Christian churches include nature in their polity, worship, and work. Book 4 will also provide an index of the major ideas running through the series. Some of the ideas in Book 3 are developed more completely, or considered in a different setting, in other books of the series.

*Ecology,* introduced here (Book 3: page 4) and then modified in its application to biblical thought (3: 48), is discussed more thoroughly in Book 2, chapter 3. There, after this biological concept is defined (2: 26), ecology is given special application within a philosophy of beauty (compare 3: 151, 178, and 2: 27). Book 2, chapter 7, critiques the role of competition in biological theories of evolution. Here (3: 222) the dangers inherent in human simplification of natural systems—a practice at the heart of agriculture—are mentioned; this warning is expanded in Book 2

(166–167) and will be discussed further in Book 4. Death may be regarded as a positive aspect of the ecology of life (3: 225–226): John Muir is particularly stimulating on this point (1: 8, 57–58), and this perspective is developed in Book 2 (30, 113, 131, 191–199).

The Priestly narrative associated predation with the fall into sin (3: 33–34), while Ezekiel and Isaiah imagined that predators would either be banished from the new covenant community or pacified within it (3: 219–220). Charles Darwin began a biological reappraisal of predation (2: 57–61), while his contemporary John Muir rehabilitated predation with deeper ethical insight (1: 78–80). Much of what we see as "savagery" in nature (3:220–222) is projection from the disorders of human society (2: 48–55). Book 2 gives a theological defense of predation (2: 28–30) and illustrates its moral beauty (2: 193–198).

*Moral beauty* (3: 9, 87) is an important theological image throughout this series. *Beauty* is defined in Book 2 (15); Part I of that book is devoted to a philosophical interpretation of beauty. Moral beauty is an engaging relationship (1: 41) distinguished from other forms of beauty by the element of conscious choice (1: 3; 2: 33). Moral beauty is also related to Jesus' notion of "purity of heart" (1: 33, 37; 2: 77–78); indeed, it expresses the character of God as it undergirds the existence of God (compare 3: 49–50 and 2: 147–149). In answer to pantheism, this philosophy gives *moral* relationships primacy over *being* (compare 3: 185–186 and 2: 127–134, 156–161). Human perception of beauty is strongly motivational (compare 3: 161–162 and 2: 20–28). We may exhibit moral beauty in our regard for nature (1: 44, 2: 3–4, 16). Indeed, we may contribute to the consciousness of the ecosystem (compare 3: 188–189, 199, 1: 43–44, and 2: 185).

Biblical language conveys the ambiguous nature of human experience of God (3: 8–9). God's presence is elusive (2: 124, 135, 145–147), and our meeting with God (3: 12–13) includes psychological projection (2: 160–161). The personal insight we draw from Scripture (3: 13–16) is part of a process of identity formation portrayed in Book 2, Part IV. The contention (3: 14) that religious differences and disagreements do not imply "relativism" is elaborated in Book 2 (156–161).

Here Christ is identified theologically with abused nature (3: 40–42); Book 2, chapter 20, argues that the doctrine of Christ's two natures allows such identification while shielding faith from pantheism. There, and in Book 1, chapter 2, nature's mediation of God's presence is examined: in circumstances as extreme as those of John Muir, nature may even become Christ for us.

The discussion of sexual anxiety here in chapter 9 builds upon the psychological theory of inhibition and repression which is developed in Book 2, chapter 9: that chapter is also background for comments on the role of repression in Adam's sin (3: 152). The suggestion here (3: 153) that repression and moral confusion may lead to political manipulation is amplified in Book 2, chapter 17.

The conviction that real knowledge requires emotional engagement (3: 179) is an important part of the psychology developed in Book 2 (18–22, 63–68). The brief suggestions here that modern sensibility represses awareness of vital qualities within other species in order to rationalize abuse of them (3: 180, 186) are thoroughly discussed in Book 2, chapter 6.

The summary of African desertification (3: 193) is expanded in Book 2, chapter 22.

Here (3: 215) it is suggested that Calvinists are disposed to images of redemption which are mechanical and coercive rather than ecological. The most important exception to this generalization, however, is Jonathan Edwards. His conviction that the experience of beauty forms the heart of the redeeming relationship lays the foundation for a profoundly ecological theology: this thesis runs throughout Book 2.

# Notes

## Chapter 1. Abuse of Nature

1. Lynn White, Jr., "The Historical Roots of Our Ecologic Crisis," *Science,* 10 Mar. 1967, 1206. White's address was subsequently reprinted in several collections of environmental essays.
2. White, "Historical Roots," 1206, 1205.
3. White, "Historical Roots," 1206.
4. White, "Historical Roots," 1206, 1207.
5. Richard Cartwright Austin, "Toward Environmental Theology," *The Drew Gateway* 48, (Winter 1977) 1–14.
6. George Mendenhall, "The Hebrew Conquest of Palestine," *The Biblical Archaeologist* 25 (Sept. 1962), 66–87 [reprinted in *The Biblical Archaeologist Reader 3* (Garden City, NY: Doubleday, 1970)].
7. See Walter Brueggemann, *The Land* (Philadelphia: Fortress Press, 1977).
8. John Howard Yoder, *The Politics of Jesus* (Grand Rapids, MI: William B. Eerdmans, 1972).
9. *The Authorized King James Version* (KJV), Westminster Study Edition (Philadelphia: Westminster Press, 1948); *The Revised Standard Version* (RSV) (New York: Thomas Nelson & Son, 1946, 1952, and 1971); *The New English Bible* (NEB) (New York: Oxford University Press, 1971); *The Jerusalem Bible* (JB) (Garden City, NY: Doubleday & Co., 1966); *The New Jerusalem Bible* (NJB) (Garden City, NY: Doubleday & Co., 1985); *An Inclusive Language Lectionary* (ILL), volumes A, B, and C, by The Inclusive Language Lectionary Committee, National Council of the Churches of Christ in the USA (Philadelphia: Westminster Press, 1983, 1984, 1985).
10. I discuss biblical use of gender in chapter 8.

## Chapter 2. Hearing the Word

1. John Donne, quoted in Robert Pattison, *On Literacy* (New York: Oxford University Press, 1982), 105–6.
2. Northrop Frye, *The Great Code: The Bible and Literature* (New York: Harcourt Brace Jovanovich, 1982), 22. Frye echoes the criticism of writing in Plato's *Phaedrus.*
3. Frye, *The Great Code,* 7.
4. Psychotherapist Erik H. Erikson masterfully portrayed the interaction of the personal and social dimensions of this process in *Young Man Luther* (New York: W. W. Norton & Co., 1958).

## Chapter 3.  Hebrews in the Land

1. George  E. Mendenhall, *The Tenth Generation: The Origins of the Biblical Tradition* (Baltimore: Johns Hopkins University Press, 1973), 220; see also 64.
2. These strategies are mentioned in the Amarna letters. See Mendenhall, "Hebrew Conquest," 77–78. Four hundred years later the prophet Elisha sadly recommended that Israel employ similar techniques against Moab: "You will cut down all their fine trees; you will stop up all the springs of water; and you will spoil every good piece of land by littering it with stones" (2 Kings 3:19, NEB).
3. Exodus 5:10–21.
4. Mendenhall, *Tenth Generation,* 122ff. The Code of Hammurabi had made provision for formal renunciation of allegiance and protection by declaring, "I hate my king and my city" (Mendenhall, "Hebrew Conquest," 71).
5. The Transjordan experience is the most obscure portion of this history, and the results were unstable. See Mendenhall, *Tenth Generation,* 25–26; see also Deuteronomy 3:18–22.
6. See Joshua, chapters 2 and 6.
7. Mendenhall, "Hebrew Conquest," 73, 81.
8. Mendenhall, *Tenth Generation,* 90n.
9. Mendenhall, *Tenth Generation,* xii–xiii; see also 18.

## Chapter 4.  Covenant Promise

1. The Inclusive Language Lectionary Committee, National Council of the Churches of Christ in the USA, *An Inclusive Language Lectionary* (Philadelphia: Westminster Press, 1983, 1984, 1985). Year A, Easter, Lesson 1 (alternate).
2. Walter Brueggemann, *Genesis, Interpretation: A Bible Commentary for Teaching and Preaching* (Atlanta: John Knox Press, 1982), 73.
3. Gerhard von Rad, in *Genesis, A Commentary* (Philadelphia: Westminster Press, 1961), summarized this documentary hypothesis as

> a fact that has become accepted in contemporary Old Testament science after almost 200 years of research: The books Genesis to Joshua consist of several continuous source documents that were woven together more or less skillfully by a redactor. The oldest source documents are known as "Yahwist" (J) and "Elohist" (E) because of their distinctive use of the name for God. The Yahwist may be dated ca. 950, the Elohist perhaps one or two centuries later. Deuteronomy (D) is literarily distinct; we have it in the book of Deuteronomy, but Deuteronomistic additions

and revisions occur also in The Book of Joshua. The latest
source is the Priestly document (P); its actual composition
(without the later additions, of course) falls in the postex-
ilic period, ca. 538–450.

The importance of these dates must not be overesti-
mated, both because they are in every instance only
guesses and, above all, because they refer only to the
completed literary composition. The question of the age of
a single tradition within any one of the source documents
is an entirely different matter. The youngest document (P),
for example, contains an abundance of ancient and very
ancient material (23–24).

For a more complete presentation of the documentary hypothesis,
see Robert H. Pfeiffer, *Introduction to the Old Testament* (New York:
Harper & Bros., 1948), 129–289, or similarly titled books by other
scholars.
4. von Rad, *Genesis,* 130.
5. The quotation from Exodus is attributable to the Yahwist. The
   optimistic perspective I attribute to the Yahwist relates to the
   character of the land, not to human nature.
6. See Isaiah 11:6–9, Ezekiel 34:25–31. Their revulsion at predation
   may project onto nature disgust derived from living amid frequent
   religious sacrifices of animals.
7. See Aldo Leopold, *A Sand County Almanac* (San Francisco and New
   York: Sierra Club/Ballantine, 1972), 137ff.; and, for a detailed study
   of Leopold's researches, Susan L. Flader, *Thinking Like a Mountain: Aldo Leopold and the Evolution of an Ecological Attitude
   Toward Deer, Wolves and Forests* (Lincoln, NE: University of Ne-
   braska Press, 1978).
8. von Rad, *Genesis,* 123.
9. Luke 5:1–11.
10. Isaiah 65:17–25; also 66:22–23.

**Chapter 5. Jesus' Baptism**

1. This text quotes Isaiah 61:1–2, and draws from Isaiah 58:6.
2. The reader may note that I characteristically refer to "Jesus" when
   considering his human activities in Roman-occupied Palestine, and
   to "Christ" when emphasizing God's engagement in these activities
   as understood by the Christian church—two perspectives on one
   person which can sometimes, though not always, be distinguished.
3. See Mark 1:9–11; Matthew 3:13–17, 4:1–11; Luke 3:21–22, 4:1–13.
4. 1 Kings 19.
5. This understanding may broaden our understanding of the two

natures of Christ, one fully God and one fully of the earth.
6. Matthew 11:16–19.
7. James I. Packer, Merrill C. Tenney, and William White, Jr., eds., *The Land of the Bible* (Nashville: Thomas Nelson, 1985), 150. See also 1 Kings 5.
8. Joshua 4; Psalm 114:3, NEB.

## Chapter 6. God Creating

1. Gerhard von Rad, *Old Testament Theology* (New York: Harper & Bros., 1962), 1: 22.
2. For comparative Egyptian and Babylonian accounts, see James B. Pritchard, ed., *Ancient Near Eastern Texts* (Princeton: Princeton University Press, 1955). Although most scholars have suggested Babylonian influence upon the story in Genesis 1, Professor George Landes of Union Theological Seminary, New York, has pointed out to me more striking parallels with the Egyptian creation tradition. Landes is also persuaded that the Genesis 1 story is more ancient than much of the material with which it was joined by Priestly editors. The day of rest which ends the story is not called a "sabbath," nor are instructions for sabbath observance attached to the seventh day, as is common in Priestly material. The Genesis 1 story may be as old as the Yahwist story.
3. Stephen Mitchell, *The Book of Job* (San Francisco: North Point Press, 1987), 81–82.

## Chapter 7. Image of God

1. Phyllis Trible, *God and the Rhetoric of Sexuality* (Philadelphia: Fortress Press, 1978), 75–97.
2. Trible, *Rhetoric of Sexuality*, 85.
3. Trible, *Rhetoric of Sexuality*, 87.
4. Year A, Trinity, Lesson 1.
5. See Deuteronomy 4:16.
6. Year B, 34–35.
7. von Rad, *Genesis*, 58.
8. Genesis 1:29–30.
9. See Colossians 1:15–23; 2 Corinthians 3:17–18, 4:4; Ephesians 4:20–24.

## Chapter 8. Moral Creativity

1. Year A, Trinity, Lesson 1.
2. This definition of *eros* derives from Paul Goodman's Gestalt psychology as interpreted by Taylor Stoehr in his introduction to *Nature Heals: The Psychological Essays of Paul Goodman* (New

York: Free Life Editions, 1977), xxii. Stoehr added that in Goodman's theory, "Eros was nothing but the self come vividly to life, not the self as distinguished from society, not the ego as distinguished from the id, but the self as the on-going interplay of the organism and its total environment, including society."

3. George M. Landes, "Creation and Liberation," in Bernhard W. Anderson, ed., *Creation in the Old Testament* (Philadelphia: Fortress Press, 1984), 144.

4. Norman C. Habel, *Yahweh versus Baal: A Conflict of Religious Cultures* (New York: Bookman Associates, 1964), 56–57, 95–100. The poetry is Habel's translation from the Ugaritic tablets.

5. Trible, *Rhetoric of Sexuality,* 45 and 53. Isaiah 63:15 illustrates how translators have let male bias obscure an important nuance. Compare Trible's version with that in the King James: "Where *is* thy zeal and thy strength, the sounding of thy bowels and of thy mercies toward me?"; the Revised Standard: ". . . the yearning of thy heart and thy compassion"; the Jerusalem Bible: ". . . the yearning of your inmost heart"; and the New English Bible: ". . . thy burning and tender love."

6. Rosemary Radford Ruether, *Sexism and God-Talk: Toward a Feminist Theology* (Boston: Beacon Press, 1983), 136–37.

7. This usage departs from that recommended by the Inclusive Language Lectionary Committee of the National Council of Churches. That committee replaced the English Bible usage of *Lord* with *Sovereign,* on the grounds that *Lord* is a masculine title of respect, as in "lords, ladies and gentlemen" (See ILL, Year A, Appendix). Most English Bibles, including the King James, Revised Standard Version, and New English Bible, continue the four-hundred-year-old tradition of English usage which translates *Yahweh,* the name of God, as LORD. Lord is also used in the New Testament to translate *kyrios,* the masculine title of respect which came to be closely associated with Jesus, as in "Lord Jesus Christ," or "our Lord." This double referent for *Lord,* the name of God and the person of Jesus, gives the word distinctive connotations in English usage which convey the biblical and Christian God as distinguished from "god" in a more general sense. *Sovereign,* recommended by the NCC committee, has political connotations which are themselves quite inappropriate: such as authoritarianism, nationalism, defensiveness, uncooperativeness, even "fading monarchy."

## Chapter 9. Sexual Anxiety

1. Genesis 29:11; book of Ruth; Hosea 2; Ephesians 5:21–33.

2. Edward W. L. Smith, *The Body in Psychotherapy* (Jefferson, NC: McFarland, 1985), 154; see also 44–45.

3. 1 Kings 12:25–33.
4. See John Gray, *1 & 2 Kings: A Commentary* (Philadelphia: Westminster Press, 1963), 290–93.
5. Genesis 12:10–20 and 20:1–18; 16:1–6 and 21:8–21; 18:1–15 and 22:1–18. In its context, the story of the near-sacrifice of Isaac appears to carry a double message: (1) that obedience to the Lord must take precedence over patriarchal hopes; (2) that by God's mercy, child sacrifice, common in Canaan, would not be required of Hebrews.
6. Dr. Eva Reich, pediatrician and psychotherapist, told me,

> I really don't think we would need sex therapy if we hadn't in the first place repressed sex.... It is the child's birthright to feel good in its body, and to have loving, affectionate, close relationships. . . . [Yet] I'm seeing the effect of birth anesthesia, and of being circumcised without anesthesia, and of separating the newborn from the mother so the baby gets cold and pale and fearful and far away. It's like a war on the newborn (Recorded January 18, 1984).

Later I heard her explain, "In the United States we are circumcising 97% of all baby boys without anesthesia, which is the greatest genital trauma you can imagine because it stays in the memory banks and [contributes to] an anxious, suspicious person who really can't expand in pleasure because the experience comes back" (recorded November 19, 1984).
7. See Genesis 34:14; Judges 14:3; Ezekiel 32:17–32.
8. Mendenhall, *Tenth Generation*, 223.

## Chapter 10. Seventh Day Delight

1. Jürgen Moltmann, *God in Creation: A New Theology of Creation and the Spirit of God* (San Francisco: Harper & Row, 1985), 278.
2. Moltmann, *God in Creation*, 279.
3. John Muir, *John of the Mountains: The Unpublished Journals*, ed. Linnie Marsh Wolfe (Madison, WI: University of Wisconsin Press, 1979), 53.
4. Walter Brueggemann, *The Message of the Psalms, Augsburg Old Testament Studies* (Minneapolis: Augsburg Publishing House, 1984), 145.
5. Revelation 5:13.
6. Edward A. Armstrong, *Saint Francis: Nature Mystic: The Derivation and Significance of the Nature Stories in the Franciscan Legend* (Berkeley: University of California Press, 1983), 242.
7. Translation by F. C. Burkitt, *The Song of Brother Sun in English*

*Rime,* quoted in Armstrong, *Saint Francis,* 228. I have changed "for," translating the Latin *per* as "by." Either rendering may interpret the ambivalent Latin word. Francis later added verses concerning forgiveness and death.

### Chapter 11. The Land

1. Brueggemann, *The Land,* 34–35.
2. Brueggemann, *The Land,* 54.

### Chapter 12. Rights for Life

1. Martin Noth, *Exodus: A Commentary* (Philadelphia: Westminster Press, 1962), 173–75. The name is suggested by the reference in Exodus 24:7.
2. Exodus 21:17.
3. Brueggemann, *The Land,* 65.
4. Exodus 21:2–11; and Deuteronomy 15:1–18.
5. See Leviticus 19:9–10, 23:22; Deuteronomy 24:19–22.
6. Phyllis Trible gives a beautiful feminist interpretation to this tale in *God and the Rhetoric of Sexuality,* 166–99.
7. See Leviticus 25:35–38. These alternative meanings are conveyed by the NEB, the RSV, and the JB, respectively. See also Brueggemann, *The Land,* 66.
8. Deuteronomy 22:10.
9. See Genesis 30.
10. Leviticus 25:6–7, NEB: "Yet what the land itself produces in the sabbath year shall be food for you, for your male and female slaves, for your hired man, and for the stranger lodging under your roof, for your cattle and for the wild animals in your country. Everything it produces may be used for food."
11. See Genesis 40–45.
12. Moltmann, *God in Creation,* 289.
13. Johannes Pedersen, *Israel: Its Life and Culture* (London: Oxford University Press, 1926), 479–80.

### Chapter 13. Jubilee

1. Leviticus 25:25–30.
2. The "fiftieth year" most probably indicates another method of counting (like the "three days" between Jesus' death on Friday and the resurrection on Sunday) and does not imply a second fallow year following the 49-year cycle. See Martin Noth, *Leviticus: A Commentary* (Philadelphia: Westminster Press, 1965), 187.
3. Leviticus 25:29–31. Scholars believe that most of the walled

Canaanite cities, like Jerusalem, were among the last areas of Palestine to fall under Hebrew control. See Noth, *Leviticus*, 184–93.
4. However, the meaning of this passage is obscure and susceptible to a variety of interpretations. See also Micah 3:1–4.
5. Numbers 36.
6. Jeremiah 34.
7. Nehemiah 10:31.

## Chapter 14. Jesus' Kingdom

1. Moltmann, *God in Creation*, 291.
2. Yoder, *Politics of Jesus*, 36.
3. "Jesus" in English transliterates the Greek name in the New Testament, which itself stands for the original Hebrew "Joshua." Joshua relates to the name of God, meaning "Yahweh is salvation," or ". . . saves," or ". . . will save." The name was common in first century Judaism. See "Jesus Christ," *The Interpreter's Dictionary of the Bible*, 4 vols. (New York: Abingdon Press, 1962), 2: 869.
4. Luke 5:1–11.
5. See Deuteronomy 23:24–25. The Pharisees' quarrel was not with snacking on another's grain, but with doing so on the sabbath. This story implies that Jesus' contemporaries had turned the sabbath into a controlling ordinance rather than a liberating one.
6. Luke 6:12–16.
7. See Jesus' conversation with the rich young ruler, Luke 18:18–30; and his parable of the unjust steward, Luke 16:1–9, which Yoder interprets brilliantly in *Politics of Jesus*, 72–74.
8. Yoder, *Politics of Jesus*, 89.
9. Jonathan Schell, from his introduction to Adam Michnik, *Letters from Prison and Other Essays*, trans. Maya Latynski (Berkeley: University of California Press, 1985), xxiii–xxiv.
10. Michnik, *Letters from Prison*, 144.
11. Schell in Michnik, *Letters from Prison*, xxix.
12. Michnik, *Letters from Prison*, 49.
13. Quoted in Michnik, *Letters from Prison*, xxviii.
14. Quoted in Michnik, *Letters from Prison*, xxviii.
15. Michnik, *Letters from Prison*, 77.
16. Michnik reflected from prison that

> Solidarity did not expect a military coup and was taken by surprise. It is not the workers who should bear the responsibility for this failure but all those (the author of this piece, for instance) who were summoned to create a political vision for the union through their intellectual work. The

theoretical reflections on systematic change—and this
should be noted — lagged behind the events. . . . Practice
preceded theory (*Letters from Prison,* 30).

17. Michnik, *Letters from Prison,* 55.
18. Mark 14:26–31, 66–72.
19. Mark 10:17–31.
20. Schell, in Michnik, *Letters from Prison,* xxxiii.
21. Mark 14:28, 16:7.

## Chapter 15. Beautiful David

1. This description refers to the first attempt, which was abandoned
   when an attendant inadvertently touched the ark and died; the
   second was equally enthusiastic.
2. See 2 Samuel 5:3, and Mendenhall, *Tenth Generation,* 208.

## Chapter 16. Solomon's Technique

1. Gray, *Kings,* 117.
2. 1 Kings 9:22, in contradiction to the passage quoted, states that only
   alien subjects were conscripted for forced labors, not the Israelites
   themselves. Judah may have been exempt from forced labor and
   even from taxation to provision Solomon's court, but Jeroboam's
   rebellion and the complaints from tribal leaders in Israel (1 Kings
   12:3–19) suggest that the northern tribes were subjected to both.
3. Brueggemann, *The Land,* 86–87.
4. See Mark 11:15–19; Mark 13.
5. Mendenhall, *Tenth Generation,* 172.
6. 1 Kings 11:14–24.
7. 1 Kings 9:10–14.
8. Brueggemann, *The Land,* 10–11.

## Chapter 17. The Serpent

1. Trible, *Rhetoric of Sexuality,* 128.

## Chapter 18. Horses and Chariots

1. Genesis 4:1–22.
2. This might account for reports of both prosperity and growing
   servitude in 1 Kings. These plows, it should be noted, did not turn
   soil over like the moldboard plow common on farms since the late
   Middle Ages. See also John Bright, *A History of Israel* (Philadelphia: Westminster Press, 1959), 196; and "Plow," *Interpreter's
   Dictionary of the Bible,* 3: 828.

3. Mendenhall, *Tenth Generation,* 173.

## Chapter 19. Pollution

1. *The Compact Edition of the Oxford English Dictionary* (Oxford: Oxford University Press, 1971), entry for "Pollute." ("Ther" was written with a single character for "th.")
2. Genesis 4:1–12.
3. Abraham J. Heschel, *The Prophets* (New York: Harper & Row, 1969), 113–14.
4. Heschel, *The Prophets,* 113.
5. I believe that the "law within them" should not be seen as a coercive spirit which removes human freedom but rather a functioning, just ecology within which the obligations and the rewards of right relationships will be plain to all, achieving freedom for all social classes as well as for the range of created species. For a more coercive interpretation see von Rad, *Old Testament Theology,* 2:213–17.

## Part V. Ecological Visions

1. Having become an aphorism, this traditional rendering is more telling than a more accurate rendering of the Hebrew, such as the NJB, "Where there is no vision the people get out of hand," or the RSV, "Where there is no prophecy the people cast off restraint."

## Chapter 20. Comparisons

1. Quoted in Joseph Epes Brown, *The Spiritual Legacy of the American Indian* (New York: Crossroad, 1982), 40 [from Melvin R. Gilmore, *Prairie Smoke* (New York: Columbia University Press, 1929), 36].
2. From *Touch the Earth,* quoted in John Hart, *The Spirit of the Earth: A Theology of the Land* (New York: Paulist Press, 1984), 48.
3. See Vine Deloria, Jr., *God Is Red* (New York, Dell Publishing, 1973); and Hart, *Spirit of the Earth.*
4. All quotations in the above paragraph are from Matthew Fox, "Creation-Centered Spirituality from Hildegard of Bingen to Julian of Norwich," in Philip N. Joranson and Ken Butigan, eds., *Cry of the Environment: Rebuilding the Christian Creation Tradition* (Santa Fe, NM: Bear & Co., 1984), 85–106.
5. I draw from Conrad Bonifazi, "Teilhard and the Natural Environment," in Joranson and Butigan, *Cry of the Environment,* 311–20. [Teilhard's words are from *How I Believe* (New York: Harper Perennial Library, 1969) 35; and from *Science and Christ* (New York: Harper and Row, 1969), 64.]

6. John B. Cobb, Jr., "Process Theology and an Ecological Model," in Joranson and Butigan, *Cry of the Environment*, 330, 333.
7. Charles Birch and John B. Cobb, Jr., *The Liberation of Life: From the Cell to the Community* (Cambridge: Cambridge University Press, 1981), 118, 107, 141.
8. J. E. Lovelock, *Gaia: A New Look at Life on Earth* (Oxford: Oxford University Press, 1979), vii.
9. Quoted in Lawrence E. Joseph, "Britain's Whole Earth Guru," *New York Times Magazine,* 23 Nov. 1986, 95.
10. Lovelock, *Gaia,* 107–108, 148.
11. Arne Naess, quoted in Bill Devall and George Sessions, *Deep Ecology* (Salt Lake City: Gibbs M. Smith, 1985), 75–76.
12. From Gary Snyder's "Four Changes" (1969), quoted in Devall and Sessions, *Deep Ecology,* 171.
13. Gary Snyder, "Good, Wild, Sacred," in Wes Jackson, Wendell Berry, and Bruce Colman, eds., *Meeting the Expectations of the Land: Essays in Sustainable Agriculture and Stewardship* (San Francisco: North Point Press, 1984), 195, 200, 205.
14. Michael P. Cohen, *The Pathless Way: John Muir and American Wilderness* (Madison: University of Wisconsin Press, 1984).

## Chapter 21. The Day of the Lord

1. See Jon R. Luoma, "Forests Are Dying but Is Acid Rain Really to Blame?" *Audubon Magazine,* March 1987, 37–51.
2. See Paul Brodeur, "Annals of Chemistry in the Face of Doubt," *The New Yorker,* 9 June 1986, 70–87.
3. See Sandra Postel, "Altering the Earth's Chemistry: Assessing the Risks," *Worldwatch Paper* 71, July 1986, 8–10.
4. Peter H. Raven, quoted in "When the Jungle Turns to Wasteland," *New York Times,* 22 Feb. 1987. See Catherine Caufield, *In the Rainforest* (New York: Alfred A. Knopf, 1985); also Jonathan Evan Maslow, *Bird of Life, Bird of Death: A Naturalist's Journey Through a Land of Political Turmoil* (New York: Simon and Schuster, 1986), about political oppression and the rainforest in Guatemala.
5. See C. Dean Fruedenburger, *Food for Tomorrow?* (Minneapolis: Augsburg Publishing House, 1984), chapter 1.
6. See Barry Commoner, *The Closing Circle: Nature, Man, and Technology* (New York: Alfred A. Knopf, 1971).
7. Lester R. Brown and Jodi L. Jacobson, "Our Demographically Divided World," *Worldwatch Paper* 74 Dec. 1986, 6, 8.
8. *Worldwatch Paper* 74, 5.
9. See Jonathan Schell, *The Fate of the Earth* (New York: Alfred A. Knopf, 1982).

10. One of the best critiques of technology as idolatry is Lewis
    Mumford's *The Myth of the Machine: The Pentagon of Power* (New
    York: Harcourt Brace Jovanovich, 1970).
11. Year C, 204.

## Chapter 22. Redemption

1. In Mark's version, the fig tree incident happens just before the
   cleansing of the temple. It is interpreted afterwards; this detached
   commentary, likely a later explanation, treats the withering of the
   tree as a sign of the power believers may exercise *over* nature, not
   in terms of covenant relationships. I see this as a misunderstanding. The parable of the vineyard, with its strong covenant flavor,
   follows shortly.
2. Jeremiah 31:27–34; 32:36–44.
3. John Gibbs observes that "only by taking 'the form of a servant' was
   Jesus 'in the form of God.' " See John G. Gibbs, "Pauline Cosmic
   Christology and Ecological Crisis," *Journal of Biblical Literature*,
   1971, 473.
4. 2 Kings 2:7–12; John 14:1–6.

## Chapter 24. Peaceable Kingdom

1. Benjamin West, 1738–1820, painted many versions of this scene,
   which are widely reproduced. The one I describe is in the Friends
   Historical Library, Swarthmore College, Swarthmore, PA. William
   Penn, after previous experience in New Jersey, founded the Pennsylvania colony in 1682. He had learned the natives' language and
   developed deep respect for them by the time he negotiated the treaty
   which opened the way for settlement at Philadelphia. Though they
   had good intentions, the Quakers were not ultimately successful in
   protecting natives from the destructive impact of rapid European
   settlement. See Penn's charming "Letter from William Penn to the
   Committee of the Free Society of Traders (1683)," in Roy Harvey
   Pearce, ed., *Colonial American Writing* (Rinehart & Co., 1950),
   467–83.
2. Johannes Pederson notes this parallel between predators and alien
   nations but draws a different conclusion about the place of the wild;
   see *Israel*, 484–85.
3. John Muir, "Wild Wool," in *Wilderness Essays* (Salt Lake City:
   Peregrine Smith, 1980), 242.
4. Moltmann, *Creation*, 212–13. Moltmann goes on, however, to limit
   his vision to "change without transience, time without the past, and
   life without death" (p. 213).

5. These images are from 1 Corinthians 15:26, 55. Paul goes on to observe, "The sting of death *is* sin" (vs. 56, KJV).

## Chapter 25. The Lamb

1. Michael Walzer, *Exodus and Revolution* (New York: Basic Books, 1985), 115. Walzer credits the phrase "ineradicable subversion" to Ernst Bloch.
2. Deuteronomy 11:10–15.
3. Jesus quoted Isaiah 56:7 and Jeremiah 7:11.
4. The Letter to the Hebrews, which compares Jesus' sacrifice with temple sacrifices, is an exception to this statement.
5. See Genesis 22:1–18.
6. Romans 8:18–23; Philippians 2:9–11; Revelation 5:13.
7. William Blake, "The Lamb," *Songs of Innocence and of Experience* (London: Oxford University Press, 1967), 8.

# Index

Aaron, 71
Abel, 164
Abigail, 132, 135
Abishag, 135
Abraham, 73, 202, 230
Absalom, 138–139, 148
Achish, 133
Adam, 31, 55, 206
Adonijah, 138, 140
Adonis, 134
Agriculture, 2, 30–31, 89, 97,
    107,113, 158, 184, 193,
    212, 218, 222
    compromised by sacrificial
        system, 228
    ethics, 92–94, 101–102, 122,
        169, 174
    not under curse, 33, 155
    polluted, 157
    redeemed, 210–211, 215
    sexual manipulation of, 62–
        64, 70–71, 74
Ahab, 91
Ahijah, 146
Ahimelech, 131
Amnon, 138
Amos, 38, 63, 127, 148, 195–196,
    210
Anat, 61–64
Animism, 2, 179–182
Anthropocentrism, 82
Armstrong, Edward, 84
Artaxerxes, 110
Author's experience, 11–12, 15,
    215

Baal, 28, 34, 45, 54, 61–64, 68,
    71–72, 74–75, 81, 91, 152,
    163, 179, 196
    of Peor, 72

Bach, 12
Bacon, Francis, 11, 186
Bathsheba, 136, 140
Beauty
    of holiness, 231
    related to ecology, 151
    See Moral beauty
Biblical ecology. See Ecology
Birch, Charles, 184–185
Blake, William, 234
Brueggemann, Walter, 5, 30, 82,
    89, 92, 99, 144, 148

Cain, 55, 157, 164
Calvinism, 43, 215
Cobb, John B. Jr., 184–185
Cohen, Michael, 188
Covenant, 4, 5, 18, 22–27,
    38–39, 41, 42, 64, 107, 109,
    111, 130, 140, 149,
    153–154, 164, 166, 172,
    189, 195–196
    ethics, 98, 132, 169
    lands, 91–93, 100, 103, 106,
        108, 113
    love, 61
    nature's inclusion in, 28–36,
        82, 87–88, 155, 157, 178,
        180, 228, 232–233
    protection of trees, 102–103
    renewal, 116–119, 123, 126,
        156, 200–201, 203, 210,
        212, 218–221, 223–225,
        229–231, 234
    rights for animals, 101–102
    violations by David, 137, 148
    violations by Solomon, 144
"Covenant Code," 97–99, 101,
    103

Creation, 43–44
    God's creativity, 45–50, 61
    See Moral creativity

Darwin, Charles, 48
David, 23, 30, 128, 129–139,
    140, 142, 144, 146, 148,
    159
Death, 79, 225–226
Deborah, 29
"Deep ecology," 179, 187
Deloria, Vine, Jr., 182
Descartes, René, 186
Donne, John, 8–9, 11

Eckhart, Meister, 182
Ecological crisis, 1–3, 190–199
Ecology
    biblical, 4, 6, 18, 26, 48–50,
        51, 87, 122, 127, 172–175,
        177–178, 180–181, 188,
        229–231
    of redemption, 210–214
    See Moral ecology
Elijah, 38–39, 91, 148, 207
Elisha, 38, 160
Eros, 60–61
Eve, 31, 174
Ezekiel, 33, 143–144, 166,
    201–203, 211, 213, 216,
    219

Fox, Matthew, 182
Francis of Assisi, 3, 84–85
Frye, Northrop, 10–11

Gaia hypothesis, 179, 186–187
Gandhi, 119
Gilmore, Melvin, 181
Goliath, 130–131

Habel, Norman, 61–62
Hagar, 73
Hart, John, 182
Hartshorne, Charles, 184

"Hebrew" defined, 22
Heschel, Abraham Joshua, 167
Hildegard of Bingen, 182–183
Hiram, 41, 142–144, 147
"Holiness Code," 103–105, 106–
    107, 112, 169
Holy land, 24, 26, 89, 104, 108,
    116, 118, 122, 126, 128,
    134, 148, 180, 188,
    200–201, 203, 205, 207,
    218, 228
    moral pollution of, 164, 166,
        169, 175
Hosea, 34, 148, 161, 165, 211,
    221

Image
    comparative uses, 55
    of God, 11, 32, 43, 51–59, 68,
        80, 84, 113, 118, 122, 152,
        174, 182, 198, 206–207,
        232, 234
    masculine and feminine,
        65–68
    relation to eros, 60–61, 77
Isaac, 73, 230
Isaiah, 33, 40, 58, 65, 66, 114,
    148, 164, 165, 203–204,
    211, 212, 218–221
Ishmael, 73

Jacob, 12, 102
Jehoash, 160
Jehoiakim, 171
Jeremiah, 15, 109, 128, 164,
    167–172, 175, 190, 197,
    199, 202, 216
Jeroboam, 71, 146, 148
Jesse, 129–130
Jesus, 1, 3, 14, 17, 35, 92, 93,
    134, 145, 197, 205, 215,
    216, 231
    baptism related to nature,
        37–42, 234
    concern for nature, 57

demands upon nature,
200–201, 234
image of God's fatherhood,
66–67
jubilee proclamation, 88,
224
kingdom, 115–126, 178,
209–210
Passover lamb, 229–230,
234
word of God, 13
Jethro, 21
Jezebel, 91
Joab, 137–138, 140
Job, 48, 95, 158–159
Joel, 198
John of Patmos, 35–36, 213, 231,
234
John the Baptist, 38–39, 41, 117,
234
John the Evangelist, 49, 229
Jonathan, 131, 133, 135
Joseph, 104
Joshua, 22–23, 42, 115–118, 123,
147
Josiah, 94, 118, 166, 171
Jubilee, 88, 106–114, 178
in the new covenant,
115–119, 122–124, 203,
224–225, 232
Julian of Norwich, 182, 186

King, Martin Luther, 119

Land, 89–96
sabbatical for, 103–105
*See* Agriculture, Covenant
lands, Holy land, Nature
Landes, George, 6
Leopold, Aldo, 34
Lipski, Jósef, 120
Lovelock, James, 186
Luke, 35, 39, 115–116
Luther, Martin, 13

Manasseh, 63
Mark, 40, 201
Matthew, 39
Mechtild of Magdeburg, 182
Mendenhall, George, 5, 20, 22,
23, 26, 75, 146, 163
Micah, 108, 228
Michal, 134–135
Michnik, Adam, 119–122
Miriam, 28
Moltmann, Jürgen, 78, 80–81,
104, 115, 224
Moral
beauty, 9, 14, 87, 94, 96, 123
creativity, 5, 43–44, 60–69
creativity completed in sabbath rest, 78
desire, 74
ecology, 18, 33, 43, 48, 51,
58, 63, 92, 103, 105, 148,
151–155, 169, 173, 175,
185, 212–213, 216–217,
228
identity, 124
Moses, 20–22, 42, 71–72, 74, 92,
94, 105, 109, 111, 117, 123,
159
Muir, John, 39, 81, 188, 198,
220, 222

Nabal, 132
Naboth, 91
Naess, Arne, 187
Nathan, 136, 140
Nature, 18, 125–126, 128, 173,
207, 214
abuse of, 1, 142, 162, 221
attractiveness, 150
comparative views of,
179–189
covenant inclusion, 28–36,
87–88, 202, 232
creativity within, 43–44
fear of humanity, 58
human sexuality within, 76

Jesus' concern for, 57
jubilee interest, 113
mastery of, 153, 174, 199
moral, not autonomous, 51
peace with, communion
    with, 93–94, 155, 199,
    205–206, 216, 222–223,
    226, 232
redeemed by Christ, 231,
    234
related to Jesus' baptism,
    37–42
renewal of, 116, 211–214,
    225
"savagery" within, 221–222
threatened by moral chaos,
    171
worship of, 82, 152
worship with, 81–85
Nebuchadnezzar, 166, 169,
    171–172, 201
Necho, 171
Nehemiah, 104, 109–111, 118
Noah, 31, 32, 157

Panentheism, 182
Pantheism, 179, 185
Passover, 227, 229–230, 234
Paul, 12, 13, 35, 57, 129, 178,
    202, 205–206, 229–230
"Peaceable kingdom," 218–226
Pedersen, Johannes, 104
Penn, William, 218
Peter (Simon), 35, 115–116, 123,
    201, 234
Plato, 10, 168
Pollution, 128, 157, 164–175,
    187, 190–191, 207, 222
Predation, 33–34, 219–222
Priestly ("P") narrative, 30–34,
    45–46, 48, 52, 54–58, 60,
    78, 106, 227
Promise, 5, 30, 32, 33
Providence, 43

Raven, Peter, 193
Reagan, Ronald, 2
Rehoboam, 63, 147–148
Relativism, 14
Ruether, Rosemary Radford, 6,
    67
Ruth, 100

Sabbath, 44, 78–85, 98–99, 114
    celebration with nature,
        81–85
    ecology, 87–88, 97, 105, 169
    ethics, 106, 111, 122, 137
    Jesus' proclamation of,
        115–117, 123
    reflection, 79–80, 108, 225
    rest, 78–79, 113, 216
    satisfaction, 80
Sabbatical, 99, 101, 108–109,
    116–118, 124, 225
    for the land, 103–105, 111,
        113, 142, 173, 219
Sacrifice, 227–230
Samuel, 130, 140
Sarah, 73
Saul, 129–135, 158
Schell, Jonathan, 119–120, 124
Sexuality, 44
    affirmed by Jesus, 76
    agricultural use, 62–64,
        70–71
    anxiety, 70–77
    circumcision, 73
    David's, 135
    deflection, 75
    eros, 60–61, 77
    God's relation to, 45, 60,
        64–68, 77
    human, created, 52–54
    moral desire, 74
    satisfaction, 75–76
    shame, 153
Sin, original, 156
Sisera, 29, 159

Snyder, Gary, 188
Solomon, 23, 41, 63, 71, 128,
     140–149, 150, 153, 158,
     160
Standing Bear, Luther, 181
Stewardship, 43

Tamar, 138
Technology, 1–4, 28, 33–34, 53,
     75, 94, 105, 126,
     157–163, 173, 189, 197,
199, 221, 228
Teilhard de Chardin, Pierre,
     183–185
Trible, Phyllis, 6, 52, 66, 154

Uriah, 136
Uzziah, 57

von Rad, Gerhard, 34, 45, 56

Walzer, Michael, 227
West, Benjamin, 218
White, Lynn, Jr., 1–3
Whitehead, Alfred North, 184
Wycliffe, John, 164

Yahweh (YHWH), 12, 21, 22, 71,
     163
     personality of, 12, 182
     use of "Lord" for the name,
     68
Yahwist ("J") narrative, 30–32,
     45, 48, 51–54, 145, 150,
     152, 155, 157, 164
Yoder, John Howard, 6, 115, 119

Zechariah, 210
Zedekiah, 109, 166, 171
Zephaniah, 166

## BIBLICAL CITATIONS

Genesis
1:1—2:4    46
1:2, NJB    46
1:3–4, KJV    46
1:11–12, NJB    46
1:20–21, NEB    46
1:22, NEB    47
1:24, NEB    54
1:25, NJB    48
1:26–28, ILL    55
1:27, ILL    60
1:28, ILL    60
1:31, KJV    54–55
1:31—2:3, author    78
2:1, NEB    58
2:5, NEB, alt.    52
2:5–6, NJB    45
2:9, NEB    52
2:15, JB, alt.    52
2:15, NJB    155
2:17, KJV    152
2:17–18, RSV    53
2:18, NEB, alt.    53
2:19, NEB    48
2:19–20, NEB , alt.    54
2:23, NEB    54
2:25, JB    70
3:1, RSV    151
3:1–3, RSV    151
3:4–6, NEB    152
3:6, NEB    150
3:12, NJB    152
3:15, NEB    154
3:16, NJB    154
3:17–19, NJB    155
4:15    55
5:1–3    55
6:8, NEB    31
6:11, NEB    31
8:21–22, NEB , alt.    31
9:1–17    32
9:2, NEB    32, 58

9:6    55
9:9–10, NEB    32
9:13–14, NEB    32
9:15, NEB    32
11:6–7, NEB    157

Exodus
3:8, KJV    18
3:8, RSV    33
12:3–13, NJB    227
15:21, ILL, alt.    28
19:5, NEB    21
19:5–6, RSV    27
19:8, RSV    21
20:4–5, JB    55
20:8, KJV    79, 87
20:14, 17, RSV    135
21:24, KJV    25
23:4–5, NEB    101
23:10–12, NEB    97
31:17    78
32:1, NEB    71
32:6, NEB    71
32:19, NEB    71

Leviticus
18:26–28, RSV    166
19:2, KJV    106
19:19, NEB    102
19:24, JB    102
20:22, JB    28–29
21:6, Wycliffe    164
25:2–5, NEB    103
25:8–10, NEB    107
25:15–17, NJB    112
25:17–18, NEB    112
25:23, NJB    26
25:23–24, JB    106
26:3–4, 6, 12–15, NJB    27
26:33–35, NEB    105

Numbers
    11:4, NEB    21
    25:1–9, NEB    72
    35:33–34, RSV    164

Deuteronomy
    6:2–3, NEB, alt.    166
    7:12–13, NEB, alt.    63
    8:7–9, NEB    94–95
    8:11–18, NEB, alt.    92
    10:12–19, NEB, alt.    74
    11:1–2, 10–15, NEB, alt.
     90
    19:14, NEB    108
    20:5–9, JB    99–100
    20:19–20, JB    103
    22:6–7, NEB    102
    23:24–25, NEB    100
    24:21–22, NEB    100
    25:4, RSV    101
    32:11–12, KJV, alt.    65
    32:18, RSV    65
    32:35–36, RSV, alt.    25

Joshua
    24:15, 24, KJV, alt.    23

Judges
    5:4–5, 20–21, NEB    29
    21:25, KJV, alt.    21

1 Samuel
    13:20, NEB    158
    16:12–13, NEB    130
    16:18, NJB    129, 134
    16:23, RSV    129
    17:34–37, NEB    130
    17:42, NEB    130, 134
    18:1–3, NEB    131
    20:41, NEB    131
    21:6, NEB    131
    22:2, JB    131
    24:11–19, NEB    132–133
    25:10, 15–17, 32–33, NEB
     132

2 Samuel
    1:20, 25–26, NEB    133
    1:26, JB    70
    6:5, NEB    134
    6:20, 21, NEB    134
    11:1, RSV    135–136
    11:24, RSV    136
    12:5–6, NEB    136
    13:39, NEB    138
    15:30, NEB    138
    18:5, NJB    138
    18:31—19:1, NJB    138
    24:9, NEB    137

1 Kings
    1:16, NEB    138
    2:46, NEB    140
    3:7–13, NJB    141
    4:21, 25, NEB    141
    4:27, NEB    141
    4:33, NEB    144
    5:1–17, NEB    142–143
    8:12–13, NEB    144
    10:4–8, NJB    146
    11:1–3, NEB    147
    11:28, NEB    146
    12:4, 14, 16, NJB    147
    14:23–24, NEB    63
    21:2–3, NEB    91

2 Kings
    13:14, NEB    161
    21:5–6, NJB    63

2 Chronicles
    26:10, NEB    57

Nehemiah
    5:1–13, NEB    110
    10:31, NEB    104

Job
    21:7–10, NEB    95
    28:1–12, 28, NEB    159
    38:28–29, NEB    65

38:39—39:6, Mitchell    47
39:5, Mitchell    48
39:19–25, NJB    160

Psalms
    8:4–6, ILL    55–56
    20:7, NJB    25
    20:7, KJV    161
    24:1, NEB    89
    37:1–4, NEB, alt.    92–93
    37:11, RSV, NEB    93
    37:27, NEB    93
    50:9–12, NEB    90
    51:1–4, KJV    136–137
    65:9–13, RSV    69
    72:1–4, 12–13, NJB    139
    84:2–4, NEB, alt.    83
    85:8–12, NEB, alt.    223–224
    96:11–13, NEB, alt.    82
    98, NJB, alt.    233
    103:22, NEB, alt.    83
    104:10–25, NEB, alt.    50
    107:33–41, NEB, alt.    18–19
    114, NEB    29–30
    119:103, 105, RSV    9
    148:1–13, NEB, alt.    83–84

Proverbs
    13:23, NEB    101
    15:25, NEB    108
    23:10–11, NEB    108
    27:23–27, JB    93
    29:18, KJV    177

Song of Songs
    2:3–6, NEB    77
    7:7–13, NEB    77

Isaiah
    4:2, NEB    203
    5:8–10, JB    112
    11    218
    11:6–9, NEB    37, 58
    11:7–9, NEB    220
    14:7–8, NJB    211

24:4–5, NEB    113
24:4–5, 7, RSV    165
27:2–6, JB    212
30:23–26, NEB, alt.    211
30:26, NEB    215
32:15, NJB    213, 215
32:16–20, JB    213
35:5–10, NEB, alt.    219–220
41:17–30, NEB, alt.    224–225
45:8, NEB    88
49:15, JB    66
55:1–3, NEB    75–76
55:10–11, NJB    10
60:19–21, NEB    204–205
61:1–4, KJV, alt.    114
63:15, Trible    66
65:17–25, NEB, alt.    203–204
66:13, NJB    65

Jeremiah
    2:7, 8, 14, 31, NEB    167–168
    2:31, RSV    167
    3:9, RSV    169
    4:23–26, NJB, alt.    171
    5:23–25, NEB    169
    8:18, 21–22, NEB    168
    9:23–25, NEB    25–26
    12:1, NEB    169
    12:4, NEB    170
    12:7–11, NEB    170
    12:11, NEB    175
    14:2–7, NEB, alt.    170–171
    20:7, Heschel    168
    20:7–9, JB, alt.    15–16
    22:29, RSV    171
    31:27, 31, 33–34,    172
    32:15, NEB    172
    32:20, Trible    66
    32:40–41, NEB    172

Ezekiel
    31:3–6, 9, NEB    143
    33:25–28, NEB    167
    34:28, NJB    219
    36:8, RSV    211

36:22–32, NEB    201–202
36:23, RSV    203
47:1–12, NJB    213–214
47:9, NJB    216
47:22–23, NJB    203

Hosea
2:16–23, NEB    34–35
2:18, NEB    221
4:1–3, JB, alt.    95, 165
10:13–14, NJB    161
13:8, NEB    65
14:8–9, NJB    211–212

Joel
1:15–20, NEB    198

Amos
2:7–8, JB    63
4:6–9, NEB, alt.    196
5:18–20, NEB    195
8:4–8, NJB    127
9:13–15, NEB    210

Micah
2:1–5, NJB    108–109
4:3, JB    161
4:4, KJV    24
4:4, NEB    113
6:6–8, KJV, alt.    228

Zephaniah
1:2–3, NEB    166

Zechariah
3:10, NEB    210

Matthew
3:2, NEB    38
4:11, JB    39
6:9–12, NJB    116–117
6:25–34, NEB, alt.    57
7:7–11, NEB    67
8:19–20, NEB    17
20:16, RSV    67
22:30, RSV    67
23:1–12    67
25:35–40, NEB, alt.    40

Mark
1:10–11, RSV    42
1:11, JB    39
1:13, JB    40
6:30–44, NJB    209
8:35–36, NEB, alt.    125
11:9–10, NJB    200
11:12–14, NJB    200
11:15–17, NJB    229
12:1–9, JB    118
12:9, NJB    200

Luke
3:8, NEB    117–118
4:14, KJV    115
4:18–19, JB, alt.    37, 115
4:21, JB    37
4:21, KJV    115
6:1–2, 5, RSV    116
6:20–21, 24–25, JB    116
6:27, RSV    101
6:27–31, NJB    117
6:35, NJB    117
12:6, JB    35
12:13–34, RSV    92
14:27–29, ILL    197
17:10, JB    80
17:21, NEB    178

John
1:3, NEB    49
1:29, RSV    229

Romans
    1:17, KJV    13
    2:1, NJB    178
    4:18, RSV    202
    8:18–21, NJB, alt.    206
    8:19–21, JB, alt.    35

1 Corinthians
    5:7–8, KJV    229
    8:4–6, JB, alt.    205
    11:25, NEB    230
    12:3, NEB    231
    15:28, NEB    183

Ephesians
    1:10, NEB    206

Philippians
    2:5–11, NEB, alt.    205–206
    2:7, RSV    57

Colossians
    1:16–17, NEB    183
    1:20, NEB, alt.    206
    3:11, NJB    122

Revelation
    5:13, JB    35, 231
    21:1, KJV    36
    22:1–2    213